AF449178

Sir Charles Grandison

Richardson reading *Sir Charles Grandison* in his grotto by Susanna Highmore. *(Permission of Pierpont Morgan Library.)*

Sir Charles Grandison

The Compleat Conduct Book

Sylvia Kasey Marks

Lewisburg
Bucknell University Press
London and Toronto: Associated University Presses

Associated University Presses
440 Forsgate Drive
Cranbury, NJ 08512

Associated University Presses
25 Sicilian Avenue
London WC1A 2QH, England

Associated University Presses
2133 Royal Windsor Drive
Unit 1
Mississauga, Ontario
Canada L5J 1K5

The paper used in this publication meets the
requirements of the American National Standard for
Permanence of Paper for Printed Materials Z39.48-1984.

Library of Congress Cataloging-in-Publication Data

Marks, Sylvia Kasey, 1943–
    Sir Charles Grandison : the compleat conduct book.

    Bibliography: p.
    Includes index.
    1. Richardson, Samuel, 1689–1761. History of
Sir Charles Grandison.   2. Ethics in literature.
3. Conduct of life in literature.   4. Didactic
fiction, English—History and criticism.   5. Social
ethics in literature.   I. Title.
PR3664.H53M37   1986   823'.6   85-47800
ISBN 0-8387-5090-7 (alk. paper)

Printed in the United States of America

For Fred

Contents

ACKNOWLEDGMENTS

SIR Charles Grandison: The Compleat Conduct Book originated during my graduate work with Henry Knight Miller at Princeton University; he has been an especially inspiring and helpful mentor and could not have introduced me to a more appropriate subject. Lawrence Lipking provided perceptive and valuable comments in the very early stages of my writing. A. Walton Litz arranged a summer travel grant from the department which enabled me to use libraries in England.

Conduct books and Richardson's letters were the object of much of my research, and I am particularly grateful for the Rare Book and Taylor Collections of Princeton's Firestone Library. Also valuable were the holdings of the Berg Collection of the New York Public Library, the Bodleian at Oxford, the Cambridge University Library, the University of London Library, the National Library of Scotland, Yale's Beinecke Rare Book and Manuscript Library, the British Library, the Cornell University Library, the Pierpont Morgan Library, the Victoria and Albert Museum, and the Northamptonshire Record Office. Many other libraries provided duplicate copies of Richardson's correspondence. During a fruitful visit to Harvard's Houghton Library, Hugh Amory and Marti Shaw offered a great deal of assistance. In London, B. C. Southam took valuable time to discuss Jane Austen's play based on *Sir Charles Grandison*. Duncan Eaves, Elizabeth Brophy, and Jocelyn Harris corresponded with me on research matters, while Mr. and Mrs. Louis Osman generously shared their hospitality and thorough knowledge of Canons Ashby with me. The final preparation of this book is the result of the able and accommodating typing of many drafts by Carolyn Kappes.

My husband Fred deserves the most thanks. Always a patient, enthusiastic, and encouraging helpmate, he constantly supplies the perfect combination of challenge and cheer. Even Sir Charles Grandison could learn a few things from him!

For permission to quote from published and unpublished sources, I wish to thank:

AMS Press, New York, for permission to quote from the 1966 reprint edition of Anna Laetitia Barbauld's *The Correspondence of Samuel Richardson.*

The British Library for permission to quote from the correspondence of Richardson, Cox Macro, and Catherine Talbot.

The Poetry/Rare Books Collection of the University Libraries, State University of New York at Buffalo, for permission to quote from Richardson's correspondence.

Cornell University Library for permission to quote from the correspondence of Lady Barbara Montagu.

Hyde Collection, Somerville, New Jersey, for permission to quote from Richardson's correspondence.

Newberry Library, Chicago, for permission to quote from Virgil B. Heltzel's *A Check List of Courtesy Books in the Newberry Library,* 1942.

Oxford University Press, London, for permission to quote from Jocelyn Harris's 1972 edition of Samuel Richardson's *The History of Sir Charles Grandison* and John Carroll's 1964 edition of *The Selected Letters of Samuel Richardson.*

The Pierpont Morgan Library, New York, for permission to quote from Richardson's correspondence and for permission to use Susanna Highmore's drawing of "Richardson Reading *Sir Charles Grandison* in his Grotto" on the book jacket.

Southern Illinois University Press for permission to quote from William C. Slattery's 1969 edition of *The Richardson-Stinstra Correspondence.*

The Trustees of the Victoria and Albert Museum, London, for permission to quote from Richardson's correspondence and the correspondence of his friends in the Forster Collection.

Yale University for permission to quote from Richardson's correspondence in the James M. Osborn Collection and in the Beinecke Rare Book and Manuscript Library.

Sir Charles Grandison

1

SIR CHARLES GRANDISON: "A CANDID EXAMINATION"

SHORTLY after the publication of *Sir Charles Grandison*, Samuel Richardson received a letter from one who signed himself BF, "a young Man, acknowledging reformation in a prison from Libertine and extravagant courses, on reading the contraste between Sir Charles's Rewarded piety and goodness, and Sir Hargrave's Despair and miserable Exit." BF writes:

> I'm now determin'd during my stay in confinement, & when in the world to make Virtue & honour to be the standard and Governour of all my actions & as real happiness must infallibly be the consequence, I shall always esteem you as the source of every Good that may hereafter accrue to [me].[1]

Such enthusiasm for *Sir Charles Grandison* would be difficult to find today. Two hundred years later Richardson's last novel has elicited the least amount of commentary among his three major works. *Grandison* is generally considered the stepbrother of Richardson's other novels, a disappointment after the triumph of *Clarissa*. Presumably it has less artistry than the earlier works; somehow, the critics now say, Richardson's didacticism interfered with the telling of a potentially exciting story. But a remark of Samuel Johnson seems to anticipate this criticism: " 'Why, Sir, if you were to read Richardson for the story, your impatience would be so much fretted that you would hang yourself. But you must read him for the sentiment, and consider the story as only giving occasion to the sentiment.' " Richardson's contemporaries and closest friends doubtless shared Johnson's view, for while they became deeply engrossed in the story, they also seemed sensible of the dictum to read for meaning. Anna Laetitia Barbauld, the first editor of Richardson's correspondence, suggests another clue that complements Dr. Johnson's assessment:

and if from any one Richardson caught, in some measure, his peculiar manner of writing, to him [Defoe] it must be traced, whose Robinson Crusoe and Family Instructor (the latter consisting of domestic dialogues,) he must have read in his youth.[2]

Significantly, Defoe's *Family Instructor* descends from the old courtesy-book tradition, examined more fully in chapter 2. What the following chapters propose is that a combination of factors, among them the need to satisfy a new class of readers, the limitations and inadequacies of older forms of courtesy literature, and Richardson's personal mission as a constant refiner of his own conduct books, resulted in one of the greatest achievements of the genre.

The connection between *Sir Charles Grandison* and the conduct-book tradition has been made but not developed. A. D. McKillop refers to *Grandison* as a "courtesy-book," reflecting the advice appropriate for the court, as well as a "conduct-book," suggesting a more general audience. Likewise, George Sherburn recognizes the debt of *Pamela II* and *Grandison* to the courtesy book. Katherine Hornbeak's discussion of the conduct book as a source for Richardson extends only to his *Familiar Letters* and *Aesop's Fables*, while Jocelyn Harris, in her introduction to the most recent edition of *Grandison*, proposes several important ideas about conduct books and this last novel. Margaret Anne Doody also suggests the connection. Finally, Phyllis Patricia Smith analyzes the relationship between the theories of educating a gentleman and *Sir Charles Grandison*. Smith goes on to examine the principal courtesy and conduct books of the period and measures *Grandison* against them. What is not developed in any of these studies is a view of *Grandison* as the most complete and compelling guide in its time to the duties, dilemmas, and moral choices faced by every member of a household under varying circumstances. That Richardson saw *Clarissa* as a conduct book is clear from a letter he wrote to Lady Bradshaigh:

> Be pleased in this case to honour the volumes with a place with your Taylor's Living and Dying, with your Practice of Piety, and Nelson's Fasts and Festivals, not as being worthy of such company, but that they may have a chance of being dipt into thirty years hence; for I persuade myself, they will not be found utterly unworthy of such a chance, since they appear in the humble guise of a novel only by way of accommodation to the manners and taste of an age overwhelmed with luxury, and abandoned to sound and senselessness.

So, too, it is clear from the prevailing tone of his correspondence that he could have made the same claims for *Grandison*. As he observes:

the present Collection is not published ultimately, nor even principally, any more than the other two [*Pamela* and *Clarissa*], for the Sake of Entertainment only. A much nobler End is in View. Yet it is hoped the Variety of Characters and Conversations necessarily introduced into so large a Correspondence, as these Volumes contain, will enliven as well as instruct.[3]

It is true that some of Richardson's readers saw his earlier works as a source of practical advice. Sarah Wescomb Scudamore planned to raise her little boy according to Locke's maxims as interpreted by Pamela. And the enthusiastic Mrs. Sarah Chapone confided to Richardson that "To my family, your writings have been of inestimable service. . . ." After reading *Pamela* she claimed that her letter-writing ability improved; but, more important, her elder daughter vowed that in doubtful points she would try to determine what a Clarissa might do and "conduct herself accordingly." Lady Bradshaigh admitted that Clarissa's regimen set a good example for herself; rising before her houseguests, she devoted the early hours of the day to correspondence.[4] Nevertheless, Mrs. Barbauld notes in her introduction to Richardson's correspondence that "the novels of Richardson were received by his admirers as manuals of instruction, and Lady Echlin [sister of Lady Dorothy Bradshaigh, Richardson's favorite correspondent], in particular, considered the morality of them, not only as the indispensible [*sic*], but as the only material point." Lady Echlin wrote to Richardson, "Can any mortal peruse your fine, delicate lesson untouched with self-reproach?"[5] Thomas Edwards, a critic and regular correspondent of Richardson, pledged a reading of all three major works at least once a year, and of *Grandison* in particular he declared that Sir Charles ". . . shall be my Master, and it will be my own very great fault if I am not the better for his lessons to the last day of my life. God reward you, my dear Mr. Richardson, both here and hereafter, for those most excellent instructions which you have given the world! You teach us both how to live, and how to die. . . . To live like Sᴿ Charles, and to die like Clarissa. . . ." Thomas Newcomb always found himself to be a better man at the conclusion of every page of Richardson's novel. If everyone had Grandison's virtues, the world would become a paradise. He added that "Pulpits have long in vain attempted to bring about this revolution;—pray continue to lend yᴿ assisting hand, to compleat it."[6]

Richardson sent a copy of *Sir Charles Grandison* to Lord Chesterfield, whose missing letter of appreciation is listed in the index to Richardson's letters in the Forster Collection. In writing to others about the novel, Chesterfield noted its extreme length, excessive conversation, and mistakes about behavior in high life. Nevertheless, he commended Richardson for his understanding of human nature and his ability to paint the "little secret movements" of the heart, adding that Richardson "would well have deserved a higher education than he has had; however, he deserves well of mankind, the object of all his writings being virtue."[7]

The literati of the period tended to echo this appreciation of a high moral purpose. *Grandison* was the subject of commendatory verse by Anna Williams, the blind poetess who was sheltered by Dr. Johnson, Thomas Edwards, William Cowper, and anonymous poets such as TRG. Even that old rake Colley Cibber, whom Lady Bradshaigh could not tolerate, wrote, "The spirited generosity of Sir Charles to the two Danbys and their sister has put me so out of conceit with my own narrow soul, that I cannot be easy for not having been myself the author of your more than moral history."[8] Tobias Smollett, an epistolary novelist himself, criticized the "superfluity and impertinence" of all three of Richardson's novels but praised the author for "inlisting the passions on the side of virtue." Adam Smith, author of *The Theory of Moral Sentiments* (1759), called Richardson a "much better instructor" than "Zeno, Chrisippus, or Epictetus," and William Shenstone felt that Richardson merited a bishopric for his writing of *Grandison*.[9]

Grandison was a great favorite of Jane Austen as well. James Austen-Leigh recalls that "every circumstance narrated in Sir Charles Grandison, all that was said or done in the cedar parlour, was familiar to her; and the wedding days of Lady L. and Lady G. were as well remembered as if they had been living friends." Austen's letters are sprinkled with references to specific details in *Grandison*. Lady Bradshaigh had once suggested to Richardson that David Garrick might make a "delightful play" from *Sir Charles Grandison*. But it was Jane Austen who wrote a little production for her family called "Sir Charles Grandison or The happy Man." Emphasizing the story line, Austen pays especial attention to Charlotte's raillery, her reluctance to marry, and the particulars of Harriet's kidnapping. The Italian scenes are eliminated, and we learn through a letter that Clementina may be persuaded eventually to marry the Count of Belvedere. Austen's intent is to entertain and provide a vehicle for family talents; thus, while the piece is reminiscent of the original *Grandison*, the moral message is absent.[10]

Among the other literary figures of the nineteenth century who praised *Grandison* was George Eliot, who wrote after reading it, "I had no idea that Richardson was worth so much. . . ." In another letter she declares "I should be sorry to be the heathen that did not like that book." Macaulay ranked Richardson's novels next to Shakespeare's plays, while Ruskin placed Richardson's works high on his list and acknowledged their effect on him for good.[11]

Applause of Richardson was not confined to English audiences. Diderot's enthusiastic eulogy is often quoted. He vowed that if need or adversity ever forced him to dispose of his library, Richardson would be retained along with Moses, Homer, Euripides, and Sophocles. De Sade, Laclos, Balzac, and George Sand all paid tribute to Richardson. Dutch translations of both *Clarissa* and *Sir Charles Grandison* were undertaken by Johannes Stinstra, and in Germany Christian Gellert completed a most satisfactory edition of *Grandison*. Gellert was extremely enthusiastic about the novel, so much so, that he was unable to put the book down and one morning read it instead of his usual sermon by Tillotson. This would have pleased Richardson! Erasmus Reich, the Leipzig bookseller who arranged for the Gellert translation and also urged Richardson in 1757 to publish his letters, was quick to note the enthusiastic reception of *Grandison* by his countrymen.[12]

Grandison, indeed, created a sensation far and wide. Christoph Martin Wieland wrote a play on the subject of Clementina in 1760 and proposed a series of letters between Sir Charles and his ward, Emily Jervois. Goethe urged readers to be Sir Charles's "devoted slave." Nor was Richardson unknown in Russia. Pushkin's library contained all three novels, and in his poem *Eugene Onegin* we learn that Tatyana's mother had been a devoted reader of Richardson. In America, *Grandison* caught the attention of evangelists. Charles Grandison Finney (1792–1875), a prominent revivalist, was president of Oberlin College. Harriet Beecher Stowe (1811–96), who set her own version of the good man in the American South, declared that *Sir Charles Grandison* was the only novel that had a place beside the Bible on the "toilet-table of godly young women." Other admirers of Richardson included John Quincy Adams's mother and Benjamin Franklin, who borrowed some of the moral sentiments collected from *Clarissa* for *Poor Richard*. Van Wyck Brooks, in his study of the culture of New England, has observed that *Clarissa* was approved reading, and "Richardson's Grandison was their beau ideal. Many a girl said she would never marry until she found his like."[13]

From the very beginning, of course, *Grandison* had its share of unappreciative readers. When the prolixity of the novel was criticized, Richardson declared that this affected him "as the Stab did Julius Caesar from his beloved Brutus." Other targets included certain newly coined words, Sir Charles's religious compromise, his apparent lack of duty in not seeking his father's permission to marry, and, on the other hand, Grandison's inimitable perfection. We do not know what Henry Fielding thought of *Sir Charles Grandison*. He was sufficiently alarmed by what he considered dangerous tendencies in *Pamela* to write *Shamela*, but he had only praise for *Clarissa*. Mrs. Chapone suspected Fielding of being the author of one of two prominent pamphlets on *Grandison: Critical Remarks on Sir Charles Grandison, Clarissa and Pamela* (1754). The author of this pamphlet admits Richardson's "intention to promote and revive the declining causes of religion and virtue," then proceeds to score him for corrupting the language, for providing little in the way of "plot, fable, or action," and for a deficient presentation of moral example through the characters. He is even annoyed at the thought that *Grandison*'s publication might have discouraged other writers, "for who could be supposed to attend to any thing else, when the lovely Harriet Byron continued in suspence, when the fate of Lady Clementina was undetermined, when it was not yet settled whether she was to marry Grandison, retire to a Nunnery, or continue crack-brain'd all her lifetime. . . ."[14]

One other pamphlet, *A Candid Examination of the History of Sir Charles Grandison* (1754), is attributed to Francis Plumer and reiterates the usual criticism of *Grandison*. Its author complains that Richardson introduces "such whining and crying and kneeling, as is very absurd, and no where in practice. . . ." At the same time, he praises Richardson for his ability to move the passions and to draw vivid scenes, and he recommends Sir Charles for his piety. Interestingly enough, too, Plumer does not label Grandison a prig but acknowledges his lively and cheerful disposition, remarking that like any ordinary young man, he must struggle with "every turbulent Passion."[15]

A number of nineteenth-century writers took a dim view of Richardson, among them Samuel Coleridge. Coleridge, whose allegiance had shifted from Richardson to Fielding, attributed the characteristics of overheated rooms to Richardson's novels. In a similar vein, one may recall Lord Byron's delight in discovering that a Tunbridge grocer was using leaves from *Pamela* to wrap bacon and cheese, or the distaste with which Anthony Trollope's older brother recalled regular evening readings of *Grandison* insisted upon by his father.[16]

A more subtle, and perhaps more substantive, change in the appreciation of Richardson's work occurred in the French translation. Dismayed by the novelist Abbé Prévost's version of *Clarissa*, Richardson wrote to Alexis Claude Clairaut that "the Abbe has left out in his Translation of Clarissa, some of the most useful and pathetic Parts of the Piece." He complained to Lady Bradshaigh that Prévost had accused him of sacrificing "his story to moral instructions, warnings, &c.—the very motive with me, of the story's being written at all." For this reason, Richardson was reluctant to have Prévost translate *Grandison;* nevertheless his cut version was one of the two available in French. Richardson was dissatisfied with both.[17] *Grandison* also suffered drastic abbreviation in its many English abridgments, another indication of the shift in attention from moral purpose to the story. In American and British editions, Sir Charles remains the epitome of goodness, but a reduction in size from seven volumes to a single volume measuring less than three by five inches and a mere half-inch thick necessarily eliminates many of the moral nuances.[18]

With the exception of Margaret Doody's extended discussion, modern criticism has pretty well neglected *Grandison,* and what criticism there is generally slights the work. Ernest Baker, author of one of the standard histories of the novel, is exceptional. He considers the technique in *Grandison* to be Richardson at his best; "if the story lacks the sustained interest of *Clarissa,* it is full of lively episodes and moving situations." But most critics would not agree with Baker; "weak plot structure," "lack of real moral tension," "monotony of movement," and "relative clumsiness" are the usual failings attributed to *Grandison.* Jocelyn Harris ascribes the apparent deficiencies of the novel to its manner of composition and suggests that Richardson wrote and revised in response to attacks leveled at the various install-ments—too many cooks spoiled the broth. Mark Kinkead-Weekes argues that "the whole novel collapses into the mode of didacticism"; the work seems further weakened because we never explore the minds of Sir Charles and Clementina. Others regard the dilemmas of the characters as trifling and less than important. Even the sympathetic Alan Dugald McKillop suggests that matters of "social embar-rassment" have been substituted for weightier tragic elements. Finally, Jean Hagstrum identifies the familial and social situations in *Grandison* as harbingers of the social change Lawrence Stone has labeled "affective individualism."[19]

Other critics view Richardson as a forerunner of later novelists such as Jane Austen, Rousseau, and Henry James. They emphasize those aspects of Richardson's work which anticipate the characters, plots, and techniques that are more fully developed in these writers. Until recently, this approach recognized the seeds of genius in Richardson's writing but generally considered his efforts inferior to what followed. Jocelyn Harris seems more on target when she describes Austen's method of "complicating" the situations found in *Grandison,* of combining, expanding, and transforming the fertile possibilities in Richardson's last novel.[20]

While these critical appraisals are illuminating, they do not account for the reasons *Grandison* is not read with the same enthusiasm today as it was in Richardson's time; perhaps the story itself has ceased to cast the same spell as it did when it was written, while the predicaments faced by the characters may not be so compelling to the modern reader. In addition, the moral dimension proves a hindrance. Current discussion of *Grandison*, may well reflect twentieth-century views of man and human nature rather than Richardson's purpose and how he achieved it. Hester Mulso Chapone, one of Richardson's correspondents, commenting on Sir Charles's perfection, expressed a similar dilemma felt by eighteenth-century readers:

> I want to hear of his faults, of his weaknesses; for some he must have: and yet is it not owing to something very bad in human nature, that mankind in general are so curious after the spots of a beautiful character, and so desirous of bringing down to their own level a fellow creature that seems soaring into a higher species?[21]

McKillop's observation that the work of Samuel Richardson, "needs not so much rehabilitation or ardent defense as candid reëxamination" applies particularly to *Sir Charles Grandison*. This study attempts such a reexamination. As John Carroll suggests, neglected areas such as humor, style, and literary allusions must be examined. Perhaps even more importantly, Richardson's repeated asseverations in his correspondence and the themes of his earlier works must also be taken more seriously, for they provide clues to his purpose in writing. His biography furnishes other insights into *Grandison*. As Thomas Edwards once wrote to Richardson, "You seem designed by Providence to be a Teacher of Mankind both by precept and example, and your patient behavior under such a load of various afflictions is no less edifying to those who have the honor of knowing you, than the morality of your writings. . . ." As a complement to studying Richardson's works, his correspondence, and his life, the characteristics of conduct literature must be recalled; it is a rich source for appreciating the format, content, and techniques employed by Richardson. And it is a tradition with which his audience was very familiar. *Sir Charles Grandison* must be placed in the context of a period that had inherited a literary tradition that gave "rise" not only to the novel but to many kinds of fiction and prose. Criminal biographies, travel narratives, scandal chronicles, and the erotic-pathetic novel took their places alongside translations and imitations of continental popular fiction, redactions of Elizabethan romances, collected sermons, reprinted conduct books, and periodical literature. At a time when more middle-class women had leisure to devote to reading, circulating libraries, begun after 1740, had extended the reading public. Richardson told Lady Brandshaigh that sales of *Grandison* were proceeding well, and that "it has been borrowed and hired by Multitudes."[22]

As we examine later in greater detail the wide range of topics treated in *Sir Charles Grandison*, it will be apparent that a significant reason for Richardson's appeal to his contemporaries was that he was in tune with his times. While no Gallup poll exists to ascertain the precise composition of Richardson's audience, we know that individual readers included Lord Chesterfield and Lady Bradshaigh, Richardson's own friends of the middle rank, BF the prison inmate, and undoubtedly real-life sisters of Pamela as well. In an age of self-improvement, there was something for everyone in *Grandison.* Richardson draws good servants temporarily corrupted by bad masters. He depicts soldiers, clergy, tutors, baronets, and all the members of a family. Merchants and new groups of landed gentry were acquiring not only wealth but respectability; refinement in matters of propriety and practical affairs had become a necessity, and a book like *Sir Charles Grandison* satisfied that need in an entertaining manner.[23]

One of the more prominent subjects treated in *Grandison* is that of courtship. Lawrence Stone's monumental *Family, Sex and Marriage* has studied the greater latitude of personal choice and privacy, particularly with regard to marriage partners, in our period. *Grandison* furnishes many case studies of the very dilemmas posed by such freedom: male and female characters of various ranks in society whose choices range from the strongly circumscribed to complete independence. Practical questions of how a courtship is to be conducted between people of different ranks, how forward to be, and how relatives may be involved all add to the complexity and completeness of Richardson's last work.

While political matters remain in the background, the issue of religion looms large, particularly marriage between a Catholic and an Anglican. The riots of 1714, 1745, and the Gordon Riots of 1780, which followed the repeal of some of the test acts against Catholics, demonstrated that beneath the surface of tolerance there was always a wave of sentiment ready to enforce the laws that had long been ignored by most citizens. Richardson, in a measured and balanced manner evident throughout *Grandison,* brings the issue out in the open.[24]

To understand *Grandison,* then, we must not only appreciate the literary conventions common to the period, but also imbibe the spirit of the times. Only thus will we be able to capture that enthusiasm for his work that caused Richardson's novel to be preempted by an imitation, *Memoirs of Sir Charles Goodville* (1753), or that sense for a best seller that prompted Richardson's own workmen to betray him and pirate the last sections of *Grandison* to Ireland. Why did Lady Bradshaigh and her husband nearly neglect their houseguests while reading *Grandison?* What was it that prompted the prisoner BF to reform his ways? Kinkead-Weekes has described *Sir Charles Grandison* as an "oddity"; if *Grandison* is read as a conventional novel, this label is probably accurate. If read with a different set of spectacles as a conduct book, we may well have before us the finest example of its kind.[25]

NOTES

1. Samuel Richardson to Lady Bradshaigh, 9 July 1754, Forster Collection XI, f. 112. Hereafter the letters "FC" designate the Forster Collection of the Victoria and Albert Museum. BF to Richardson, 2 May 1754, FC XV, 3, ff. 41–41v; Lady Bradshaigh to Richardson, 6 August 1754; FC XI, f. misnumbered 115.

2. Monographs devoted to *Clarissa* flourish: Terry Castle, *Clarissa's Ciphers* (Ithaca: Cornell University Press, 1982); Terry Eagleton, *The Rape of Clarissa* (Oxford: Basil Blackwell, 1982); Carol Houlihan Flynn, *Samuel Richardson: A Man of Letters* (Princeton: Princeton University Press, 1982); Christina Marsden Gillis, *The Paradox of Privacy: Epistolary Form in Clarissa* (Gainesville: University of Florida, 1984); William Beatty Warner, *Reading Clarissa* (New Haven: Yale University Press, 1979). For Johnson's insight see James Boswell, *Life of Johnson*, ed. R. W. Chapman, corrected J. D. Fleeman (London: Oxford University Press paperback, 1970), p. 480. For Mrs. Barbauld's clue, see Samuel Richardson, *The Correspondence of Samuel Richardson*, ed. Anna Laetitia Barbauld, 6 vols. (1804; reprint, New York: AMS Press, Inc., 1966), 1:xx. Hereafter *Correspondence* designates Mrs. Barbauld's edition.

3. Alan Dugald McKillop, *Samuel Richardson* (Chapel Hill: University of North Carolina Press, 1936), 206 and 234; George Sherburn, "Samuel Richardson's Novels and the Theatre: A Theory Sketched," *Philological Quarterly* 41 (January 1962): 325–26; Katherine Hornbeak, "Richardson's *Aesop*," *Smith College Studies in Modern Languages* 19 (January 1938): 30–50; Katherine Hornbeak, "Richardson's *Familiar Letters* and the Domestic Conduct Books," ibid., 1–29; Jocelyn M. Harris, "*Sir Charles Grandison* and the Little Senate: The relation between Samuel Richardson's correspondence and his last novel" (Ph.D. diss., University of London, 1968), Appendix C, 431–36; Samuel Richardson, *The History of Sir Charles Grandison*, ed. Jocelyn Harris, 3 vols. (London: Oxford University Press, 1972), 1:xviii–xxi. Hereafter the letters "SCG" designate the Harris edition. Margaret Anne Doody, *A Natural Passion* (Oxford: Clarendon Press, 1974), 246–52; Phyllis Patricia Smith, "The Eighteenth-Century Gentleman: Contributing Theories and Their Realization in Sir Charles Grandison" (Ph.D. diss., Radcliffe, 1947); Richardson to Lady Bradshaigh, 15 December 1748, *Correspondence*, 4:237–38; SCG 1:4.

4. Mrs. Scudamore to Richardson, 12 March 1758, *Correspondence*, 3:331; Sarah Chapone to Richardson, 23 April 1751, FC XII, 2, f. 3; Sarah Chapone to Richardson, 12 October 1750, FC XII, 2, f. 4; Lady Bradshaigh to Richardson [early November 1749?], *Correspondence*, 4:264. Doubtful dates follow T. C. Duncan Eaves and Ben D. Kimpel, *Samuel Richardson* (Oxford: Clarendon Press, 1971), Appendix, "Richardson's Correspondence," 620–704.

5. *Correspondence*, 1:ccix; Lady Echlin to Richardson, 23 February 1754, *Correspondence*, 5:3.

6. Thomas Edwards to Richardson, 15 January 1755, *Correspondence*, 3:111–12; Thomas Edwards to Richardson, 28 January 1754, FC XII, 1, f. 88v; Thomas Newcomb to Richardson [late October 1754], FC XV, 4, f. 39.

7. "Mr. Leake to Mr. R. Lord Chesterfield's pleasure on Receiving Grandison," FC XV, 3, f. 1; Chesterfield's remarks are quoted in McKillop, *Richardson*, 219–20.

8. Thomas Edwards to Richardson, 1 March 1754, FC XII, 1, f. 95v; Richardson to Thomas Edwards, 7 March 1754, FC XII, 1, f. 75; Anna Williams, *Verses Addressed to Mr. Richardson, on his History of Sir Charles Grandison* (London: n.p., 1753); Thomas Edwards's poem faces the title page of Richardson's *The History of Sir Charles Grandison*, 2d ed., 6 vols. (London: S. Richardson, 1754); William Cowper, "An Ode on Reading Mr. Richardson's 'History of Sir Charles Grandison,' " FC XVI, 2, f. 14; TRG, "An Ode to Mr. S. Richardson. Occasioned by his history of Sr. Charles Grandison." 23 August 1754, FC XV, 4, ff. 35–36; Colley Cibber to Richardson, 19 November 1753, *Correspondence*, 2:177; Lady Bradshaigh to Richardson, 29 March 1751, *Correspondence*, 6:93–94.

9. Smollett quoted in McKillop, *Richardson*, 181; Frederic T. Blanchard, *Fielding the Novelist* (New Haven: Yale University Press, 1927), 557 and 113.

10. James Edward Austen-Leigh, *Memoir of Jane Austen*, ed. R. W. Chapman (Oxford: Clarendon Press, 1951), 89; Jane Austen to Cassandra Austen, 14 September [1804], Jane Austen, *Jane Austen Letters 1796–1817*, ed. R. W. Chapman (London: Oxford University Press, 1955), 57; Jane Austen to Cassandra Austen, 15 September [1813] and 11 October 1813, Jane Austen, *Jane Austen's Letters to her sister Cassandra and others*, ed. R. W. Chapman, 2 vols. (Oxford: Clarendon Press, 1933), 2:322 and 344; Jane Austen, *Northanger Abbey*, vol. 5 of *The Novels of Jane Austen*, 3d ed. (London: Oxford University Press, 1933), 30, 41–42; Lady Bradshaigh to Richardson, 20 November 1753 in 27 November 1753 begun 28 October 1753, FC XI, f. 48; Jane Austen, *Jane Austen's 'Sir Charles Grandison,'* ed. B. C. Southam (Oxford: Clarendon Press, 1980).

11. George Eliot to Sara Sophia Hennell, 13 October [1847], George Eliot, *The George Eliot Letters*, ed. Gordon S. Haight, 9 vols. (New Haven: Yale University Press, 1954–78), 1:240; George Eliot to Bessie Rayner Parkes, 30 October 1852, *Eliot Letters*, ed. Haight, 2:65; Blanchard, *Fielding*, 389 and 385–86.

12. Blanchard, *Fielding*, 154; Clara Linklater Thomson, *Samuel Richardson* (London: Horace Marshall & Son, 1900), 272; John Carroll, ed., *Samuel Richardson* (Englewood Cliffs: Prentice-Hall, 1969), Introduction, 9; Christian F. Gellert to Count Hans Moritz de Buhl of Martinskinker, 3 April 1755, Yale Speck Collection G24b.B755.4:3, typescript translation of German original; Eaves and Kimpel, *Richardson*, 415; Samuel Richardson, *Selected Letters of Samuel Richardson*, ed. John Carroll (Oxford: Clarendon Press, 1964), 3. Hereafter *Selected Letters* designates Carroll's edition, which is frequently cited in this study because of its availability. Erasmus Reich to Richardson, 10 May 1754, *Correspondence*, 5:297–98.

13. Thomson, *Richardson*, 287; Blanchard, *Fielding*, 113; Alexander Pushkin, *The Letters of Alexander Pushkin*, trans. J. Thomas Shaw, 3 vols. in 1 (Madison: University of Wisconsin Press, 1967), 274, n. 11; Alexander Pushkin, *Eugene Onegin*, trans. Walter Arndt (New York: E. P. Dutton & Co., Inc. paperback, 1963), st. 2, l. 29, p. 51; other references to Grandison in the poem: st. 2, l. 30, p. 51; st. 3, l. 9; st. 3, l. 10, p. 65; Blanchard, *Fielding*, 267 and 259 n.76; Eaves and Kimpel, *Richardson*, 420; Van Wyck Brooks, *The Flowering of New England 1815–1865* (New York: E. P. Dutton and Co., Inc., 1936), 56–57.

14. Richardson to Lady Bradshaigh, 9 November 1756, FC XI, f. 197; Eaves and Kimpel, *Richardson*, 127–32, 294–95, and 409; [Alexander Campbell?], *Critical Remarks on Sir Charles Grandison, Clarissa and Pamela* (London: J. Dowse, 1754), 3, 12, 11, 17, and 6.

15. [Francis Plumer?], *A Candid Examination of the History of Sir Charles Grandison* (London: Dodsley, 1754), 11 and 22.

16. Mark Kinkead-Weekes, *Samuel Richardson, Dramatic Novelist* (London: Methuen and Co. Ltd., 1973), 423; Frank Kermode, "Richardson and Fielding," in *Essays on the Eighteenth-Century Novel,* ed. Robert Donald Spector (Bloomington: Indiana University Press, 1965), 67; Diary of Lord Byron, 4 January 1821, in *The Poetical Works, Letters and Journals, of Lord Byron: with Notices of His Life,* ed. Thomas Moore (London: n.p., 1844), British Library press mark C.44.g, 41:395–96; Thomas Adolphus Trollope, *What I Remember* (New York: Harper & Brothers, 1888), 42 and 155.

17. Richardson to Alexis Claude Clairaut, 5 July 1753, in *Byron,* ed. Moore, facing p. 396, sheet #68; Richardson to Lady Bradshaigh, 24 February 1753, *Correspondence,* 6:244–45; Eaves and Kimpel, *Richardson,* 415–16; Clairaut apparently liked one of the translated volumes he had read, Richardson to Alexis Claude Clairaut, 12 September 1755, Liverpool Public Library; Frank Howard Wilcox, "Prévost's Translations of Richardson's Novels," *University of California Publications in Modern Philology* 12 (11 January 1927):341–411.

18. Some abridgments are Samuel Richardson, *The History of Sir Charles Grandison, Abridged from the Works of Samuel Richardson, Esq; Author of Pamela and Clarissa* (London: F. Newbery, n.d.); Samuel Richardson, *The History of Sir Charles Grandison, Abridged* (Boston: Samuel Hall, 1794); Samuel Richardson, *The History of Sir Charles Grandison, Abridged* (Philadelphia: Mathew Carey, 1794); Samuel Richardson, *The History of Sir Charles Grandison,* ed. Mary Howitt (London: George Routledge and Sons, [1873?]).

19. Ernest A. Baker, *Intellectual Realism: from Richardson to Sterne,* vol. 4 of *The History of the English Novel* (London: H. F. and G. Witherby, 1930), 56; Elizabeth Bergen Brophy, *Samuel Richardson, The Triumph of Craft* (Knoxville: University of Tennessee Press, 1974), 88, 72; John Samuel Bullen, *Time and Space in the Novels of Samuel Richardson* (Logan: Utah State University Press, 1965), 24; Cynthia Griffin Wolff, *Samuel Richardson and the Eighteenth-Century Puritan Character* (Hamden, Conn.: Archon Books, 1972), 3; Harris, "*Grandison* and the Little Senate," 6–7; Kinkead-Weekes, *Richardson,* 367; McKillop;, *Richardson,* 213; Jean Hagstrum, *Sex and Sensibility* (Chicago: University of Chicago Press, 1980), 214–18.

20. Noel David Berggren, "Grandisonian Depths: A Study of Richardson's Last Novel" (Ph.D. diss., Yale, 1968); McKillop, *Richardson,* 251, 263–64, and 278; Eaves and Kimpel, *Richardson,* 605–6; Jocelyn Harris, "Pride, Prejudice, and 'Grandison'" (Paper delivered at the American Society for Eighteenth-Century Studies Meeting, Washington, D.C., 10 April 1981); Jocelyn Harris, "'As if they had been living friends': *Sir Charles Grandison* into *Mansfield Park,*" *Bulletin of Research in the Humanities* 83 (Autumn 1980): 360–405.

21. Hester Mulso Chapone to Susanna Highmore, 20 July 1751, *Correspondence,* 2:267.

22. McKillop, *Richardson,* vii; Carroll, ed., *Richardson,* Introduction, 19; Thomas Edwards to Richardson, 18 June 1755, FC XII, 1, f. 142; John J. Richetti, *Popular Fiction Before Richardson* (Oxford: Clarendon Press, 1969), 2; Kinkead-Weekes, *Richardson,* 3; Baker, *The Novel of Sentiment and the Gothic Romance,* vol. 5 of *History,* 16; Ian Watt, *The Rise of the Novel* (Berkeley: University of California Press paperback, 1971), 42–43; Richardson to Lady Bradshaigh, 8 April 1754, *Selected Letters,* 301; Lady Bradshaigh to Richardson, 21 May 1754, FC XI, f. 100.

23. Helen Sard Hughes "The Middle-Class Reader and the English Novel," *Journal of English and Germanic Philology* 25 (1926): 362–78; Watt, *Rise,* chap. 2; J. H. Plumb, *England in the Eighteenth Century* (Harmondsworth, Middlesex, England: Penguin Books Ltd., 1980), chaps. 1–3; Boris Ford, ed., *From Dryden to Johnson,* vol. 4 of the *New Pelican Guide to English Literature* (Harmondsworth, Middlesex, England: Penguin Books Ltd. 1982), pt. 1; Roy Porter, *English Society in the Eighteenth Century* (Harmondsworth, Middlesex, England: Penguin Books Ltd., 1982); Lawrence Stone, *The Family, Sex and Marriage* (New York: Harper & Row, Publishers, 1977), 394–95; Jan Fergus, "The Clay Circulating Libraries," (Paper delivered at the New York Eighteenth-Century Seminar Meeting, New York City, 22 March

1984) has begun to assemble information that should add to our knowledge of the eighteenth-century reading audience.

24. [Daniel Defoe], *A Tour Through the Whole Island of Great Britain*, 7th ed., 4 vols. (London: J. & F. Rivington, 1769), 1:287, comments on a community of Benedictines who live undisturbed near Winchester, and the foreign visitor, Monsieur César de Saussure, *A Foreign View of England in the Reigns of George I. & George II.*, trans. Madame Van Muyden (New York: E.P. Dutton and Company, 1902), 327–28, observes the same tolerance with regard to Sunday worship in London.

25. Eaves and Kimpel, *Richardson*, 375–83; Richardson to Elizabeth Carter, 2 October 1753, Berg Collection, New York Public Library; Lady Bradshaigh to Richardson, 28 October in 27 November 1753, FC XI, f. 43; Kinkead-Weekes, *Richardson*, 280 and 391.

2

OLD SPECIES OF WRITING

IF *Sir Charles Grandison* is a response to a social context, it reflects the forms and themes of a literary context as well. We shall glance briefly at this context before examining the conduct-book tradition, the most significant source for Richardson's last work. While Richardson lacked a formal classical education, he nevertheless printed and probably proofread a large number of learned works, from Elizabeth Carter's translation of Epictetus to James Thomson's *Seasons* and Edward Young's *Night Thoughts, Centaur Not Fabulous,* and *Conjectures on Original Composition.* Richardson's printing activities as well as the circle of his acquaintance, which included such figures as Aaron Hill, Thomas Edwards, and Dr. Johnson, suggest that traditional themes and literary concerns were very much a part of his milieu. Moreover, it requires little stretch of the imagination to see that traditional themes and forms are reflected in all that he wrote. Though there is no proof that Richardson ever read Ben Jonson's *To Penshurst* or Andrew Marvell's *Upon Appleton House,* for example, these country-house poems capture a spirit that can be found in *Grandison.* The same may be said for the complimentary verse epistle. Like Pope's Man of Ross, Sir Charles provides dowries that enable less fortunate women to marry respectably and creditably. With a dowry, Miss Awberry can wed the reformed footman William Wilson, who now will have sufficient means to join his sister's business. Sir Charles presents a generous portion to the misled Miss Obrien, and "if she made a good wife, would be further kind to her." He urges Mrs. Giffard, his uncle's former mistress, to bestow part of her annuity "upon young creatures of your sex, as an encouragement to them to preserve that chastity, which you, with your eyes open, gave up." Grandison also intends to use part of the Danby legacy for "little fortunes" to help girls who were marrying "honest men of their own degree."[1]

The well-run household and the kind of estate depicted in *To*

Penshurst are important in *Grandison*, too. Harriet has learned her lessons well from Grandmother Shirley at Shirley Manor, and while living at Selby House, she assumes direction of domestic duties gracefully and efficiently. Sir Charles is skilled in estate management, and Grandison Hall is a model of taste and orderliness. His servants are loyal and trustworthy. Harriet remarks, "Don't you see, by the silent veneration and assiduities of the servants of Sir Charles Grandison, how much they adore their master?" Reminiscent of Pope's *Epistle to Burlington* is Harriet's description of Sir Charles:

> He has a great taste, the doctor tells us, yet not an expensive one; for he studies situation and convenience; and pretends not to level hills, or to force and distort nature; but to help it, as he finds it, without letting art be seen in his works, where he can possibly avoid it. For he says, He would rather let a stranger be pleased with what he sees, as if it were *always* so; than to obtain comparative praise by informing him what it was in its former situation.

As in Marvell's *Upon Appleton House*, the genteel past of Grandison Hall and the Grandisons is apparent to Harriet as she muses on the family portraits in the long gallery.[2]

But *Sir Charles Grandison* is more than a prose version of the country-house poem, epistle dedicatory, or verse epistle, all of which complimented good men. As an epistolary work, *Grandison* capitalizes on the rage for letter fiction. It might be said that the eighteenth century was an age of the letter, as well as of the diary and journal. One has only to think of Pepys and Evelyn early in the period and Chesterfield and Lady Mary Wortley Montagu later; Richardson himself published a letter-writing manual early in his career. The cultivation of personal letter writing was accompanied by a great vogue for epistolary fiction. From the beginning of the seventeenth century until the second half of the eighteenth, French salon romances in translation used letters either as a format or as a means of advancing the plot. Letters were lost and found, forged, misdirected; they both incriminated and absolved.[3]

But while *Grandison* is written in the epistolary manner, and letters cause some turn in the action, their importance in this respect is minimal: they do not lead to intrigue. Charlotte tempts Harriet with a letter she has discovered from her brother to Dr. Bartlett. This, however, is as far as it goes. Harriet resists, as does Sir Charles when he finds one of Harriet's letters in the garden—quite different from the conventional behavior in epistolary fiction! Interestingly enough, in a novel in which several love affairs are developed, there is little correspondence between the lovers themselves. We never see the letters exchanged between Charlotte and Captain Anderson, who has employed the services of a surrogate letter writer. Nor do we see the incriminating letter actually written by Anderson, which reveals his illiteracy and convinces Charlotte that the relationship should be broken. Eventually, Sir Charles must bargain for the written promise Charlotte has made to Anderson and wishes to retract, just as he had to negotiate for his dead father's incriminating letters to the Obrien family. Nor does the correspondence help us discover the inner workings of Clementina or Grandison in the same way that we are able to understand Clarissa or Harriet. Richardson was accustomed to the epistolary form, but the public nature of the letters and the atmosphere of debate in *Grandison* distinguish it from the introspective *Clarissa*.

The relationship between *Sir Charles Grandison* and the drama has been noted as frequently as its connection with the epistolary form. It is perhaps suggestive that *Sir Charles Grandison* was written when there was a lag in dramatic writing, partially caused by the Licensing Act of 1737. One finds a list of dramatis personae at the beginning of the work as well as frequent lapses into dramatic dialogue. Harriet writes: "By the way Lucy, you are fond of plays; and it is come into my head, that, to avoid all *says-I's* and *says-she's*, I will henceforth, in all dialogues, write names in the margin. . . ." Frequently the narrative, in parentheses or in the comment of a character, will provide what might be considered a stage direction: "Disgrace, Sir, was your portion, Sir (half out of breath)—What would you, Sir?—Why this visit? What am I to do?"[4]

Furthermore, the characters in *Sir Charles Grandison* have much in common with earlier dramatic works. The sentimental drama, for example, is an obvious legacy. Capitalizing on the tide of opinion against such plays as William Wycherley's *The Country Wife* (1675) and George Etherege's *The Man of Mode* (1676), Colley Cibber's *Love's Last Shift* (1696) signaled a change in emphasis. Rather than laughing at men's vices, the audience would be moved to tears by natural goodness or goodness newly acquired through reformation. John Harrington Smith identifies those plays which follow the sentimental lead of Cibber as "exemplary" drama: "the use of characters as examples for conveying edification." Richard Steele's *The Conscious Lovers* (1722), with its exemplary hero young Bevil, was written "To Chasten Wit, and Moralize the Stage"; Steele declares "that the whole was writ for the sake of the Scene of the Fourth Act, wherein Mr. *Bevill* evades the Quarrel [duel] with his Friend." Fielding's *The Temple Beau* (1730) repeats the situation when Vermoil checks Valentine's impulse to fight a duel. Richardson's model hero, too, is confronted with challenges from Sir Hargrave, the General, and the Count of Belvedere, all of which he refuses for reasons of principle. And *Sir Charles Grandison* does not lack for characters who are reformed.[5]

Ernest Bernbaum has identified other character types that were repeated many times over in the sentimental comedy of 1696–1704. They appear with variations in *Grandison*. "The sorely-tried but loyal wife" can be seen in Sir Charles's mother, while "the maiden faithful to her absent lover" is illustrated in an extended way in Harriet, Clementina, and Caroline Grandison. Mrs. Oldham is another version of "the pitiable forsaken mistress finally restored to respect," and "the repentant young prodigal" is seen in Jeronymo and, in a modified form, in Everard Grandison and Sir Hargrave's friends. Grandison and his friend Beauchamp are good examples of "the nobly generous friend"; Lord W. is a variation of "the wayward but reclaimable husband," since he is reclaimed before his marriage.[6]

Ira Konigsberg, in his analysis of dramatic influence on the novels of Richardson, notes that there are no literary sources for either the Sir Charles Grandison and Harriet plot or the Sir Charles and Clementina story, although he suggests a connection between the madness of Shakespeare's Ophelia and Clementina. He, too, finds parallels between individual characters in the earlier drama and in *Grandison*. The progenitors of the pedant Walden can be found in Richard Steele's Cimberton in *The Conscious Lovers* (1722) and in the Reverend James Miller's Haughty in *The Humours of Oxford* (1730). The pretty but proud Miss Cantillon is traced to Narcissa in Colley Cibber's *Love's Last Shift* (1696) and Lady Fancyfull in Vanbrugh's *The Provok'd Wife* (1697). Sir Hargrave follows in the footsteps of his rakish forebears and the comic fops from the restoration stage. Konigsberg finds Charlotte, as most critics do, a very intriguing character, but Harriet is rather unfairly described as an "indistinct" dramatic heroine and "little more than a love-sick female waiting to be claimed by her hero." This assessment ignores her sense of humor as well as her verbal and social adeptness.[7]

The Italian section of the novel, woven together with injunctions from the dead in two grandfathers' wills, lengthy debates among the powerful members of an old family, suicide and madness, a confidante who spirits messages hither and yon, and eavesdroppers behind every wall, contains the outlines of Jacobean revenge tragedy. But still another dramatic influence that has not been suggested is that of the heroic drama, the drama in which heroes and heroines are torn by seemingly irreconcilable choices. Dryden's *All for Love* (1678) evinces the violence and inflated rhetoric that are hallmarks of these plays.

Otway's *Venice Preserved* (1682) and *The Orphan* (1680) portray characters who experience divided loyalties. Fielding poked fun at the excesses of this kind of drama in *Tom Thumb* (1730). Even Lady Bradshaigh worried that Richardson had an inordinate penchant for scenes of death and distress. With teasing exasperation she wrote, "In short, -I think- you had better kill them *all.* and (like Tom Thumb the great.) make it the most 'Tragical Tragedy, that ever was Tragedized.'"[8]

In fact, Richardson suggests the dilemmas of heroic drama in a much milder form in *Grandison*. Clementina is torn between her love for, or gratitude to, Grandison and her religion and country. Sir Charles balances between a moral conviction that he must marry Clementina and his ties to Protestantism, England, and ultimately Harriet: "But, O my Religion and my Country! I cannot, cannot renounce you! What can this short life give, what can it promise, to warrant such a sacrifice!" Harriet must determine between a potentially unrequited love and the proposals of extremely eligible suitors; she also expresses reservations about Grandison's "divided heart." Charlotte must choose between her knowledge of the kind of man she should marry, bearing in mind her rank and fortune, and the importunities of Captain Anderson. Later, her sense of honor prohibits her from breaking her word to him. As Grandison avers to Anderson: "My sister is a woman of honour. She thinks herself bound by it; and she is content to lead a single life to the end of it, if you will not acquit her of this promise." Even the agreeable Lady L. finds it difficult to acquiesce in the demands of an unreasonable father while being addressed by the unexceptionable Lord L. But none of these situations is insoluble; they do not result in violence, suicide, or murder. Clementina's cousin, Laurana, commits suicide for reasons of jealousy and not because she cannot choose between two impossible alternatives. Grandison, Harriet, Charlotte, and all the others are extricated from the horns of their dilemmas. And while Clementina's scruples are not entirely resolved, we see her at least in a state of sane abeyance.[9]

But literary detective work to establish indebtedness for dramatic plots, characters, themes, or format does not completely explain the uniqueness of *Sir Charles Grandison*. Nor does it entirely account for Richardson's motive for structuring and writing *Grandison* as he did. Fiction in Richardson's time had not solidified into a particular form in accordance with absolute rules. Thus, while we might lump Defoe, Fielding, and Richardson together as novelists, we must also grant that Defoe's work is akin to the spiritual autobiography, and Fielding's origins lie in the epic and romance tradition. Richardson and

Fielding both regarded themselves as innovators of a "new species of writing."[10]

Just what was this "new species of writing," and from what sources did it spring? Many attempts were made to define and evaluate the precise nature of the new forms. As early as 1691 William Congreve in his preface to *Incognita* tried to differentiate the romance from the embryonic novel:

> Romances are generally composed of the Constant Loves and invincible Courages of Hero's, Heroins, Kings and Queens, Mortals of the first Rank, and so forth; where lofty Language, miraculous Contingencies and impossible Performances, elevate and surprize the Reader into a giddy Delight which leaves him flat upon the Ground. . . . Novels are of a more familiar nature; Come near us, and represent to us Intrigues in practice, delight us with Accidents and odd Events, but not such as are wholly unusual or unpresidented, such which not being so distant from our Belief bring also the pleasure nearer us. Romances give more of Wonder, Novels more Delight.

Dr. Johnson, writing many years after Congreve, also distinguishes between the two forms, the romance defined as "A military fable of the middle ages; a tale of wild adventures in war and love," and the novel as "A small tale, generally of love." French heroic romances of the seventeenth century by such writers as La Calprènede and de Scudéry were based on the medieval forms. They were available to English readers well into the eighteenth century, and their improbability was often criticized. Richardson's Pamela declares,

> for either they dealt so much in the *marvellous* and *improbable*, or were so unnaturally *inflaming* to the *passions*, and so full of *love* and *intrigue*, that most of them seemed calculated to *fire* the *imagination* rather than to *inform* the *judgment*. . . . And what is the instruction that can be gathered from such pieces, for the conduct of common life?

In like manner, Hester Mulso Chapone chastises Elizabeth Carter for reading romances, saying that they are

> the worst of all the species of writing: unnatural representations of the passions, false sentiments, false precepts, false wit, false honour, and false modesty, with a strange heap of improbable, unnatural incidents mixed up with true history, and fastened upon some of the great names of antiquity, . . . at least of such as I have read, which have been mostly French ones.[11]

The novel, too, conveyed a slight taint of the disreputable. Some women writers were reluctant to be known as novelists. Richardson corresponded with a number of ladies wary of the propriety of such a calling. Anna Meades did not want the notoriety accorded a female novelist, nor did Mrs. Sarah Chapone: "A Female Author is so rare a Character." And Lady Barbara Montagu, the liaison between Richardson and her anonymous friend who was publishing a collection of stories by reformed prostitutes, asked not to be mentioned "in regard to the Novel, for by giving less assistance than this upon a like occasion I had it attributed to myself." The novel as a form was treated with reservation by other writers. Fanny Burney's preface to *Evelina* admits that young ladies might profit by the "annihilation" of novels; but "since the distemper they have spread seems incurable . . . surely all attempts to contribute to the number of those which may be read, if not with advantage, at least without injury, ought rather to be encouraged than contemned."[12]

The merits of popular fiction to excite attention were not lost on Richardson. *Grandison* begins *in medias res:* Harriet has just gone off to London, and her suitors are in suspense. Her abduction by Sir Hargrave, imprisonment by a widow with two daughters, and Sir Hargrave's attempts to force marriage on Harriet are details worthy of a romance. Following her rescue, Harriet is left to the care of Grandison's sister at Lord and Lady L.'s "castle" in Colnebrook. Later, Sir Charles playfully remarks, "Do you know, Mrs. Reeves, that I have found my third sister? Was she not stolen from us in her cradle?" Harriet recollects some of her dreams since the kidnapping:

> But when fancy is more propitious to me, then comes my rescuer, my deliverer: And he is sometimes a mighty prince (dreams then make me a perfect romancer) and I am a damsel in distress. The milk-white palfrey once came in. All the Marvelous takes place; and lions and tygers are slain, and armies routed, by the puissance of his single arm.

The tone of this comment suggests that Richardson may have used the romance merely to initiate the reader into the story, possibly even to poke fun at the romance conventions, since once the abduction and rescue are sorted out, different generic expectations predominate. As Clara Reeve, author of *The Progress of Romance,* observed: "The business of Romance is, first to excite the attention; and secondly, to direct it to some useful, or at least innocent, end. Happy the writer who attains both these points, like Richardson!"[13]

If *Grandison* is not entirely indebted to the romance, neither is its hero entirely conventional. Richardson once observed of the *Iliad:*

> I am afraid this poem, noble as it truly is, has done infinite mischief for a series of ages; since to it, and its copy the Eneid, is owing, in a great

measure, the savage spirit that has actuated, from the earliest ages to this time, the fighting fellows, that, worse than lions or tigers, have ravaged the earth, and made it a field of blood.

His intention seems to have been one of offsetting this spirit by creating a hero who bears a closer resemblance to Richard Steele's ideal as described in *The Christian Hero* (1701). Steele, arguing that Christianity surpasses pagan philosophy as a guide to right conduct, demonstrates the ineffectuality of pagan morality in the lives of Cato, Caesar, and Brutus. Their lives are contrasted with the heroic elements in Christ's life and the true gallantry of the early Christians, particularly of St. Paul. Steele writes,

> when you've said a Man's Meek and Humble, you've acquainted us, that such a Person has arrived at the hardest Task in the World in an universal Observation round him, to be quick to see his own Faults and other Mens Virtues, and at the height of Pardoning every Man sooner than himself.

Grandison's encounter with the volatile Major O-Hara and Captain Salmonet, followed by his repeated avowals of dissatisfaction with his momentary lapse in self-control in the presence of those two, echoes Steele:

> You cannot imagine, my dear Dr. Bartlett, how much this idle affair has disturbed me: I cannot forgive myself—To suffer myself to be provoked by two such men, to violate the sanction of my own house!

Steele urges "extensive Magnanimity" to enemies as well as friends. Here one recalls Sir Hargrave's henchmen, who are incredulous when they hear Grandison's position against dueling. Mr. Jordan remarks, "I never saw an hero till now." But the Christian Hero, Steele writes, is faced not only with enemies, but also with circumstances beyond his control:

> For, since Accidents are not in our Power, but will (in spite of all our Care and Vigilance) befall us; what remains, but that we accommodate our selves so far, as to bear 'em with the greatest Decency and handsomest Patience we are able?

Grandison frequently expresses such sentiments. In his attempts to do right or simply to offer no grounds for censure, he has entangled himself in a delicate and complicated relationship with the Porretta family. The reader could draw further parallels between Steele's ideal and Grandison, but it is sufficient to say that both writers were proposing a new and exceptional model for a generation of readers different from those of the Restoration period.[14]

This new audience was also absorbed in the periodical essay, especially the *Spectator.* Grandmother Shirley observes, "The reading in fashion when I was young, was Romances. You, my children, have, in that respect, fallen into happier days. The present age is greatly obliged to the authors of the Spectators." Periodical readers who read about Amanda's plight in *Spectator* 375 would not have been surprised by *Pamela.* Such instructive fictional episodes accompanied general discussions of matters of conduct. The evils of dueling, the dangers of the masquerade, the absurdity of hoops and patches, and the problems of pin money were debated, as well as topics traditionally included in courtesy and conduct literature, such as education for women and the management of servants. As Joseph Collet in remote Sumatra wrote to the *Spectator:*

> The Bible has the first place in our Study as teaching me the whole compass of my Duty to God and Man; Mr. Lock who first taught me to distinguish between Words and things has the next place; Mr. Steele who had taught me a more easy and agreeable manner of practising Vertue it self, precedes all Others.[15]

The themes, the gallery of characters, and the conduct of various callings of society in periodical literature all find a place in *Grandison;* indeed, the author wrote to Aaron Hill that

> The Spectators did some Good, as to prescribing to the Tastes of -these- + that + Many—But that Work has been published some time: And a Son of Thunder is wanted to rouse the Public out of -their- its Stupidity, and tell -them- it what -they- it should, and what -they- it should not, approve of.

Following in the tradition of the *Spectator, Grandison* was commended for being "a living system of manners," "yᵉ most complete System of life & manners & yᵉ best calculated for yᵉ amendment of head & heart, that ever has been exhibited in Prophane writing. . . ." One writer claimed that *Grandison* might "supply the place of a Tutor, and boarding school: Young persons may learn how to act in all the important conjunctures, and how to behave Gracefully, properly, and Politly [*sic*] in all Common Occurrences of life."[16] And this, too, was the task undertaken by the conduct books. What needs to be emphasized is that *Grandison* is obviously more than a collection of periodical essays, and herein lies the clue to the "new species of writing." It transcends even as it transforms every familiar genre of writing.

But before we examine Richardson's transformation of conduct literature in the next chapter, a survey of its origins, development, content, and form is in order. In Richardson's novel *Pamela II* (1741), his newly married heroine escorts her sister-in-law on a visit of charity to neighboring poor cottagers. Among the books provided for them, besides the Bible, the *Book of Common Prayer,* and a catechism, is Richard Allestree's *The Whole Duty of Man* (1658), one of the most popular English conduct books of the seventeenth and eighteenth centuries. Different from the manuals we dust off to clarify the fine points of etiquette, yet closely resembling our modern syndicated advice columns, *The Whole Duty of Man* springs from a long tradition of courtesy and conduct literature written to form behavior and character. Familiar examples that come immediately to mind are the Proverbs of Solomon, Baldassare Castiglione's *Courtier* (1528), Thomas Elyot's *Boke Named the Governour* (1531), Polonius's advice to Laertes in *Hamlet,* and Chesterfield's *Letters to His Son* (1774).[17]

Castiglione's *Courtier,* an Italian work, marks the first significant courtesy work. His four dialogues are lessons in the requisite accomplishments and behavior of the gentleman and lady in court. Castiglione and such French and Italian courtesy writers as La Rochefoucauld, Giovanni della Casa, and Baltassar Gratian were translated and adapted for English audiences. But England produced her own courtesy writers, too. Elyot's *Governour,* for example, illustrates the practical and often specialized tendency of English courtesy literature. Elyot tells us *how* the great nobleman is formed and focuses on his education. In England, advice was directed not only to the nobleman in court, as described primarily in the courtesy book, but also to the nobleman or member of the gentry who might reside on a country estate. Other manuals prescribed the conduct of merchants, tradesmen, and even apprentices in the ordinary workaday world. Thus, the conduct book, the domestic household manual, and the vade mecum took their places alongside the older courtesy books to meet the requirements of a different audience.

The backgrounds of the authors also reflect the variety in English courtesy and conduct literature. Traditionally, a nobleman wrote for his peers, and the classic example of this is the *Basilikon Doron* (1599) of James I, written for his son, Prince Henry. *Basilikon Doron* follows a typical pattern of setting forth the young prince's duties toward God and his potential responsibilities as a king; the book also serves as a guide to prudent conduct in social situations as well as in matters of dress and proper recreations. Other nobles who wrote were the Marquis of Argyle, Sir Matthew Hale, Sir George Mackenzie, the Marquis of Halifax, and Lord Chesterfield, who was Halifax's grandson. Besides authors from the ranks of the nobility, military men such as Captain Edward Panton and Colonel James Forrester took up the pen, as did a number of clergymen, including Stephen Penton, Denis Grenville, Gilbert Burnet, William Law, John Dalton, and the Jesuit William Darrell. Roger Ascham, who was Queen Elizabeth I's mentor and author of *Scholemaster* (1570), John Locke, and Jean Gailhard are among the tutors who composed instructive works.

Describing the form and content of the typical conduct book is an elusive task. Moral exhortation and directions for right conduct found their way into many kinds of literature so that there is often a fine line beteeen a courtesy or conduct book and other kinds of literature that offer advice. Sermons, for instance, are not conduct books, but their authors frequently expressed many of the same concerns. Devotional manuals fall into a similar category: Richard Baxter's *The Catechizing of Families* (1683) is designed to be read aloud by the master of the household to his children and servants. Samuel Richardson's fictional Clarissa writes to her friend Miss Howe that one of the books her family deigns to send her after her escape with Lovelace is Lewis Bayly's *Practice of Piety* (1613, 3d ed.), a devotional manual.[18] Another vehicle of moral instruction is the character-essay, a brief sketch of a virtue, vice, occupational type, or other human quality. Joseph Hall, Sir Thomas Overbury, and John Earle were seventeenth-century popularizers of the form. One edition of *The English Theophrastus* (1702), a late outgrowth of the character-essay, cynically describes a country squire as one "whose Ancestors have been Wise and Provident, and rais'd an Estate by Ingenuity and Industry, and given their Posterity after 'em Means and Leisure to be Fools."[19] A different approach to character formation is found in the publications of societies for the reformation of manners. These societies took strong positions against drinking, swearing, and violating the Sabbath. A 1702 tract attributed to Daniel Defoe on this subject and another of 1699 ascribed to Josiah Woodward enumerate statutes and penalties for transgressions and reveal a zealous concern for the spiritual welfare of others.[20] Still another means of inculcating moral principle is that of storytelling. *Aesop's Fables* has a long tradition in this regard, and Sir Roger L'Estrange, whose translated work was frequently reprinted well into the eighteenth century, has especial praise for this method:

Children are but *Blank Paper,* ready indifferently for any Impression, good or bad. . . . What was it that brought even *David himself* to a Sight and Detestation of Sin in the Matter of *Uriah,* and to a Sense of his Duty, but the Prophet *Nathan's* telling him a story at a Distance.

But L'Estrange's end was not simply moral instruction; "reflections" appended to each story frequently underscore his royalist sympathies.[21]

A more popular approach to instruction can be found in *The New Help to Discourse* (1669?), thought to be written by William Winstanley. This interesting manual is Emily Post, Dale Carnegie, the *Farmer's Almanac,* and the *Book of Knowledge* all rolled into one. Employing a question-and-answer format, the author discusses whether the sea is higher than the earth, notes that pointing is impolite, and urges the reader to cover his mouth when yawning or sneezing. Burning questions of conduct were also treated in John Dunton's *Athenian Gazette* (1691). One reader inquired, in rather timeless manner, "Whether it is lawful for two unmarried Persons, each consenting, to cohabit, &c. since Marriage was a thing set up by Man?"[22]

But those books written to advise a son, daughter, nephew, or pupil come closest to the typical courtesy or conduct book, and it is these that exhibit the greatest diversity in form. Lord Halifax in *The Lady's New-years Gift* (1688), reprinted many times throughout the eighteenth century, advises his daughter under the headings of "Religion, Husband, House and Family. Servants, Behaviour and Conversation, Friendships, Censure, Vanity and Affectation, Pride. Diversions, Dancing." Thomas Fuller's *Introduction ad Prudentiam* (1727), essentially a list of over 3,000 maxims to assist his son, aims not at "great Men, Politicians, Preachers, Pleaders, Warriors, . . . but to such as are in a middle Station, between great Riches and great Poverty; and therefore nothing is to be look'd for here but what relates to common Men and common Life." Denis Grenville's *Counsel and Directions Divine and Moral* (1685) is written in the epistolary form to a nephew just about to enter Oxford. A clergyman, Grenville pays especial attention to spiritual reading, religious exercises, education, travel, and the evils of prodigality.[23]

The variety of method chosen by conduct-book writers is quite wide. Edward Panton, for example, in *Speculum Juventutis* (1671), undertakes a discussion of some of the usual topics, including the nature of nobility and the advantages of education. Being a military man, he pays particular attention to the rules to be observed not only at court and in the family but also in camp, and he speaks out strongly against the practice of dueling. Panton sweetens his message, however, by setting his discussion in a castle, where three guests comment on the story of Sisaras and Valinda. To cite another example, William Law's *A Serious Call to a Devout and Holy Life* (1728), a work that made a lasting impression on Samuel Johnson, examines the case histories of fictional characters to make its instructive point. Mundanus, for example, is a character who knows his trade but not how to pray; Classicus is a learned man who lacks religious devotion. A similar approach is the use of biblical and classical figures for purposes of illustration. Drawing on the lives of such worthies as Deborah, Esther, Lucretia, and Clotilda, the author of *Female Excellency, or the Ladies Glory* (1688) declares to his reader, "Men have the advantage of education . . . if Women had the same helps, I dare not say but they would make as good returns, of which there have been many famous instances in former Ages."[24]

Regardless of the background and method of the author or the rank of his audience, common threads run through all courtesy and conduct works. This is evident in a cursory examination of two books written for two different audiences: Henry Peacham's *The Compleat Gentlemen* (1622), intended for the "Person of Honor," and Richard Allestree's often reprinted *The Whole Duty of Man* (1658), composed "for the Use of All, but especially the Meanest Reader." Peacham's work is, in fact, extremely complete, going beyond the usual discussions of the definition of nobility, education, suitable recreations, and travel to include sections on drawing, painting, limning, heraldry, and even the lives of Italian painters. Yet he is not simply interested in forming a polished nobleman. At the outset he maintains that "if a Prince be the Image of God, governing and adorning all things," he ought "to out-run the rest in a vertuous race, and out-shine them in knowledge." The duties and obligations Peacham views as necessary for the good and worthy noble are quite similar to those delineated by Allestree for men in ordinary ranks of life: "The three great Branches of Man's Duty, to God, Ourselves, our Neighbour."[25] The spheres of activity and particulars may be different, but the emphasis in both Peacham and Allestree remains on the individual's duties and responsibilities in his particular station.

Perhaps the common denominator that seems to exist among all conduct and courtesy books can best be illustrated by the biblical Ecclesiasticus or Sirach. General enough to apply to anyone, it treats of duties to God, parents, family, and neighbor. A good mix of worldly wisdom and spiritual admonition is evident in topics ranging from friendship, proper use of the tongue, wealth, and table etiquette to self-control, prudence, avoidance of sin, and preparation for death. The concluding chapters contain the stories of Old Testament figures worthy of imitation. If one wishes to read a model conduct book, reading Ecclesiasticus is a handy way to do it.

Literary forms change subtly, not suddenly, and the literature of courtesy and conduct is no exception. This is evidenced in the works of Daniel Defoe, whose significance lies not only in the universal appeal of his advice but also in his method. His *Family Instructor* (1715) included both average citizens and the offspring of George I among its readership and taught basic catechetical truths by means of dialogues between a child, who asks perceptive questions, and his parents, who know their religion but do not practice it. Defoe shows what the duties of parents should be and writes additional sections for masters and servants as well as husbands and wives. The dialogues are far from dry, and the sustained narrative captures our interest and builds suspense: what will happen to the good servant in the religiously indifferent household and to the religiously indifferent servant in the truly Christian household? Defoe's *Religious Courtship* (1722) pursues the religious theme even further and engages our attention in the affairs of three sisters who have been exhorted on their mother's deathbed to marry truly religious men and men of their own Protestant faith. Can an indifferent Protestant be reformed? What happens when a devout Protestant unwittingly marries a fervent Catholic? These are the questions Defoe poses in works that seem poised between the conduct book and the novel as we know it today.[26]

It cannot be denied that conduct books such as Allestree's *The Whole Duty of Man* retained their popularity and were reprinted throughout the eighteenth century. But Defoe's works and such conduct books as Richard Steele's *The Ladies Library* (1714) suggest that something was happening to the old courtesy and conduct book. One modern critic has called Steele's work "an 'omnibus' of conduct books of the seventeenth century, offered to readers of the eighteenth." The reader detects bits and pieces in it culled from Jeremy Taylor, Richard Allestree, and other prominent writers. In gathering up the advice of the past, this anthology serves almost as a silent transition between the old form and its various replacements. The popular periodical essays in the *Spectator* would answer many of the questions and pursue many of the issues covered by the earlier courtesy and conduct books. These essays and fictional creations like Sir Roger de Coverley and his friends would be the new arbiters of taste in the arts, dress, and right conduct.[27]

Conduct literature would also take shape in other new forms, among them Samuel Richardson's handbook of letter writing, an early work designed to teach not only correct epistolary form but also "How to Think and Act Justly and Prudently, In the Common Concerns of Human Life." Richardson's preface indicates that the contents of the model letters will embrace the usual topics of conduct literature. But buried in this manual are two letters, number 138: "A

Father to a Daughter in Service, on hearing of her Master's attempting her Virtue" and number 139: "The Daughter's Answer." These two letters ultimately formed the germ of Richardson's *Pamela,* a work that would mark a turning point in prose fiction. It would also provide a potentially new garb for conduct literature and ultimately result in a "new species of writing."[28]

NOTES

1. William M. Sale, Jr., *Samuel Richardson: Master Printer* (1950; reprint, Westport, Conn.: Greenwood Press, Publishers, 1978), p. 155:no. 470; pp. 209–11:nos. 87, 179, 150; pp. 217–21; pp. 221–22:nos. 487 and 488; see *Epistle To Bathurst,* ll. 263–74; Thomas Edwards to Richardson, 15 April 1756, *Correspondence,* 3:133; on the Wilson-Awberry affair see *SCG,* 1:392; on Miss Obrien 1:377; on Mrs. Giffard 2:51; on Miss Danby 1:455; on other dowries 2:11.

2. Harriet's preparations for the Porrettas in *SCG,* 3:370 parallel those of Penshurst's lady in *To Penshurst,* ll. 75–88; on Grandison's servants see *SCG,* 2:32; *Epistle to Burlington,* ll. 99–168; on Sir Charles's taste see *SCG,* 2:160–61; on Grandison's estate see *SCG,* 3:272–73; the portraits are mentioned in *SCG,* 3:278–79.

3. Robert Adams Day, *Told in Letters* (Ann Arbor: University of Michigan Press, 1966); Eaves and Kimpel, *Richardson,* 437–38, point out that Richardson was urged to publish his own letters; Helen Sard Hughes, "English Epistolary Fiction Before *Pamela,*" in *The Manly Anniversary Studies in Language and Literature* (Chicago: University of Chicago Press, 1923), 156–57; Katherine Gee Hornbeak, "The Complete Letter-Writer in English 1568–1800," *Smith College Studies in Modern Languages* 15 (April–July 1934): iii–150; Herbert Davis, "The Correspondence of the Augustans," in *The Familiar Letter in the Eighteenth Century,* ed. Howard Anderson, Philip B. Daghlian, and Irvin Ehrenpreis (Lawrence: University of Kansas Press, 1966); for various estimates of the number of epistolary works in the eighteenth century see Day, *Told in Letters,* 2; F. G. Black, "The Technique of Letter Fiction in English from 1740 to 1800," *Harvard Studies and Notes in Philology and Literature* 15 (1933), 291; Natascha Würzbach, *The Novel in Letters* (London: Routledge and Kegan Paul, 1969), ix; Day, *Told in Letters,* 23, 24, 28, 86; examples of early epistolary fiction are *Five Love-Letters from a Nun to a Cavalier,* trans. L'Estrange in Würzbach, *Novel,* 1–21; John Littleton Costeker, *The Constant Lovers* in Würzbach, *Novel,* 103–47; Aphra Behn, *Love-Letters between a Noble-Man and his Sister* in Würzbach, *Novel,* 187–282.

4. The dramatic antecedents have been traced in Ira Konigsberg, "The Dramatic Background of Richardson's Plots and Characters," *PMLA* 83 (March 1968): 42–53; Ira Konigsberg, *Samuel Richardson and the Dramatic Novel* (Lexington: University of Kentucky Press, 1968); see also Sherburn, "Samuel Richardson's Novels": 325–29; John A. Dussinger, "Richardson's *Clarissa:* 'A Work of Tragic Species' " (Ph.D. diss., Princeton, 1964); *SCG,* 1:273 and 269.

5. Jeremy Collier's *A Short View of the Immorality and Profaneness of the English Stage* (1698) is the most famous diatribe against dramatic looseness on the Restoration stage; Archbishop Tillotson, too, took a dim view of the theater: "How will men attend for several hours to a lewd and extravagant play, and sit not only with patience, but with delight to hear things spoken, which are neither fit to be spoken nor heard?" Sermon 212, "Of diligence in our general and particular calling," John Tillotson, *The Works of the Most Reverend John Tillotson, Lord Archbishop of Canterbury,* 12 vols. (London: C. Hitch et al., 1757), 11:72; John Harrington Smith, *The Gay Couple in Restoration Comedy* (Cambridge: Harvard University Press, 1948),

231; Richard Steele, *The Conscious Lovers,* in *Eighteenth Century Comedy,* ed. Simon Trussler (London: Oxford University Press, 1969), "Prologue," p. 86, l. 28 and "Preface," p. 83; other heroes and men of sense who act as correctives to the Dorimants and Horners of Restoration drama can be found in such characters as Sir Friendly Moral in Cibber's *The Lady's Last Stake* (1707), Gaywit in *The Modern Husband* (1732), Eustace in Theophilus Cibber's *The Lover* (1731), Bellamy in Dr. Benjamin Hoadly's *The Suspicious Husband* (1747), and Lewson in Edward Moore's *The Gamester* (1753); see Konigsberg, *Richardson,* 49–50.

6. Ernest Bernbaum, *The Drama of Sensibility* (Boston: Ginn and Company, Publishers, 1915), 95.

7. Konigsberg, *Richardson,* 48, 53–54, 51–53.

8. Nathaniel Lee, *The Rival Queens,* ed. P. F. Vernon (Lincoln: University of Nebraska Press, 1970), xviii; Hazel M. Batzer Pollard, *From Heroics to Sentimentalism* (Salzburg: Institut für Englische Sprache und Literatur, 1974), 35; Lady Bradshaigh to Richardson, 22 February 1754, FC XI, ff. 83v–84. In quotations, a word preceded and followed by a hyphen has been deleted by the writer; a small cross before and after a word indicates an addition by the writer.

9. On Clementina see *SCG,* 2:163–64; on Sir Charles 2:177; on Harriet 2:492; on Charlotte 1:434; Earl Wasserman, "Johnson's *Rasselas:* Implicit Contexts," *Journal of English and Germanic Philology* 74 (January 1975): 1–25, suggests another source for the idea of choice between two alternatives: the common pattern of Hercules at the crossroads.

10. Henry Fielding, *The History of Tom Jones. A Foundling,* intro. and commentary Martin C. Battestin, ed. Fredson Bowers, 2 vols. (Middletown, Conn.: Wesleyan University Press, 1975), 1:77; Richardson to Aaron Hill, 5 January 1746/47, *Selected Letters,* 76; Richardson to Aaron Hill, 26 January 1746/47, *Selected Letters,* 78.

11. William Congreve, "Preface to *Incognita,*" in *Novel and Romance,* ed. Ioan Williams (London: Routledge & Kegan Paul, 1970), 27; Samuel Johnson, *A Dictionary of the English Language,* 2 vols. (London: J. and P. Knapton et al., 1755), 2:n.p.; Samuel Richardson, *Pamela,* intro. M. Kinkead-Weekes, 2 vols. (London: Everyman's Library, 1974), 2:454, 443, 452, Letter 102. Hereafter, *Pamela II* refers to vol. 2 of this two-volume edition. Mrs. [Hester Mulso] Chapone to Miss Carter, 31 July [?], R. Brimley Johnson, ed., *Bluestocking Letters* (London: John Lane, 1926), 173–74.

12. Anna Meades to Richardson, 19 January 1757, British Library Add. Ms. 28097, ff. 1–2; Eaves and Kimpel, *Richardson,* 351; Sarah Chapone to Richardson, 12 October 1750, FC XII, 2, f. 4v; Lady Barbara Montagu to Richardson, 31 January 1759, Cornell University; Frances Burney, "Preface to *Evelina, Or, A Young Lady's Entrance into the World,*" in *Novel and Romance,* ed. Williams, 302.

13. *SCG,* 1:148 and 285; Clara Reeve, "Preface" to *The Old English Baron,* 2d ed., 1778, in *Eighteenth-Century British Novelists on the Novel,* ed. George L. Barnett (New York: Appleton-Century-Crofts, 1968), 136.

14. Richardson to Lady Bradshaigh [late November 1749?], *Correspondence,* 4:287; Richard Steele, *Tracts and Pamphlets by Richard Steele,* ed. Rae Blanchard (Baltimore: John Hopkins University Press, 1944), 1 and 37; *SCG,* 2:63, 68, 67; *Steele,* ed. Blanchard, 56; *SCG,* 1:264; *Steele,* ed. Blanchard, 47–49; *SCG,* 2:196; 3:68; Addison Ward, "The Noblest Work of God: Studies in Augustan Social Ideals" (Ph.D. diss., Yale, 1957), attempts to determine what the ideal man was like in the eighteenth century.

15. *SCG,* 3:398; Donald F. Bond, ed. *Spectator,* 5 vols. (Oxford: Clarendon Press, 1965), 3:411–13, no. 375; 1:44, no. 10; 1:lxxxvi.

16. Richardson to Aaron Hill, 7 November 1748, *Selected Letters,* 100; Philocalus to the reader, n.d., FC XV, 4. f. 45; Frances Grainger to Richardson, 23 May 1754, FC XV, 3, f. 49; Anonymous to Richardson, n.d., FC XV, 3, f. 61, 2v.

17. Richardson, *Pamela II,* 183, Letter 37; Fielding's Joseph Andrews has also read the Allestree book; see [Henry Fielding], *The History of Joseph Andrews,* 2 vols. (London: A

Millar, 1742), 1:11; [Richard Allestree], *The Whole Duty of Man* (London: W. Mount and T. Page, 1741). Allestree's work was first published in 1658; the British Library catalogue lists fifty-five different editions between 1658 and 1819. For a fuller treatment of courtesy and conduct literature, see John E. Mason, *Gentlefolk in the Making* (1935; reprint, New York: Octagon Books, 1971); Virgil B. Heltzel, comp., *A Check List of Courtesy Books in the Newberry Library* (Chicago: The Newberry Library, 1942) has catalogued well over a thousand in the Newberry collection. His definition of courtesy literature is useful:

> I should apply this term to any work, or significant part of a work, which sets forth for the gentleman (or gentlewoman) first, the qualities or criteria, inherent or acquired, which he must possess; second, his formation (including his various interests, exercises, recreations, and amusements) and his education; and third, his conduct. Under the first head I have in mind works which deal with such matters as, to mention but a few examples, birth, wealth, honor, arms, learning, and good breeding; under the second, works concerned with sports (hunting, angling, riding, etc.), or with recreations such as parlor games, music, art, and poetry, or with the aim and method of education, or with advice about the studies to be pursued; under the third, works treating moral and social conduct and obligations in human intercourse or works on the pursuit of an occupation or profession, such as the ministry, the law, diplomacy, warfare, farming, or the management of a household or an estate. (vii–viii)

Gertrude E. Noyes's bibliography of courtesy literature is restricted to the seventeenth century and contains close to five hundred entries; her introduction is also useful; Gertrude E. Noyes, *Bibliography of Courtesy and Conduct Books in Seventeenth-Century England* (New Haven: Tuttle, Morehouse and Taylor Co., 1937). Rules of etiquette as known today were not ignored, but they were not a prominent subject. Among the few works that cover etiquette matters are W[illiam] W[instanley], *The New Help to Discourse*, 8th ed. (London: Peter Parker, 1721); [Antoine de Courtin], *The Rules of Civility* (London: J. Martyn and J. Starkey, 1678); and J[ean] Gailhard, *The Compleat Gentleman* (London: John Starkey, 1678). The terms *courtesy* and *conduct book* are used in this study interchangeably, but perhaps it is useful to think of those books directed particularly to members of the court and nobility as "courtesy" books and those for a general audience as "conduct" books. All titles are abbreviated from those actually on the title page.

18. Richard Baxter, *The Catechizing of Families* (London: T. Parkhurst and B. Simmons, 1683), A3; Samuel Richardson, *Clarissa*, ed. John Butt, 4 vols. (New York: Everyman's Library 1976), 2:256, Letter 74; [Lewis Bayly], *The Practise of Pietie*, last corrected edition (Amsterdam: Jo. Stofford, 1649).

19. *The English Theophrastus*, 3d ed. (London: William Turner and John Chantry, 1708), 59.

20. [Daniel Defoe], *An Account of the Progress of the Reformation of Manners*, 11th ed. (London: J. Downing 1702); [Josiah Woodward], *An Account of the Societies for Reformation of Manners* (London: B. Aylmer, 1699).

21. Sir Roger L'Estrange, *Fables of Aesop*, 8th ed. corrected (London: A. Bettesworth et al., 1738), preface, n.p.

22. W[instanley], *The New Help to Discourse*, 29, 144, 136; [John Dunton], *The Athenian Gazette* (London: John Dunton, 1691), 1:5 (Tuesday, April 7, 1691), Question 3.

23. [George Savile, Marquis of Halifax], *The Lady's New-years Gift: or, Advice to a Daughter*, 2d ed. (London: Matt. Gillyflower and James Partridge, 1688), quoted from the full title; Thomas Fuller, M.D., *Introductio ad Prudentiam*, 3d ed. (London: W. Innys, 1743), 1: xiv; idem, 2d ed. (London: W. Innys and R. Manby, 1740), vol. 2; [Denis Grenville], *Counsel and Directions Divine and Moral* (London: Robert Clavell, 1685).

24. Capt. Edward Panton, *Speculum Juventutis* (London: Charles Smith and Thomas Burrell, 1671); William Law, *A Serious Call to a Devout and Holy Life* (London: William Innys, 1729),. 254 and 256; Boswell, *Life*, ed. Chapman, 50–51; R. B. [Nathaniel Crouch], *Female Excellency, or the Ladies Glory* (London: Nath. Crouch, 1688), dedication to the Reader, n.p.

25. Henry Peacham, *The Compleat Gentleman*, 3d impression (London: Richard Thrale, 1661), quoted from the full title and pp. 18–19; [Allestree], *Whole Duty*, quoted from the full title and p. 1.

26. Paul Dottin, *The Life and Strange and Surprising Adventures of Daniel Defoe*, trans. Louise Ragan (New York: Macaulay Co., 1929), 196; [Daniel Defoe], *The Family Instructor*, vol. 1, 16th ed. (London: H. Woodfall et al., 1766); [Daniel Defoe], *The Family Instructor*, vol. 2, 8th ed. (London: H. Woodfall et al., 1766); [Daniel Defoe], *Religious Courtship* (London: E. Matthews et al., 1722).

27. Joyce Hemlow, "Fanny Burney and the Courtesy Books," *PMLA* 65 (September 1950): 732–61, discusses in some detail the publication of courtesy books for ladies in the latter half of the eighteenth century; Katherine Hornbeak, "Richardson's *Familiar Letters* and the Domestic Conduct Books," *Smith College Studies in Modern Languages* 19 (January 1938): 8.

28. Samuel Richardson, *Familiar Letters on Important Occasions*, intro. Brian W. Downs (London: George Routledge and Sons, Ltd., 1928), 164–65.

3

THE COMPLETION OF MY WHOLE PLAN

RICHARDSON'S earliest writing ventures, alluded to in the conclusion of the last chapter, mark the beginning of a lifelong effort to write conduct books. If social currents and literary genres contributed to the creation of *Sir Charles Grandison*, events in Richardson's own life, his style of correspondence, and, most important of all, the works he published before *Grandison* form a part of the piece as well. Richardson refined the instructive element of each of his books, and in the process, the traditional scope and methods of the conduct book. The results in *Grandison* are a truly comprehensive and compelling conduct book in terms of the many examples afforded to the reader.

Several pictures of Richardson emerge from his correspondence. His amusing self-portrait in a letter to Lady Bradshaigh describes a short, plump man, subject to "sudden tremors" and dizziness. His countenance, he has been told, has "nothing in it severe or forbidding." Other letters, particularly those to Dr. George Cheyne, reveal a man subject to chronic physical ailments. Richardson claimed that his constitution had been quite good originally, and that he had not been intemperate. However, he had exhausted himself in helping others: "Indifferent as my own Health is, I am too susceptible to the Griefs of my Friends." Johannes Stinstra, Richardson's Dutch publisher, speculated that Clarissa's Belford might be Richardson's fictional counterpart, and there may well be some truth in this. On the one hand, Richardson insisted that he "never was a Belford," and he told Mrs. Chapone that he never

> was in a bad house in my Life nor in Company with a lewd Woman. Drunkards & such were always odious to me. . . . I never to this Day, have been at a Masquerade. But of all of these kind of Diversions, & of all those sort of Persons I have heard Talk; & it was not hard from Dislike of such, to conceive enough to paint them in strong colours.

44

On the other hand, judging from his correspondence, making the connection between his fictional characters and their creator seems perfectly valid. Richardson, like Belford and Grandison, did take charge of the affairs of many of his friends. He managed some business matters for the Bradshaighs, Sir Roger noting that he himself was unaccustomed to such things. Richardson looked after the orphans of various relatives and was called upon by Dr. Delany to help the infamous and destitute Laetitia Pilkington, whose story could easily have found a place in *Grandison.* Her own description of Richardson's behavior parallels what one would expect from Sir Charles. Even Dr. Johnson was rescued from financial straits by Richardson. Lady Bradshaigh noted "a certain positiveness . . . in your temper, allways to do 'right and proper things.'" To an anonymous admirer who wishes he could do more good, Richardson responds, ". . . the Will to do good, according to our Power, is all that is required of us."[1]

The harmony and activity of Selby House in Harriet's Northamptonshire seem to reflect Richardson's own home, which in fact was often called "Selby Lodge." Catherine Talbot, writing about Parson's Green, Richardson's retreat after 1754, says that

> His Villa is fitted up in the same style his Books are writ. Every Minute detail attended to, yet every one with a view to its being useful or pleasing. Not an inch in his Garden unimproved or unadorned, his very Poultry made happy by fifty little neat Contrivances, his House prepared not for his Family only but for every friend high or low to whom Air & Recess may be of Benefit.

Many of Richardson's female correspondents, such as Sarah Wescomb, frequently asked to become his "adopted" daughters, and they in turn addressed him as "Papa." The familial relationship is affirmed constantly in *Sir Charles Grandison* between individuals who are not related by blood; and this is unique among all his works except the correspondence. Harriet, soon after her rescue from the clutches of Sir Hargrave Pollexfen, becomes a "sister" to the Grandison girls and their brother. Sir Charles becomes a brother and son in the Porretta family. Sir Rowland Meredith is adopted as Harriet's father, while Dr. Bartlett is "another Grandfather." By the end of the novel, several families have been united into one large harmonious group extending all the way from Northamptonshire to Grandison Hall to Colnebrook to London and several cities in Italy.[2]

It might also be said that Richardson well understood the concept of the divided heart, so often touched upon in *Sir Charles Grandison.*

Could one be as happy with a second love after being disappointed in or deprived of one's first love? Richardson wrote to Lady Bradshaigh that he had lost eight children and his first wife. The second Mrs. Richardson does not seem to have had a lively cast or an especially literary bent, but she and her husband were apparently happy together. Of both wives Richardson says,

> I cherish the Memory of my lost Wife to this Hour, and as to the second, when I assure you that I can do so without derogating from the Merits of, or being disallowed by my present; who speaks of her on all Occasions as respectfully, and as affectionately, as I do myself.

We may recall that Harriet Byron seems to have a similar capacity to speak of Clementina in the same sympathetic manner.[3]

Richardson began his letter-writing career as a youngster. In a letter to Stinstra he relates that as a mere youth of eleven he wrote a letter admonishing a widow of fifty whose religious zeal tended to provoke quarrels. At the age of thirteen he composed love letters for several young ladies in his neighborhood. Later, as an apprentice, Richardson engaged in correspondence with a gentleman who "was a Master of the Epistolary Style," and who, if he had lived, had "intended high things" for the young man. This gentleman wrote mostly narrative accounts of his adventures abroad.[4] Richardson's enthusiasm for letter writing never waned, as evidenced by the six huge folios at the Victoria and Albert Museum, and while this is the largest collection of his correspondence, it represents but a fraction of the letters that are scattered or lost. Richardson was just as busy a letter writer as were Pamela, Clarissa, and Harriet.

His correspondents constituted a varied group. Though not all were prominent, they were, nevertheless, not undistinguished. Among the literary figures were Aaron Hill, Thomas Edwards, Edward Young, and Colley Cibber. Richardson's female correspondents included the classical scholar Elizabeth Carter, the bluestocking Hester Mulso, as well as other lesser-known women such as Susanna Highmore, Frances Grainger, and Sarah Wescomb. Lady Dorothy Bradshaigh, one of his steadiest correspondents, acted as a sensible and astute sounding board during the composition of *Grandison*. He lent his correspondence with her to others among his friends, and he told her that she might show his letters to anyone she wished so long as no copies were made. In 1757, when urged by his German publisher, Erasmus Reich, to publish his correspondence, Richardson expressed concern for the reputation of his female correspondents. To Lady Bradshaigh he wrote:

There is, on every Acc!, greater Reason for your Ladiship's Delicacy than there is for mine. Do you, therefore, severely watch over me, & resolve to please yourself. . . . Never was there a more Innocent Correspondence carried on between Man & Woman, nor perhaps as y! Ladiship took ye Lead, a more instructive one for young Women, who wish to be tho! prudent and good.

He, and other correspondents who agreed to publication, disguised their names and locations and blotted out sections they thought might be incriminating. Lady Bradshaigh was assured that her "pasted-over Passages are safe; for I defy anybody to read or loosen them." Discretion in correspondence is an important issue in *Grandison*. Caroline Grandison engages in a secret correspondence with Lord L. before their marriage, and Charlotte writes secretly to Captain Anderson. But both sisters are taken to task for this. Harriet asks, "Ah! Lady L. was this *quite* right, tho' it came out happily in the event? Does not concealment always imply somewhat wrong?" And Sir Charles advises Charlotte, "Most young women, who begin a correspondence with our designing Sex, think they can stop when they will. But it is not so." Grandison writes to Clementina as a brother and with her mother's permission; he regards a correspondence with the tempestuous Lady Olivia as imprudent unless she, too, will regard him as a brother. The correspondence in *Grandison* is definitely a public one. Letters are shared many times over, and some are enclosed within letters which are enclosed within still others. Harriet allows Grandison to read only parts of her correspondence; Dr. Bartlett has discretionary power over those portions of Sir Charles's correspondence from Italy which will be seen by the English contingent. Thus, in several ways, letter writing as a way of life in *Grandison* mirrors Richardson's own life.[5]

One can go further. Richardson's correspondence taken as a whole anticipates the style, method, and even the incidents of his fiction. Often the letters assume the mode and tone of a dialogue. This is particularly noticeable in his debates with Sarah Chapone, Hester Mulso, Frances Grainger, and Lady Bradshaigh. Each repeats, or quotes at length, the statements of the other writer. Lady Bradshaigh claimed that she always wrote with Richardson's last two letters before her and beside these her own response. In *Grandison*, characters often refer back to previous letters, frequently quoting them, and then answering. Charlotte does this when she replies in her usual spirited manner to Harriet's admonitions. Lady Bradshaigh had commented that familiar letters ought not to be edited too carefully ". . . for shou'd they not appear Extempore, and just as the thoughts flow'd at the time of writing? . . . as to Eligance, the very word *Familiar* takes off the expectation." Richardson agreed.[6]

Lively depiction of incidents by Richardson and his correspondents occurs often. In a letter to Thomas Edwards, Richardson describes the misfortune of Miss Highmore,

> who has often set the Hearts of young Fellows on Fire, and warmed herself by it, the other day sat herself in a Blaze with her torturing curling Irons.

In another letter we learn that a sermon destined for Richardson's eye by the precocious son of a proud Mrs. Chapone has been devoured by the rats. When Richardson asked Lady Bradshaigh to edit their correspondence for possible publication, she writes,

> You wou'd have laugh'd Sir, to have seen me, looking with the sagacity of an author, one pen in my mouth, another, in my Hand, one for writing, the other, for Scratching out, and often thro' eagerness, diping my pen in the paste & my finger in the Ink. Sometimes, Stamping my foot, in anger; as it were to keep myself in awe, at others, starting up, out of patience.

And when she asked Richardson to write more after *Grandison,* he answered:

> My vanity lifted up its head upon it: It looked at me, as if for leave to rise. It actually got upon its feet—Lie down, said I, and stamped,—It shook itself, -and- again -lay- + laid + down, and fell asleep.

Other lively accounts are to be found in his correspondence with Laetitia Pilkington, Hester Mulso, and Frances Grainger.[7]

A particularly interesting exchange of letters occurred not long after the publication of *Grandison* between the author and one Eusebius Silvester. The letters reveal a patient, trusting Richardson, one who was willing to give an imposter a chance but yet not afraid to state his own case boldly. Silvester, attracted by a lawyer in *Grandison* with a name identical to his own, began to write flattering comments to Richardson and sought his financial aid for projects that later failed. Before he realized that Silvester had taken advantage of him, Richardson had responded to his problems with paternal interest and good advice, reminiscent of that found in his *Apprentice's Vade Mecum* and other correspondence to young friends who sought his counsel. To Silvester he cautioned:

> Aim not at too much. Content yourself with the Station you are in; It is not an unhappy one; yet keep your mind prepared, if your Prospects are

more encouraging, to receive enlarged Blessings: But be not impatient if the Fruit you wish to gather, ripen not so fast as you would have it.

Exasperated by Silvester's procrastination in paying his debts, Richardson drew up a little document called, "My Observations on Mr. Silvester's State of his Affairs," a balance sheet explaining Silvester's problems and Richardson's side of the matter.[8]

A similar balance sheet is found in connection with Richardson's disapproval of his daughter's marrying a Dr. Ditcher of Bath. Irked that his brother-in-law and his own wife apparently negotiated the whole affair behind his back, and further concerned that the doctor, not being a man of business, would leave a prospective widow nothing in the way of negotiable goods, Richardson composed an analytical document. Almost in dialogue form, the document expresses his reservations about the marriage, his irritation at not being consulted earlier, and his wish that his wife not be troubled now with the arrangements he has made. Though nearly a legal brief, the prose is lively, and the reader's curiosity is aroused to learn the eventual outcome of the marriage. Richardson wishes to make it clear that "Mr. D. has had *full* Justice already done him" and hopes his "other Girls may have the like done for them. . . ." *Grandison* contains several such documents. Harriet draws up a balance sheet comparing her situation with that of Clementina. Grandison composes an agreement to be signed by all members of the Porretta family setting out the terms for Clementina's year of decision. Sir Charles also legalistically argues in favor of Clementina's marrying rather than entering a convent. Even Harriet's wedding date is determined in debate and submitted for approval in written form. Thus, potentially dry or ordinary situations in Richardson's own life assume lively and dramatic dimensions under his pen and anticipate his fiction.[9]

The thumbnail biography that Richardson wrote for Stinstra reveals that his father had

designed me for the Cloth. I was fond of his Choice: But while I was very young, some heavy Losses having disabled him from supporting me as genteelly as he wished in an Education proper for the Function, he left me to choose at the Age of Fifteen or Sixteen, a Business; having been able to give me only common School-learning[.] I chose that of a Printer, tho' a Stranger to it, as what I thought would gratify my Thirst after Reading.

Although Richardson was forced to abandon his career as a preacher, he never abandoned the practice of preaching. Characteristic was the concern he shared with Dr. Johnson about the corrupting influence of current romances on the young: ". . . do I not write with hopes to improve the younger world. . . ." Cox Macro had written to Richardson that young people needed a "prudent Director," since they "will always be reading Something." It seemed to Macro that Richardson answered this calling. He had expressed scorn for sensational writers such as Mrs. Pilkington, Constantia Phillips, Mrs. Manley, and Mrs. Haywood, as well as "some Men, who, accommodating themselves to the vile Taste of the present Times, regard only what is most likely to fill their Pockets." Lady Bradshaigh might have been overly lavish in her enthusiasm when she said that Richardson should have been a bishop, but others, too, recognized the merits of his methods. Edward Young observed:

> When the pulpit fails, other expedients are necessary. I look on you as a peculiar instrument of Providence, adjusted to the peculiar exigence of the times; in which all would be *fine gentlemen,* and only are at a loss to know what it means. While they read, perhaps, from pure vanity, they do not read in vain; and are betrayed into benefit, while mere amusement is their pursuit.[10]

There is no evidence that Richardson foresaw the entire body of his writing when he first began; he only admitted to an overall plan in the preface to *Sir Charles Grandison.* But by that time his total corpus does, in fact, give the impression of having evolved from a larger design. This impression may be underscored by Richardson's continued efforts to write instructive works whose kinship lay with the conduct book. And each of his works improves upon the last in the complexity of conduct-book issues treated and in the increasing sophistication with which those issues are developed. Richardson's first conduct book, *The Apprentice's Vade Mecum* (1733), was based on a letter he wrote to his nephew Thomas Verren Richardson and is indicative of his particular concern for youth. It follows the tradition of advice literature extending from the Marquis of Halifax and the Marquis of Argyle to writers such as John Barnard and Caleb Trenchfield, who composed manuals for their apprentice sons. The first two sections describe the duties of apprentices to their masters, the dangers of the theater, the importance of manners, the responsibilities of friendship, and the necessity of avoiding evil in general; the third part consists of arguments against deism.

Richardson's interest in the instruction of youth expanded further when he undertook a revision of L'Estrange's *Aesop's Fables* (1739). He felt that his task was to choose fables appropriate "for the instruction of the youth of both sexes, at the same time that we hope it will not be found unworthy of the perusal of persons of riper years and understandings." He endeavored to reduce the size of the book in view of "the *hands* and *pockets* for which it was principally designed." The political overtones are removed, and the notion of duty found in the *Vade Mecum* is stressed again: children are to be taught "what they ought to do," then how to do it, and finally, "the love and practice of doing their duty." Not all of Richardson's revisions are dramatic, but Fable 240, adapted from L'Estrange's Fable 495, "a most ludicrous one," as Richardson labels it, illustrates a subtle change in tone and emphasis. Richardson's story features a profligate who resolves reformation during illness but reneges on his resolution when he recovers. The episode is reminiscent of other fictional deathbed scenes, with their attendant joy or terror, depending on the tenor of the individual's life. In Richardson's later novels, for example, Clarissa's death is contrasted with Belton's and Sinclair's, and the final moments of Lady Grandison and Sir Harry Beauchamp are compared with those of Sir Hargrave Pollexfen, Sir Thomas Grandison, and Lorimer.[11]

Richardson's next work, a letter-writing manual entitled *Letters Written To and For Particular Friends On the Most Important Occasions* (1741), was commissioned by two booksellers, John Osborn and Charles Rivington. Such handbooks were not unusual; but Richardson makes clear early in the preface that he is not simply composing a guide to the correct forms of letter composition. His principal aim is to

> inculcate the principles of virtue and benevolence; to describe properly, and recommend strongly, the social and relative duties; and to place them in such practical lights, that the letters may serve for rules to think and act by, as well as forms to write after.

It is well known, of course, that *Pamela* is foreshadowed in letters 138 and 139. But snatches of *Clarissa* and *Grandison* can be found, too. Letter 62 tells the tale of a young girl in London for the first time unwittingly lured off to a brothel. Letters 149 to 160 are travel letters describing the city of London. The virtues of trade are sung in Letter 1, and we recall the Danbys in *Grandison*. An indulgent mother admits her failing to her son in Letter 3, reminding the reader of Lovelace and Lorimer, reprobate sons of indulgent mothers. Letters, discussing good conversation, the duties of servants, courtship, and Richardson's particular concern for "Orphans and ladies of independent fortunes" anticipate the issues addressed in the later works. All three major novels, for example, contain variations on the theme of the woman without parental guidance. Pamela is forced to do without her parents' advice, Clarissa is locked out from the counsel of good people because of waylaid letters, and Harriet, not without advisers, has nevertheless been left on her own as far as courtship and marriage are concerned. And the warning in Letter 67 against the "wild assertion" that a rake makes a good husband was subsequently debated in *Grandison* and in Richardson's letters to Lady Bradshaigh. The manual also points to Richardson's later fiction because it groups several letters together to create short narratives, thereby enhancing the reader's interest.[12]

Richardson stated that *Pamela* grew out of the *Familiar Letters* and that he had "almost accidentally slid into the writing of Pamela." Nevertheless, the work created a sensation. Alexander Pope and Dr. Benjamin Slocock praised it; Fielding attacked it in *Shamela*. Why did Richardson write in such a way? One answer is to see *Pamela* in terms of other kinds of literature of the period. The salon romances, often titillating and salacious, had captured the fancy of the youth Richardson worried about.

> I thought the story, if written in an easy and natural manner, suitably to the simplicity of it, might possibly introduce a new species of writing, that might possibly turn young people into a course of reading different from the pomp and parade of romance-writing, and dismissing the improbable and marvellous, with which novels generally abound, might tend to promote the cause of religion and virtue.

But even if we take Richardson at his word, there are objections. Is Pamela really a sly minx? Should one expect virtue to be rewarded here on earth? Is it a good example for a maidservant, however superior, to marry out of her rank? Richardson had opened a Pandora's box, which he tried to close in *Pamela II*.[13]

This sequel, almost at the opposite extreme of *Pamala I*, goes out of its way to instill wholesome precepts. A string of adventures engages the new Mrs. B., and many of the questions Richardson considered later are already anticipated: can a reformed rake be truly reformed? How does one raise children? What benefits are to be gained from the Grand Tour? What are the merits and demerits of romances and plays? How does one treat an unfaithful husband? A reader could learn much from *Pamela II*, but artistically, the work is not compelling. The suspense of Clarissa's dilemma and the courtship in *Sir Charles Grandison* are not matched by the effect of Mr. B.'s momentary dalliance in *Pamela II*. In addition, Pamela's new position in a higher rank and her advice to her parents in their now exalted circumstances would have been fruitful material for a conduct book. Indeed, Richardson presents variations of these subjects in *Sir Charles Grandison*. But there is some stiffness in the portrayal as Pamela becomes more of a curiosity for her new relatives and their friends and an awkward yardstick of behavior for her parents.

In any case, *Pamela II* proved an ineffective corrective. The exact origins of Richardson's next novel, *Clarissa,* are unclear, but it has been analyzed as a tragedy, a descendant of the erotic-pathetic novel, and, of course, as the forerunner of the modern psychological novel. Again, *Clarissa* treats the same issues Richardson has been confronting and will confront all along: parental control over the choice of spouse, the practicability of reclaiming a rake, marriage for money, as well as marriage to an incompatible person, and the running of a household. Included in the picture are such issues as the management of servants, mutual duties of parents and children, dueling, and the dangers of a deathbed repentance. We also begin to see Richardson's technique of instructive contrasts. Belford, the reformed rake, acts as a foil to the debauched Lovelace; one observes the dissimilar deathbed scenes of Sinclair, Lovelace, and Clarisssa. Other examples would include the bad sister Arabella and the good sister Clarissa; the lively, slightly irreverent daughter Anna Howe and the dutiful Clarissa; the corrupt clergyman Brand pitted against Dr. Lewen. The reader will encounter repetitions of characteristic situations, as, for instance, the imprudent actions that lead Pamela and Clarissa astray. This was intended as a warning to the reader. Pamela repeatedly delays her departure from Mr. B.'s home until it is impossible for her to escape. Likewise, Clarissa begins a correspondence with Lovelace in the hope that she may avert killing and tragedy; but eventually she, too, finds herself inextricably entangled in Lovelace's web. The theme is continued in *Grandison*. Harriet goes off to a masquerade, an activity frowned upon in the *Spectator,* as well as in Fielding's *Amelia.* The Porrettas are castigated both by the fictional Harriet and the real Lady Mary Wortley Montagu for their lack of discretion in permitting Sir Charles to stay in their home where the affections of two young people were so likely to be engaged. Though "honour, and laws of hospitality, were Mr. Grandison's Guard," one wonders whether Sir Charles does not share some of the blame for this imprudence.[14]

The key point to be made here is that *Clarissa* turned out to be something of a disappointment to Richardson when readers often seemed to miss his purpose:

> I am afraid, Madam, that the Inattention of the Story-Lovers and Amusement-Seekers will not suffer half of those Lessons or Instructions in this Piece to be observed, for the Sake of which the whole was written.

Misunderstandings were legion. Some critics misinterpreted Clarissa's goodness and Anna Howe's disrespectful liveliness: "Can it be, that to the one we know we are superior, and therefore are not Jealous?" Two of his most "ingenious" and "attentive" readers had accused him of favoring forced marriages. The most obvious and serious misconception to arise from *Clarissa* centered upon the character of Lovelace. Richardson wrote:

> I thought I had made him too wicked, too Intriguing, too revengeful, (and that in his very first Letters) for him to obtain the Favour and good Wishes of any worthy Heart of *either* Sex. I try'd his Character, as it was first drawn, and his last Exit, on a young Lady of Seventeen. She shewed me by her Tears at the latter that he was not very odious to her for his Vagaries and Inventions. I was surprized; and for fear such a Wretch should induce Pity, I threw into his Character some deeper Shades.

Lady Echlin, along with other readers, wanted to see Lovelace reformed by the end of the novel. But Richardson defended his approach on the ground that Belford was the example of a reformed rake he wished to present to the reader; ". . . reformation is not, cannot, be an easy, a sudden thing, in a man long immersed in vice." And he was equally adamant about not rewarding "a Rake *so* atrocious!" with Clarissa's hand: "How had the moral of my Work, in that Case, been destroyed!" Aaron Hill voiced another objection. Richardson must not portray Lovelace as "a less delicate and amiable Character than he might have been," since an extremely evil figure would not be convincing: ". . . no young Woman, who shall read him will suppose *her* Lover such a base and wicked one as *he* (by choice) will seem to her to be." Nevertheless, Richardson persisted, and Mark Kinkead-Weekes has shown how succeeding editions underscored Lovelace's diabolical qualities.[15]

No less troubling to Richardson was the fact that Hickman, the apparent alternative to Clarissa's Lovelace, struck his correspondents as unappealing. Miss Grainger had said that while she would be indifferent to a Hickman in real life, she would choose him over a Lovelace just to prove that Richardson's moral had had its effect on her. Richardson cautioned her against too much presumption in her ability to recognize such a rake and reform him.

> If Mr. Hickman's respectful Love, if his worthy Character, if his beneficent Disposition, if his Perseverance, will not give him a Preference for the sake of *those good Qualities*—What shall I say?—

Anne Donnellan was not sympathetic to a Hickman either, claiming that a woman who married such a man runs the risk of being the husband rather than the wife. Lady Bradshaigh was fond of Lovelace and conducted a long discussion by letter with Richardson on the merits of a "moderate rake." "A Man may deserve the name of a rake, without being quite an abandoned profligate; as a man may sometimes drink a little too much, without being a sot." She would like the "dress and address of such a man, without his vices," a "man who has seen the world," "without suffering a corruption of morals." She recalls Anna Howe's impression of Lovelace at Colonel Ambrose's ball and wonders why a good man has to be formal, disagreeable in manner, and lacking in amiable appearance.[16]

The time was thus ripe to fashion a powerful corrective to *Clarissa*. As early as 1741 it was suggested that Richardson write "a Book made up a little more of important Transactions, that we may be better Judges how to Act in them; the History of a Man, whose Life would be the Path that we should follow." Lady Bradshaigh was one of the first to urge Richardson to draw a good man. Even before Richardson had introduced his hero in the novel, she speculated about his mien:

> I am willing to think Miss Byron happened to see him first at church, and was struck with his behaviour. Who would not? To see a man, in person like Lovelace, in an act of sincere devotion: only think of that!

Richardson sought advice about his good man from a variety of correspondents. To Miss Highmore he insisted, "He must be wonderfully polite; but no Hickman! How can we hope that ladies will not think a good man a tame man?" Harriet once wrote that if Sir Charles had been wicked, his great ability to manipulate people would render him extremely dangerous. Richardson, of course, recognized Lovelace's good qualities. Thus when we compare the male protagonists of *Grandison* and *Clarissa*, it seems as though the verbal skills and ability to control people possessed by Lovelace are reposed in Sir Charles. This tends to offset the lackluster quality found in the goodness of a Hickman. Sir Charles is frequently described as charming, manly, vivacious, and in possession of a particularly gracious manner. He is admired by "over a score of young women." He adroitly engages the cooperation of a petulant Lady Beauchamp, disarms the volatile Lady Olivia, counsels and bears with the recalcitrant Everard, and reforms an antagonistic Lord W. He avoids several duels and is able to socialize with rakes without demeaning himself. Grandison resembles Lovelace in that everything seems to be under control when he is in charge. At the same time, the dissolute qualities of a Lovelace are dispersed among many characters: Merceda, Bagenhall, Jordan, Pollexfen, Sir Thomas Grandison, Lord W., Jeronymo, Lorimer, Fenwick, and Greville. This diffusion tends to render the rakes more humorous and less deserving of attention and regard. When the reader recalls Sir Hargrave Pollexfen's continual preening before a mirror and excessive attention to his appearance, and then his subsequent encounter with Grandison that leaves him partially toothless, a black patch over his lip, it is difficult to find Sir Hargrave particularly admirable.[17]

Richardson admitted that he used this method of combination to create Lovelace in the earlier novel, having in mind a man whose best qualities he gave to Mr. B. in *Pamela* and whose worst he gave to Lovelace "made still worse by mingling the worst of two other Characters that were as well known to me." He elaborated further in a letter to Mrs. Chapone:

> But tho I have had Ideas of this or that Person before me in *parts* no one Person Man or Woman sat before me for the *Whole* of any of my Pictures so that I was out of Fear of being supposed to have it in my Thought either to flatter or affront any Person breathing. . . . Indeed I put the Iniquity of two or three bad Characters together in my Mind in order to draw his [Lovelace's].

The same technique is evident in the creation of Harriet Byron. Mrs. Chapone exprssed her admiration for Harriet and remarked on "the diversity yet sameness in the characters of Clarissa and Harriet." Richardson said that he had "designed her to keep the middle course, between Pamela and Clarissa; and between Clarissa and Miss Howe; or rather, to make her what I would have supposed Clarissa to be, had she not met with such persecutions at home, and with such a tormentor as Lovelace."[18]

Besides those characters who mingle the traits of individuals from earlier novels, others appear to be direct descendants from previous works, an observation made in *Critical Remarks on Sir Charles Grandison* (1754). Lady Davers in *Pamela* becomes Anna Howe, the forerunner of Charlotte Grandison. Lady Bradshaigh called Charlotte "another Lovelace" because of the wittiness of her insolence. Hickman seems to be repeated in Lord G., though Richardson felt Hickman's fault was "Formality: Lord G. is a Fashionist, and no Formalist." Pedants are among the characters in *Clarissa* and *Grandison*: Brand puts himself in a bad light and further complicates the action, while Walden provides the opportunity for a discussion of the Ancients and Moderns controversy and shows Harriet at her liveliest best. The indulgent but harried and oppressed mother seen in Mrs. Harlowe is transported to a foreign setting in the figure of the Marchioness della Porretta. Both are devoted to their daughters but lack the strength to take a firm position in families dominated by forceful men and other shrewd, cruel women, such as Arabella and the Sforza ladies. Mrs. Jewkes in *Pamela* and Sinclair in *Clarissa* are transformed into the milder Mrs. Awberry of *Grandison*. Lovelace's servant, Joseph Leman, is Wilson in *Grandison*, whose lapse is momentary and who soon reforms. Rosebud in *Clarissa* is seen in Miss Obrien, whose eager relatives are anxious for a liaison with Sir Thomas Grandison. In *Grandison*, that whole episode becomes an occasion for a lesson and much moralizing. Clarissa and Clementina are subject to the legal wills of grandfathers. Clarissa's grandfather puts her in possession of an estate, which results in increased greed on the part of the Harlowes. The Porrettas fear that if Clementina follows her inclination to retire to a convent, the property of her two grandfathers will pass out of their control. Finally, Richardson himself suggests a thematic connection between *Clarissa* and *Grandison*. In a letter to Stinstra he identifies Sir Charles's father as "a married Lovelace, as to Gaiety and Immorality," and so we see what might have happened had Clarissa married Lovelace. The continuity is suggested in another way. When urged to marry Lovelace, Clarissa, quoting from Ecclesiasticus, declares "For who *can touch pitch, and not be defiled?*" Harriet uses the very same passage to explain why she cannot possibly give encouragement to Greville. But the theme takes on different dimensions when Clementina expresses similar sentiments about Sir Charles: she fears a different kind of defilement in the loss of her Catholic faith under the influence of a good and exemplary Protestant husband.[19] *Sir Charles Grandison*, then, does seem to be an expansion, continuation, and development of the themes, characters, and situations that interested Richardson throughout his life—in fact, the working out of the last part of his plan.

Yet, while *Grandison* bears an unmistakable resemblance to Richardson's previous work, it is unique both in content and form. First of all, unlike *Pamela* and *Clarissa*, it portrays episodes in high life. Actually, Richardson had now rounded out his approach to the writing of conduct literature by appealing to readers of every rank, from his *Apprentice's Vade Mecum* for the young apprentice, *Aesop's Fables* for children, and *Familiar Letters* for "Country Readers," to *Pamela* for young servant girls.[20] *Clarissa* depicts a family of the middle rank contending with the aristocracy, while *Grandison* portrays Harriet, of a middling but old family, Clementina, of a higher rank than Grandison, and Grandison himself, a member of the baronetcy founded by James I.

Grandison is also distinguished from *Pamela* and *Clarissa* because part of it is given a foreign setting. The Italian section provides a typical description of the problems of an Englishman abroad on the Grand Tour. Conduct books warned against the dangers to faith and morals encountered on such trips. Defoe's *Religious Courtship* treats the subject of an interfaith marriage, while his *New Family Instructor* tells the story of a young English Protestant who converted to Catholicism while abroad, despite parental admonitions. One of Richardson's critics indicated that such occurrences were enough of a problem in real life to warrant worrying about what kind of example Grandison was setting by engaging in a religious compromise with the Catholic Porrettas.[21]

We may also be able to account for the Italian setting in another way. Elizabethan and Jacobean plays were often set in the lurid and hysterical Italian world, and contemporary travel accounts tended to reinforce this image of Italy. Jean Gailhard attributed qualities of suspicion, cunning, and revenge to the Italian temper, while Roger Ascham concluded that nine days in Venice afforded "more liberty to sinne, then in London he ever heard of in nine years." Defoe wrote in his *True-Born Englishman* that "Lust chose the Torrid Zone of Italy, / Where Blood ferments in Rapes and Sodomy. . . ." There is a certain frantic quality to the Italians in *Grandison*, what with disguises, eavesdropping, suicide, straitjackets, and wildly disordered scenes.[22]

But the contrast is not always to the disadvantage of the Italians. Perhaps in an attempt to temper the current perception, Richardson depicts women of superior intellectual attainments; Clementina is constantly acclaimed for her greatness of soul. Mrs. Hester Thrale, on a trip to Bologna, immediately recalled Richardson's *Grandison* and reflected that he had captured the right spirit in his depiction of Italian character. This is not surprising for, although Richardson never visited Italy, in the interests of accuracy he did consult persons familiar with life on the Continent. The French translator de Freval had given him hints about what a good man might encounter in France and where worthy people were to be met. Once, when Lady Bradshaigh had taken exception to Grandison's account of the box on the ear and caning, he quickly rejoined,

> I will only add, that a very ingenious and learned Italian, who is well acquainted with the Manners of every Nation in Italy, had made no manner of Objection to this little Story; on the contrary, had complimented me, that I have been in Italy.

Possibly this Giuseppe Baretti, friend of Edward Young, Anna Williams, and Mrs. Thrale. There is a notation in Richardson's correspondence that Baretti corrected the spelling of Jeronymo's name. Baretti also authored a book on Italian life that indicates that not all Italian girls were locked up in convents and were, in fact, discouraged by their parents from entering them. He describes educated women who speak Italian and French and who discuss trade and politics without being considered forward. Baretti's work was intended to be a corrective to common misconceptions of Italians, and perhaps that is what Richardson was trying to do in *Grandison*.[23]

Catholics, of course, were viewed unsympathetically in England. Nevertheless, there are no sneaking Jesuits or odd abbesses in *Grandison*. Throughout all the difficulties the Italians create for him, Sir Charles maintains that he respects good people of all persuasions. This view seems to reflect Richardson's own attitude. In a letter to Alexis Claude Clairaut, Richardson says that he has tried to be zealous in presenting the Catholic and Protestant characters fairly. As a matter of fact, he has been told by one clergyman that he is more of a Catholic than a Protestant. Richardson's tolerance is illustrated in his preface to *Aesop's Fables;* he urges readers to make allowances for accusations that L'Estrange was a papist because he lived in difficult times. Another instance of Richardson's unbiased temperament occurred during his publication of the *Universal History.* John Swinton had apparently written a fiery attack against Mohammed. Richardson grants that Swinton should "be zealous in the Christian Cause" but chides him for mixing too much passion with his reason: "a Gentleman and a Scholar should [not] have given such way to his Resentment. . . ." Richardson once wrote that he himself had very nearly married a "violent Roman Catholic lady . . . a zealous professor." This may partially account for his sympathy toward Catholics.[24]

Grandison diverges from *Pamela* and *Clarissa* in form as well as content. In the first place, it is less confessional in tone and approach, much less of a spiritual autobiography or interior spiritual analysis. Pamela's letters and journal reveal her inner state of mind. She writes with the idea of eventually looking back "upon the Dangers she had escaped" so that she "might examine and either approve of, or repent for, her own Conduct in them." Ultimately, she recognizes pride as the source of her difficulty, and her writing to the moment enables the reader to follow her innermost reasoning. *Clarissa* follows much the same pattern. There are a few editorial comments, and letters from Belford, Anna Howe, Lovelace, Mrs. Norton, and Arabella serve as a contrast and commentary on Clarissa's plight. They also furnish information for the reader to which Clarissa does not have access. But it is primarily Clarissa's spiritual journey that links all of these letters.

As in *Pamela,* we are able to follow the soul-searching of an individual who believed she might be able to influence Lovelace and who
ultimately realizes that her pride is the root of her problems.[25]

Grandison, on the other hand, is more of a debate or discussion of
questions regarding morality and conduct. Clementina's soul, which
would be an interesting one to plumb, is never fully revealed, and we
must be satisfied with letters more nearly approaching legal briefs. We
will never entirely know what happened to her from the time she first
met her brother's rescuer to the moment she finally owns that she
cannot marry Sir Charles because of the risk to her soul. Grandison
furnishes us with few letters, and we know that at times he is in
anguish over the whole Italian situation, but Sir Charles never writes
to the moment about his first encounter with Clementina or Harriet.
The reader is permitted to see slightly more of Harriet's heart; as a
matter of fact, some readers criticized her for being overly frank. But
there is no conversion or spiritual renewal. Harriet and Sir Charles
are already good; the question is how should a good person respond
to the difficult situations of life.[26]

Thus, while Grandison embraces the epistolary form, it is not
composed in the spirit of writing to the moment of Richardson's
other novels. Details and descriptions may be "minute," but in many
instances events are recalled at second and third hand. Pamela's and
Clarissa's letters are intercepted with unfortunate consequences and
an increase of suspense. But in *Grandison* letters are shared and
discussed, not stolen or intercepted, and so that kind of suspense is
eliminated. Richardson himself suggests the change in his method. In
Clarissa

> The Subject of one Letter arose often out of another. It was necessary it
> should. In the new Work (except one or two Letters of each of the
> Respondents, as I may call them) the Answers to the Letters of the
> *Narratist* are only supposed, & really sunk.[27]

In some respects, Harriet, as the major correspondent and orga-
nizer of the materials in the novel, is the real conduct-book writer.
Her correspondence from London to Lucy Selby in Northamptonshire reminds us of the model letters in Richardson's manual.
Even more important are her letters detailing discussions and debates
on matters of conduct. These, too, hark back to traditional conduct-
book methods. William Darrell's *Gentleman Instructed,* for example,
is a series of debates carried on by several visitors in a castle. Defoe
also makes use of instructive dialogues in his *Religious Courtship* and
Family Instructor. In *Grandison* Harriet writes to Lucy about an

enclosed conversation describing Lady L.'s confrontation with her father, Sir Thomas Grandison:

> I thought, my Lucy, that the conversation I have attempted to give, wou'd not, tho' long, appear tedious to you; being upon a *new* subject, the behaviour of a free-liver of a father to his grown-up daughters, when they came to have expectations upon him, which he was not disposed to answer. . . . I am sure, my grandmamma, and my aunt Selby, will be pleased with it; because it will be a good supplement to the lessons they have constantly inculcated upon us.

Selby House, Shirley Manor, and eventually Grandison Hall are depicted as places of instruction. After a visit to Northamptonshire, Charlotte admits that Aunt Selby admonishes "with so much good sense, and her praise and her cautions were so delicately insinuated, that I began to think, it was almost as pretty to be good as to be saucy." Emily, as a "second Harriet" in Northamptonshire, will also have the benefit of this instruction, and now that Harriet and Sir Charles are married Grandison Hall will be another school. Richardson intended his readers to engage in the discussions, too. He admitted that "Many things are thrown out in the several characters, on purpose to provoke friendly debate; and perhaps as trials of the reader's judgment, manners, taste, and capacity."[28] Besides contributing to an atmosphere of discussion and debate, Harriet's commentary serves as a gloss on the narrative, quite similar to the moral attached to an Aesop's fable or a Quarles' emblem. A good example of this is Harriet's commentary on Mrs. Oldham's story. At one point she remarks of Sir Thomas's mistress, "What an humbling thing is the consciousness of having lived faultily, when calamity seizes upon the heart!" But in a spirit of charity and fairness, she later chastises the Grandison sisters' cold and unforgiving demeanor toward Mrs. Oldham. On another occasion she observes of Sir Thomas's behavior that "rakish men make not either good husbands, or good fathers; nor yet good brothers." Again, however, she represents a balanced approach when she cautions against filial disobedience even when the commands of parents like Sir Thomas are "unnatural." Harriet also fills the role of monitor, particularly to the recalcitrant Charlotte. Richardson confided to Lady Echlin that Charlotte's criticism of old maids, for example, "was thrown into Lady G.'s Character on purpose . . . to be corrected by Harriet." Perhaps this is why Harriet, in her roles as observer and monitor, is constantly hunting for faults in Sir Charles's character. Even if her own views on such subjects as education and dress differ from those of Sir Charles, she finds little if anything to censure, and Richardson explains that he intends "to make her shine by her cordial approbation, as she goes along, of every good action of her beloved." Harriet admits to Lucy that she has omitted some parts of an especially stimulating after-dinner conversation because, "my point is, to let you into the character and sentiments of Sir Charles Grandison: And whenever I can do them tolerable justice, I shall keep to that point." Harriet's brief character-essays also provide opportunities for commentary. The pedant Walden, for example, is labeled "quaint and opinionated," while the masculine Miss Barnevelt appears an "odd creature," a woman "out of character." Miss Clements is "plain; but of a fine understanding, improved by reading." Harriet even has fun at her own expense, another indication of her fairness, by writing a character-essay of herself from the points of view of the very people she has just described. Thus, Harriet becomes not only the principal arbiter of conduct but also, as will be shown in the final chapter, one of the principal examples, a rather unique role in conduct literature.[29]

As noted earlier, the conduct book may assume any number of forms: lists of maxims, dialogues, letters of advice, case histories, and plain prose, to name but a few. Of these, the dialogue form seems to play the largest role in *Grandison,* and it is a form often used by other conduct-book writers. Darrell in *The Gentleman Instructed* likens his book to a play: ". . . for indeed it is a sort of *Drama,* written in Dialogue, without *Numbers*" designed to applaud virtue and expose vice. Defoe echoes this in *The Family Instructor:*

> The whole Work being designed both to divert and instruct, the Author has endeavour'd to adapt it as much as possible to both those Uses, from whence some have called it *A Religious Play.* . . .
> As to its being called a *Play, be it called so if they please;* it must be confess'd, some Parts of it are too much acted in many Families among us.

In addition to this, Defoe identifies the form of his *Religious Courtship* as "Historical Dialogues," and Fénelon's *Instructions for the Education of a Daughter* presents model dialogues, as does Adam Petrie's *Rules of Good Deportment.* The latter even prescribes stage directions; a young girl receiving a proposal of marriage should accompany the suggested response "with blushing."[30]

Richardson's distinctive contribution to the dialogue form, as found in so many earlier conduct books, is an enlarged cast of characters and situations, as well as a more thorough analysis of familiar issues. Children, for example, must be dutiful to parents. But what if the parents are unreasonable, as Sir Thomas Grandison is; or irresponsible, as Mrs. O-Hara is; or have left a female ward to her own discretion, as in Harriet's case? Situations are multiplied in order to bring the largest number of questions under consideration. How does a son handle a wayward and wenching father or uncle? How does he extricate his sister from the clutches of an illiterate soldier? And how does he propose to a girl who knows he has been committed to another woman? Can a girl find happiness with a man she thinks has a divided heart; and what should be the attitude of a lively, intelligent, witty wife to a good, devoted, but rather mild husband? There are frequent debates about a course of action. The Selbys wonder if they are being overly punctilious in their behavior toward Sir Charles as he courts Harriet. What length of time is proper between his initial formal declaration and the day of marriage? The dialogue form also illustrates for the reader how one might respond to various questions of conduct. In dialogues Sir Charles explains his position on dueling, and Harriet makes a wonderful showing in her Ancients versus Moderns debate with Walden. Sir Charles is repeatedly faced with situations calling for debate. He must constantly spar with zealous members of the Porretta family as well as with other difficult characters. Richardson apparently read sections of *Grandison* aloud to a sympathetic audience at North End, and it is this, coupled with the dialogue form he inherited from the conduct books, that most likely accounts for the dramatic quality of *Grandison*. What is written for the ear tends to be livelier than what is written for the mind only.

Another technique inherited from the conduct book and upon which Richardson expanded is that of the exemplum. Thomas Fuller, for example, sets forth the characteristics of the good wife and then discusses Augustine's mother Monica; a description of the good husband is illustrated by the biblical Abraham. In other books, a figure proposed for imitation might be contrasted with its opposite. Defoe develops this approach in his *Religious Courtship*. On her deathbed a mother asks that her three daughters marry, first, only men of religious conviction, and second, only men of their own Protestant faith. One daughter is courted by a religiously indifferent man, the second unwittingly marries an Italian Catholic, and the third marries a man of her own faith. The three parallel situations act as foils to one another, each of them serving to increase the subtlety and complexity of the instruction.[31]

Grandison, replete with such foils, forms something of a giant prism in that the polar opposites usually found in conduct books become more shaded and complicated. Many women love and admire Sir Charles. Clementina's high-minded love and Emily's youthful infatuation are often contrasted, and episodes involving each of them are frequently narrated in adjacent letters. Emily is proposed as a model for Clementina, just as Clementina is suggested as a model for Emily. Clementina and Harriet are often paired and referred to as "mirrors" and "sister-excellence." Both love the same man, both have relatives anxious for the match, and both fall ill at the thought of the impossibility of marriage with Sir Charles. Lady Bradshaigh recognized the difference between the two, however: Clementina's *"frantick zeal"* stands in opposition to Harriet's *"undisturb'd reason."* One sets off the other; they are "two different beauties." Beyond this, Olivia forms a contrast both with Clementina and Harriet. She is a more vengeful Italian than Clementina but, like Harriet, she is independent of parental control. She and Clementina make impetuous sea voyages to England, but while Olivia is willing to give up her religion, Clementina is not. Lady Bradshaigh recognized that one purpose of introducing Olivia was "to heighten your other Characters, particularly Your Heros." Richardson added that Olivia was a test for Grandison's character. Even Clementina and Charlotte provide an instructive contrast as two women who do not marry their first loves. Several other stories in the work are mentioned but never developed: the Selby courtship, Olivia's background, and Mrs. Beaumont's history. Each of these would undoubtedly have provided an instructive contrast to the major story line. Mrs. Beaumont's story, which exists in manuscript form, would definitely have been an appropriate addition to *Grandison.* Having been robbed of her inheritance by her uncle and guardian, Mrs. Beaumont faces a dilemma that complements the circumstances of Emily Jervois, whose guardian is watchful of her character and fortune. In addition, Mrs. Beaumont is loved by an Italian who is already engaged to another Italian, which contrasts nicely with the Sir Charles-Harriet-Clementina triangle.[32]

The same use of multiple foils may be seen among the male characters. Young Beauchamp is often called a second Sir Charles. Sir Hargrave, Greville, and Fenwick, each in his aggressive pursuit of Harriet, are contrasted with the serious, shy Mr. Fowler, who must be prompted by his warm-hearted uncle; Mr. Orme, an ailing neighbor; and Lord D., who has an anxious and forthright mother. Lord D. and Sir Charles are both kept in suspense by the women they admire. Finally, Sir Charles on the Grand Tour and in the company of a bad tutor is set off against the rakish Lorimer and his tutor, the good Dr. Bartlett.[33]

In presenting the notion of relative duties, so important in conduct books, Richardson expands the conventional use of foils. We see, for example, several representatives of the same calling. The patient, long-suffering mother of Sir Charles is diligent in carrying out her responsibilities toward her children and is clearly in the mold recommended by the Marquis of Halifax. Clementina's mother is devoted, too, but is unable to exert herself against more powerful family members. Emily Jervois's mother, Mrs. O-Hara, is inebriated and irresponsible before her conversion. New mothers are seen in Lady L. and Charlotte; the role of surrogate mother to the orphan Harriet is filled by Grandmother Shirley and Mrs. Selby; and the potential behavior of a prudent mother-in-law is illustrated in the character of Lady D.

Richardson broadens the scope of his work further by portraying one person in several roles. Sir Charles discharges his filial duty alike to a good mother and a dissolute father. We see him as a brother to his orphaned sisters and as a nephew to a rakish uncle. He is friend to the good Beauchamp, as well as to the reformed Jeronymo, and eventually to Greville and Sir Hargrave. He is likewise a suitor to two women and is even cast in the role of "widower-bachelor." But regardless of the role, Sir Charles is beset by trials, and Richardson shows him as the supreme example of one who fulfills his duty to the utmost. As Lucy Selby said of Sir Charles and Harriet on their wedding day: "We were all considered but as Satellites to the Planets that passed before us."[34]

One must not be misled by Richardson's statement that he never wrote according to a plan. Whatever Richardson's method, *Sir Charles Grandison* is not entirely formless; nor is the main body of Richardson's writing disconnected. He had come a long way from his comments on *Pamela II* in 1742:

I must own I am so great an Enemy to the French Marvellous, that I only aimed, to give the Piece such a Variety, as should be consistent with Probability, and the general Tenor of a genteel Married Life. . . . And I labour'd hard to rein in my Invention, and made it a Rule with me to avoid unnecessary Digressions, & Foreign Episodes; and indeed, had so much Matter upon my Hands to give probable Instances of what a good Wife, a tender Mother, a faithful Friend, a Kind Mistress, and a worthy Neighbour shou'd do.

Grandison is far more subtle, complex, and analytical as a conduct book than anything that came before, whether by Richardson or anyone else—nothing less, in fact, than a new species of conduct book.[35]

NOTES

1. The details of Richardson's life have been ably studied by McKillop, Eaves and Kimpel, and, most recently, in Carol Houlihan Flynn's intriguing book, *Samuel Richardson: A Man of*

Letters; Richardson to Lady Bradshaigh, [late November 1749?], *Correspondence,* 4:290–91; for the Cheyne letters, see Charles F. Mullett, ed., "The Letters of Doctor George Cheyne to Samuel Richardson (1733–1743)," *The University of Missouri Studies* 18 (1943): 5–137. Hereafter, *Cheyne* designates Mullett's edition. Richardson to Sarah Wescomb, 11 September 1753, *European Magazine* 54 (August 1808): 94; Richardson to Lady Bradshaigh, 30 May 1754, FC XI, f. 105; Johannes Stinstra to Richardson, 24 December 1753, William C. Slattery, ed., *The Richardson-Stinstra Correspondence and Stinstra's Prefaces to Clarissa* (Carbondale: Southern Illinois University Press, 1969), 61. Hereafter *Stinstra* designates Slattery's edition. Richardson to Stinstra, 20 March 1754, *Stinstra,* 71; Richardson to Sarah Chapone, 11 January 1751, *Selected Letters,* 172–73; see also Richardson to Stinstra, 2 June 1753, *Selected Letters,* 233; Sir Roger Bradshaigh to Richardson, 18 October 1756, FC XI, f. 193; Richardson to Miss Sutton, 20 August 1750, *Correspondence,* 4:123; Eaves and Kimpel, *Richardson,* 471–72, 175–79; for the Laetitia Pilkington-Samuel Richardson letters, see *Correspondence,* 2:113–57; Eaves and Kimpel, *Richardson,* 337; Lady Bradshaigh to Richardson, 24 November in 27 November 1753, FC XI, f. 48; Richardson to Anonymous, 27 January 1742, FC XVI, 1, f. 85.

2. Susanna Highmore, "Original pencil sketch of Richardson reading at Selby Lodge, N. End Rd. Hammersmith," Pierpont Morgan Library; Cecil Roberts, *And So to Bath* (New York: Macmillan Co., 1940), 11; Catherine Talbot to [Mrs. A. Berkeley?], 9 October 1756, British Library 39311, ff. 84b–85; Sarah Wescomb to Richardson, 30 December 1755, FC XIV, 2, ff. 53–54; some individuals whom Richardson helped or consoled are discussed in Eaves and Kimpel, *Richardson,* pp. 201–2, 444, 485, 539; Richardson to Miss Righton, 14 December 1756, FC XIV, 2, f. 1–2 and 2; Richardson to Mrs. Scudamore, 3 January 1757, FC XIV, 2, f. 75; Richardson to Lady Echlin, 4 May 1756, Yale University; Richardson to Aaron Hill, 29 October 1742, *Correspondence,* 1:84; *SCG,* 1:90 and 228.

3. Richardson to Lady Bradshaigh, 15 December 1748, *Selected Letters,* 109–10; Richardson to Lady Echlin, 12 September 1754, Hyde Collection, f. 2.

4. Richardson to Stinstra, 2 June 1753, *Stinstra,* 26–27, 25.

5. Eaves and Kimpel, *Richardson,* 225 and 437; Richardson to Frances Grainger, 28 February 1750, British Library 33964, f. 366b; Richardson to Lady Bradshaigh, 22 July 1750, *Correspondence,* 6:27; Richardson to Lady Bradshaigh, 2 January 1758, FC XI, f. 227–28; Richardson to Mrs. Scudamore, 1 September 1758, FC XIV, 2, ff. 5–6 and 5–6v; Lady Bradshaigh to Richardson, 21 April 1758, FC XI, f. 241; Richardson to Lady Bradshaigh, 23 May 1758, FC XI, f. 242v; Richardson to Lady Bradshaigh, 19 November 1757, *Selected Letters,* 335–37; see *SCG,* 1:333; on Charlotte see 1:438–39; on Sir Charles and Clementina see 2:602 and 636; on Sir Charles and Olivia see 2:370 and 650–51.

6. Lady Bradshaigh to Richardson, undated section of 27 November 1753, FC XI, f. 41; for Richardson's discussion on parental authority with Sarah Chapone see Sarah Chapone to Richardson, 22 February 1752, FC XII, 2, ff. 58–61; Richardson to Sarah Chapone, 2 March 1752, FC XII, 2, ff. 38–45; Sarah Chapone to Richardson, [March 1752?], FC XII, 2, ff. 47–57; Richardson to Sarah Chapone, 18 April 1752, FC XII, 2, ff. 62–73. For Richardson's extended discussion with Frances Grainger see Richardson to Grainger, 20 December 1748, Pierpont Morgan Library; Richardson to Grainger, 5 December 1749, Hyde Collection; Richardson to Grainger, 21 December 1749, *Selected Letters,* 136–41; Richardson to Grainger, 22 January 1749/50, Yale University; Richardson to Grainger, 1 February 1749/50, Pierpont Morgan Library; Richardson to Grainger, 28 February 1750, British Library, 33964, ff. 365–66; Richardson to Grainger, 29 March 1750, *Selected Letters,* 150–57; Richardson to Grainger, 8 September 1750, Houghton Library, fMS Eng 870 (38). For Richardson's extended discussion with Hester Mulso see Mulso to Richardson, 12 October 1750, 10 November 1750, 3 January 1750/51, Hester Mulso Chapone, *The Works of Mrs. Chapone,* 4 vols. (London: John Murray, 1807), 2:29–34, 37–85, 89–143.

7. Richardson to Thomas Edwards, 21 February 1752, FC XII, 1, f. 42; Sarah Chapone to

Richardson, 24 November 1750, FC XII, 2, ff. 16v and 17; Lady Bradshaigh to Richardson, 21 April 1758, FC XI, ff. 241 and 241v; Richardson to Lady Bradshaigh, 14 February 1754, FC XI, f. 81v.

8. Richardson to Eusebius Silvester, 15 May 1756, FC XIV, 4, f. 22v; Samuel Richardson, "My Observations on Mr. Silvester's State of his Affairs," FC XIV, 4, f. 28.

9. Samuel Richardson, "Private Thoughts on Mr. Ditcher's Proposal and Address," Yale University, p. 3 and cover sheet; *SCG*, 2:158; 3:374–76.

10. Richardson to Stinstra, 2 June 1753; *Stinstra*, 24; Richardson to Bishop Hildesley, 13 July 1754, *Correspondence*, 5:127; Richardson to David Graham, 3 May 1750, FC XV, 2, f. 85; Cox Macro to Richardson, March 1754, British Library 32557, f. 175; Richardson to Sarah Chapone, 6 December 1750, FC XII, 2, f. 7v–8; Lady Bradshaigh to Richardson, 3 March–22 March 1754, FC XI, f. 95; she also recommended that Richardson write sermons, Lady Bradshaigh to Richardson, 28 October in 27 November 1753, FC XI, f. 44; Edward Young to Richardson, 14 March 1754, *Correspondence*, 2:32–33; this is echoed in Mary Heylin to Richardson, 24 November 1747, FC XV, 2, f. 3.

11. Richardson to Stinstra, 2 June 1753, *Stinstra*, 30; [Samuel Richardson], *Aesop's Fables* (London: J. F. and C. Rivington, n.d.), xii, x, iii, xiv, 191–92; Sir Roger L'Estrange, *Fables*, 538–39.

12. Richardson, *Familiar Letters*, xxvii–xxix.

13. Richardson to Stinstra, 20 March 1754, *Selected Letters*, 298; Richardson to Aaron Hill, [1 February 1741?], *Selected Letters*, 40–41; perhaps the best study of the response to *Pamela* is Bernard Kreissman, *Pamela-Shamela* (Lincoln: University of Nebraska Press, 1960).

14. Some of these ideas have been suggested in Donald L. Ball, *Samuel Richardson's Theory of Fiction* (Hague: Mouton, 1971), 309, and Morris Golden, "Richardson's Repetitions," *PMLA* 82 (March 1967): 64–67; *SCG*, 2:156–57 and 187; Lady Mary Wortley Montagu to Lady Bute, 20 October [1755], Lady Mary Wortley Montagu, *The Complete Letters*, ed. Robert Halsband, 3 vols. (Oxford: Clarendon Press, 1967), 3:91.

15. Richardson to Lady Bradshaigh, 15 December 1748, *Selected Letters*, 116; Richardson to Sarah Chapone, 2 March 1752; *Selected Letters*, 204; Richardson to Sarah Chapone, 18 April 1752, FC XII, 2, f. 65; Richardson to Lady Bradshaigh, 15 December 1748, FC XI, f. 9; Richardson to Lady Echlin, 17 May 1754, *Selected Letters*, 302; Richardson to Lady Bradshaigh, 6 October 1748, *Correspondence*, 4:190; Richardson to Lady Echlin, 14 February 1755, Berg Collection; Richardson to Lady Echlin, 17 May 1754, *Selected Letters*, 302; Aaron Hill to Richardson, 23 January 1747, FC XIII, 3, f. 83v; M. Kinkead-Weekes, "*Clarissa* Restored?" *Review of English Studies*, n.s., 10 (May 1959): 156–71.

16. Richardson to Frances Grainger, 20 December 1748, Morgan Library; Anne Donnellan to Richardson, 17 August 1750, *Correspondence*, 4:18; Lady Bradshaigh to Richardson, 10 October 1748, *Correspondence*, 4:180; Lady Bradshaigh to Richardson 25 November 1750, *Correspondence*, 6:42–44; Lady Bradshaigh to Richardson, 29 March 1751, *Correspondence*, 6:90–93.

17. Eusebius to Mr. Rivington, 2 February 1740/41, FC XVI, 1, ff. 47v–48; Lady Bradshaigh to Richardson, 16 April 1751, *Correspondence*, 6:114–15; Richardson to Susanna Highmore, 4 June 1750, *Correspondence*, 2:235–36; *SCG*, 2:272 and 1:297; Richardson to Edward Moore, 3 October 1748, *Selected Letters*, 89, Gerald A. Barker, "The Complacent Paragon: Exemplary Characterization in Richardson," *Studies in English Literature* 9 (Summer 1969): 518; on Pollexfen, see *SCG*, 1:45, 200, and 224.

18. Richardson to Aaron Hill, 26 January 1746/47, *Selected Letters*, 79; Richardson to Sarah Chapone, 25 March 1751, *Selected Letters*, 181; Sarah Chapone to Richardson, 10 December 1753, FC XIII, 1, f. 94; Richardson to Lady Bradshaigh, 24 March [1751?], *Correspondence*, 6:85.

19. [Campbell?], *Critical Remarks*, 25; Lady Bradshaigh to Richardson, 1 November in 27

November 1753, FC XI, f. 45; Richardson to Lady Bradshaigh, 8 February 1754, *Selected Letters*, 280; some of these ideas have been suggested by Ball, *Richardson's Theory* and Golden, "Richardson's Repetitions"; Richardson to Stinstra, 2 June 1753, *Stinstra*, 30; Richardson, *Clarissa*, 3:520, Letter 131; Ecclesiasticus 13:1; *SCG*, 1:26 and 2:564–65.

20. Richardson to Stinstra, 2 June 1753, *Selected Letters*, 232.

21. Richardson to [Cox Macro?], 22 March 1754, British Library 32557, ff. 176 and 176b.

22. Gailhard, *Compleat Gentleman*, pt. 2, p. 144; Ascham's remarks are noted in Thomas Fuller, B.D., *The Holy State* (Cambridge: John Williams, 1642), 159; [Daniel Defoe], *The True-Born Englishman* (n.p., 1700), 6.

23. Hester Lynch Piozzi, *Observations and Reflections Made in the Course of a Journey Through France, Italy, and Germany*, 2 vols. (London: A. Strahan and T. Cadell, 1789), 1:265; Lady Mary Wortley Montagu, on the other hand, thought Richardson did not know Italy, Lady Mary Wortley Montagu to Lady Bute, 20 October [1755], Lady Mary Wortley Montagu, *Complete Letters*, ed. Halsband, 3:91; Jean Baptiste de Freval to Richardson, 17 April 1751, *Correspondence*, 5:278–79; *SCG*, 1:259; Lady Bradshaigh to Richardson, 3 March–22 March 1754, FC XI, f. 90v; Richardson to Lady Bradshaigh, 8 April 1754, *Selected Letters*, 299–300; on Baretti see Edward Young to Richardson, 20 September 1753, *Monthly Magazine* 40 (1 September 1815): 134, Letter 71; Anna Williams and Mary Masters to Richardson, 30 October 1753, FC XV, 3, f. 17; "Index to Correspondence," FC XV, 3, f. 1a; Joseph Baretti, *An Account of the Manners and Customs of Italy*, 2 vols. (London: T. Davies et al., 1768), 2:8–9, 127; on the Italian background see J. C. Hilson and Rosalind Nicol, "Two Notes on 'Sir Charles Grandison,'" *Notes and Queries*, n.s., 22 (November 1975): 493; A. D. McKillop, "On *Sir Charles Grandison*," in *Richardson*, ed. Carroll, 124; Alan Dugald McKillop, *The Early Masters of English Fiction* (Lawrence: University of Kansas paperback, 1968), 82.

24. *SCG*, 2:155; Richardson to Alexis Claude Clairaut, 5 July 1753, British Library C.44.g, facing p. 396, sheet no. 68; [Richardson], *Aesop's Fables*, preface, p. vi; Richardson to Benjamin Kennicott, [November ?] 1754, Osborn Collection, Yale, ff. 1–2; Richardson to Lady Bradshaigh, [ca. 1 October 1755], *Selected Letters*, 323; see also Roger B. Dooley, "The Catholic in the Eighteenth-Century Novel" (Ph.D. diss., Catholic University, 1956) and Frank David Kievitt, "Attitudes Toward Roman Catholicism in the Later Eighteenth-Century English Novel" (Ph.D. diss., Columbia, 1975); it is intriguing to think of Richardson's Hammersmith country home in such close proximity to one of the few Catholic strongholds in England, while Lady Bradshaigh lived in one of the most populous Catholic counties, Lancashire; Bernard Ward, *The Dawn of the Catholic Revival in England 1781–1803*, 2 vols. (London: Longmans, Green, and Co., 1909), 1:xxiv, xxvi, and 34.

25. Samuel Richardson, *Pamela*, ed. T. C. Duncan Eaves and Ben D. Kimpel (Boston: Houghton Mifflin Company, 1971), p. 94, Letter 31.

26. On Harriet's frankness see Lady Bradshaigh to Richardson, 27 November 1753, FC XI, f. 45.

27. For other discussions of Richardson's method see Janet Gurkin Altman, *Epistolarity* (Columbus: Ohio State University Press, 1982) and Brophy, *Richardson;* Richardson to Stinstra, 2 June 1753, *Selected Letters*, 234–35.

28. Richardson, *Familiar Letters*, pp. 72–76, Letter 62 and pp. 193–220, Letters 149–60; McKillop has suggested that the discussions are comparable to medieval courts of love, McKillop, *Richardson*, 198; for Harriet as editor see *SCG*, 1:348–49; on Selby House 2:515; on Grandison Hall 3:437; on debate in *SCG* see Richardson to Lady Echlin, 10 October 1754, *Correspondence*, 5:34; Richardson to Lady Bradshaigh, 12 November 1753, FC XI, f. 39; Richardson to Lady Bradshaigh, 8 December 1753, *Selected Letters*, 257.

29. For Harriet on Mrs. Oldham see *SCG*, 1:363; Harriet on the Grandison sisters 1:371; on reformed rakes 1:342; on unnatural commands 1:321; other examples of Harriet's moralizing may be found in *SCG*, 1:342 and 355; Sir Charles, too, moralizes after an account, see 2:48 and 52; Harriet as monitor 3:267 and 1:194; and Richardson to Lady Echlin, 12 September 1754,

Hyde Collection; Richardson to Hester Mulso, 3 September 1751, *Selected Letters*, 189–90; Harriet on Sir Charles *SCG*, 1:430; Harriet as character writer 1:42–43 and 68–72.

30. [William Darrell], *The Gentleman Instructed*, 6th ed. (London: E. Smith, 1716), Dedication; [Defoe], *Family Instructor*, 16th ed. (1766), 1:vi; [Daniel Defoe], *Religious Courtship* (London: E. Mathews, et al., 1722), Preface; Francois de Salignac de la Mothe Fénelon, *Instructions for the Education of a Daughter*, trans. and rev. George Hickes (Edinburgh: James Reid, 1750), 47–55; Adam Petrie, *Rules of Good Deportment* (Edinburgh: n.p., 1720), chap. 9, p. 98.

31. Fuller, B.D., *Holy State*, chaps. 1–4.

32. On foils see *SCG*, 3:418 and 155; Lady Bradshaigh to Richardson, 3 November in 27 November 1753, FC XI, f. 45v; Lady Bradshaigh to Richardson, 30 June 1754, FC XI, f. 106v; on Olivia see *SCG*, 2:364–65, 117, and 630; Lady Bradshaigh to Richardson, 31 October in 27 November 1753, FC XI, f. 44v; Richardson to Lady Bradshaigh, 8 February 1754, *Selected Letters*, 278; Samuel Richardson, *History of Mrs. Beaumont*, in *Correspondence*, 5:301–48; the manuscript is in the Pierpont Morgan Library and four additional letters in the possession of Alan Dugald McKillop, Eaves and Kimpel, *Richardson*, 425, n. 18.

33. *SCG*, 1:440 and 463.

34. *SCG*, 2:647 and 3:57; for Lucy's comment see *SCG*, 3:224.

35. On writing with a plan see Richardson to Aaron Hill, 29 October 1746, *Selected Letters*, 71; Richardson to Lady Bradshaigh, [April–October?] 1751, *Correspondence*, 6:117; Richardson to William Duncombe, 22 October 1751, *Selected Letters*, 194–95; Sarah Chapone to Richardson, 18 November 1751, FC XII, 2, f. 32v; Richardson to Sarah Chapone, 22 November 1751, *Selected Letters*, 195; Richardson to Stinstra, 2 June 1753, *Selected Letters*, 235; Stinstra to Richardson, 24 December 1753, *Correspondence*, 5:258; Richardson to Stinstra, 20 March 1754, *Selected Letters*, 298; Richardson to Hildesley, 21 February 1755, *Correspondence*, 5:132; for Richardson on *Pamela II* see Richardson to Dr. Cheyne [January 1742?], FC XVI, 1, f. 58.

4

THE COMPLEAT GENTLEMAN

HAVING considered *Sir Charles Grandison* in its critical and social context, in its relation to other kinds of literature, the conduct book in particular, and in light of Richardson's own background, we may now proceed to comment on how the author treats specific conduct-book issues and how he draws a unique kind of hero.

Following its publication, *Grandison* evoked a sharp response from its readers. Richardson wrote to Lady Echlin, "A Time will come, and perhaps it is not far off, when the Writer of certain moral Pieces will meet with better Quarter from his very Censurers. His Obscurity, a Man in Trade, in Business, pretending to draw Characters for Warning to one Set of People, for Instruction to another—Presumptuous!—"Richardson's dual intention, to jog the consciences of those already noble and provide models for those with rising aspirations, suggests something of the mix and change in the nature of courtesy literature found by W. Lee Ustick in his study of seventeenth-century works. In many ways Grandison harks back to an older aristocratic tradition in which the nature of nobility, the formation of the young man, his education and recreation, and his larger responsibilities to his family and the state were important. At the same time, we see the same emphasis on duty and on the responsibilities one has to one's superiors, peers, and inferiors found in the conduct books directed toward a more general audience.[1]

Among the first topics treated in the traditional conduct book is the origin and nature of nobility. By traditional criteria, inherited nobility, originating from the virtuous and glorious action of a family ancestor, was the only true nobility. Sir Charles himself, as a baronet, holds a rank created fairly recently by James I, while his uncle Lord W. is a peer, as are his brothers-in-law, Lord L. and Lord G. Sir Thomas, Sir Charles's father, rather petulantly notes the difference between his rank and Lord L.'s. The Porrettas, too, represent a high rank as Italian aristocrats. Charlotte Grandison says of her brother's attitude toward rank that he "regards the heart, rather than the head, and much more than either rank or fortune, tho' it were princely; and yet is not a leveller, but thinks that rank or degree intitles a man who is not utterly unworthy of both, to respect." At the same time, Sir Charles expresses the concern of Richardson's time that the nobility had strayed far from the virtuous qualities of its ancestors. Sir Charles commends Clementina's mother for being "illustrious by descent, and still more so for her goodness of heart, sweetness of temper, and prudence." But he upbraids the erring Jeronymo, "Are you determined to sit down satisfied with the honour of your ancestors? Your progenitors, and every one of your family, have given you reason to applaud their worthiness: Will you not give them cause to boast of yours?" And he chastises the volatile Olivia in a similar vein:

> Your situation in life, your high birth, your illustrious line of ancestors, are so many calls upon *you*, in whom the riches and the consequences of so many noble progenitors centre, to act worthy of their names, of their dignities, of your own; and of the dignity of your Sex. The world looks up to you (your education, too, so greatly beyond that of most Italian Ladies) with the expectation of an example—

Charlotte, too, reflecting on the wayward Everard, asks what is nobility "where descendants depart from the virtue of the first enobling ancestor!" Besides his cousin Everard, Grandison's family has two other cases of irresponsible nobility. Lord W., Sir Charles's widowed uncle, a gouty man of about fifty, is under the spell of his housekeeper. And Grandison's own father, having engaged in numerous affairs, has fathered two children by his housekeeper, and at the time of his death has a treaty under way for an intrigue with the young Miss Obrien. Sir Hargrave Pollexfen and his henchmen Bagenhall, Merceda, and Jordan are also unreformed. Even after Sir Charles has apparently had some good effect on them, he finds himself rescuing three of them on the Continent from the angry kinsmen of women they had seduced.[2] The conduct-book writers frequently blamed the behavior of characters like Pollexfen and his friends on indulgent parents and faulty education. And faulty education might lead to a related problem among the nobility: a younger brother dependent on the bounty of an elder brother when, with proper education, he might have done quite well in business. The *Spectator's* Will Wimble is a good example of this, and Richardson offers similar cases for consideration. Everard Grandison "knows nothing of figures, or business of any kind" and "had been brought up in idleness." Bagenhall is a younger brother who succeeded to an elder brother's fortune but "was brought up to no business." The death of Lord W.'s father left him independent at too early an age, while Greville had a good education but makes "a jest" of the "pious precepts" of his father. Sir Thomas's waywardness is attributed to his being a poet, and Harriet observes "that to be a poet, requires an heated imagination, which often runs away with the judgment." Lord G. is no rake, but Charlotte takes exception to his education. She admits that "he spells pretty well, for a Lord" but thinks he has been brought up to be idle and criticizes his collecting of shells, moths, butterflies, and china. It does take time for Charlotte to appreciate a husband who has been "brought up as an only son" and whose "education has not given him a turn to significance."[3]

The opposite extreme of the nobleman deficient in education is, of course, the pedant, and conduct books warned against this type, too. Walden is Richardson's example in *Grandison*. But, characteristic of Richardson's approach, several characters represent a middle way. Lord D. "has learning, and is allowed to have good sense, which every *learned* man has not." Young Mr. Beauchamp, too, is learned and prudent, while Sir Charles has had the benefit of a good tutor in Dr. Bartlett and a "foundation that was so nobly laid, by the best and wisest of mothers." He has studied law and husbandry and, in a discussion which nicely balances out Harriet's debate with Walden, defends learning from a theoretical as well as practical point of view: "The knowledge of the Latin language, in particular, let me say, is of singular use in the mastery of every science." He has obviously studied history, a subject regarded as indispensable by the conduct-book writers, since he argues from history in his discourse against dueling and draws upon historical examples in his conversation.[4]

Travel abroad, a part of the young man's education, was treated with reservation by the conduct-book writers, because there was a danger that the young man would return corrupted in habits, religion, and morals. A good governor or companion was important, but, as Jean Gailhard observes, "some governors need governors themselves." Unfortunately, Mr. Creutzer, Grandison's tutor, is depraved and attempts to lure his young charge from the path of virtue. In Turin, Grandison meets Dr. Bartlett, who is trying to govern his profligate pupil Mr. Lorimer. Grandison is eventually allowed to dismiss Creutzer, and Lorimer dies lacking the comfort of a repentant conscience.[5]

Harriet Byron exhibits skepticism regarding travel, partially colored, undoubtedly, by the fact that Sir Charles's travels resulted in a conflict in his affections. She notes that there is nothing to see but ruins, which one can better appreciate from reading books. She points to Charlotte's ease and politeness of manner acquired "without stirring out of the kingdom." Sir Hargrave has been abroad, but "he must have carried abroad with him a great number of follies, and a great deal of affectation, if he has left any of them behind him." Lord W. congratulates Grandison on his apparent improvement from travel, adding that "nine parts in ten of those who go abroad, ought to be hanged up at their fathers doors on their return." Dr. Bartlett assures Harriet that travel abroad can result in greater affection and esteem for one's own country if the traveler is cautious and circumspect. In fact, Grandison appears anxious to settle permanently in England. He joins the Selbys and Harriet on an excursion through the English countryside, a trip reflecting Pamela's view that "England abounds with curiosities, both of art and nature, worth the notice of the diligent inquirer, and equal with some of those we admire in foreign parts. . . ."[6]

Grandison and young Beauchamp are obviously sensible travelers in spite of the fact that both have been practically exiled due to unpleasant family matters in England. As a matter of fact, Grandison has been abroad eight or nine years, far longer than the usual three. Grandison writes letters home describing his travels, as recommended by the conduct-book writers, and has traveled beyond Europe to Asia and Africa, as well. He is respected abroad and even has friends among the College of Cardinals. But while he is morally uncorrupted from the Grand Tour, he is involved in a romantic entanglement that causes great distress, both to himself and to an Italian family. Jean Gailhard had cautioned against falling in love, which can result in "great straits and difficulties." Mrs. Beaumont and Harriet both suggest that the Porrettas were partially to blame for allowing Grandison, nobly as he acted, to be in such close proximity to a young woman. In any case, Richardson's warning is clear: individuals acting properly and with the best intentions may yet entangle themselves in difficult circumstances.[7]

Richardson, like traditional conduct-book writers, goes beyond the specifics of education to treat the intangible quality essential to a true gentleman. Fielding called it Good Breeding or "the Art of pleasing, or contributing as much as possible to the Ease and Happiness of those with whom you converse." Chesterfield would describe it as Je Ne Sçay Quoy:

It is in my opinion a compound of all the agreable qualitys of body and mind, in which no one of them predominates in such a manner as to give exclusion to any other. It is not mere wit, mere beauty, mere learning, nor indeed mere any one thing that produces it, though they all contribute something towards it. It is owing to this *Je ne scay quoy* that one takes a liking to some one particular person at first rather than to another. One feels oneself prepossessed in favour of that person without being enough acquainted with him to judge of his intrinsick merit or talents, and one finds oneself inclined to suppose him to have good sense, good nature, and good humour. A genteel address, gracefull motions, a pleasing elocution, and elegancy of style, are powerful ingredients in this compound. It is in short an extract of all the *Graces.*

A distinctive manly grace and amiable manner are attributed to Sir Charles, even when he is seated on the floor. Harriet calls him "one of the most unreserved of men, as well as one of the most polite. He makes not his guests uneasy with his civilities: But you see freedom and ease in his whole deportment; and the stranger cannot doubt but Sir Charles will be equally pleased with freedom and ease, in return." He is handsome, but Harriet adds that even if this were not so, his manner would make him "very agreeable." Sir Charles has a way of disarming all those he encounters. Lady Beauchamp, antagonistic initially to Grandison's effort to reconcile young Beauchamp with his father and herself, is surprised that a man with Grandison's reputation for goodness is not grave, formal, bashful, or sheepish. Sir Charles flatters gracefully and is free "but not *impertinent.*" And he can be equally agreeable in the company of rakes without degrading himself. In conversation, a commonly treated topic of conduct books, Sir Charles goes out of his way to draw out reluctant speakers by introducing topics familiar to them, by leading the shy individual into the discussion, and by generally steering the conversation so that everyone appears at his best. We see him relieving Harriet's embarrassment, alleviating the fear of the Danbys, and lessening the awkwardness of all the Italians as they join him in a dinner of reconciliation. Even in the easily missed habit of smiling rather than laughing we find him setting the best example. Chesterfield particularly speaks against laughter as one of "the distinguishing characteristicks of the vulgar and the ill-bred." Thus, Sir Hargrave and the pedant Walden are examples of characters who engage in immoderate laughter, while Sir Charles only smiles, and he does so frequently.[8]

Taste in dress, another subject treated by the conduct-book writers, is closely connected with the overall impression made by a gentleman. The author of the *Art of Complaisance* urged that "Our Cloaths ought to be proper and sutable, not superfluous; and according to the fashion then in use, without being fantastick, in too much affecting new, or counterfeiting gravity in obstinately following the old. . . ." Lord Chesterfield would also avoid singularity. Fuller warned against wearing clothes beneath one's own rank, and the *Spectator* told the story of a man dressed beneath his quality who was deservedly treated roughly. At the other extreme, Matthew Hale advised against being "sick for every new Fashion," and Jeremy Taylor soberly admonishes the reader not "to lay a snare for a Soul" through one's apparel. Again, Richardson provides examples from one end of the spectrum to the other. Harriet comments on Sir Hargrave:

> The taste of the present age seems to be dress: No wonder, therefore, that such a man as Sir Hargrave aims to excel in it. What can be mis-bestowed by a man on his person, who values it more than his mind? But he would, in my opinion, better become his dress, if the pains he un-doubtedly takes before he ventures to come into public, were less appar-ent.

Everard "dresses very gaily" and is "at the *head* of the fashion." Lord G. is "a gay-dressing man" but is governed by "fashion, rather than his inclination." Charlotte's other admirer, Sir Walter Watkyns, "out-does him in Foppery." Sir Charles dresses to the fashion so as not to appear singular and admits that perhaps he is a bit more flamboyant than he would normally like to be. He tells Harriet that his father "loved to be dressed," and that he does not want to "discredit his magnificent spirit" before his friends and tenants.[9]
A final word is in order respecting other gentlemanly accomplish-ments. Some of the courtesy books advocated such skills as dancing, music, and various exercises such as fencing and riding. There is plenty of dancing in *Grandison*. Grandmother Shirley regards danc-ing as a healthful exercise and sponsors several balls. Grandison is acknowledged the finest dancer in England, and Charlotte suggests that it might be called a science. Sir Charles also plays the violin and harpsichord and sings, Beauchamp joining in on the violin, Lord L. on the bass viol, and Lord G. on the German flute. Besides this he paints and is an expert horseman. All in all, in education, behavior, and gentlemanly skills, Grandison measures up quite well to the standards suggested by the courtesy writers.[10]
While whole conduct books were not devoted to particular voca-tions, except for those directed to apprentices, sections were often given over to a brief discussion of the qualities, strengths, drawbacks, and obligations of various callings. Richardson has depicted examples of potential callings for men. Tutors, for example, are represented in Dr. Bartlett along with his profligate opposite, Mr. Creutzer. Respon-sible men were hard to come by; Lady Echlin had expressed concern

to Richardson about finding a good tutor for her nephew at Oxford: "a discreet, good clergyman I want for that purpose; would much rather choose a real good Christian, than what the world calls a clever learned man." Mr. Lowther is Richardson's representative of the medical profession. He must try to patch up the work performed on Jeronymo by an unskillful Cremonese surgeon, followed by one from Bologna and another from Padua, a "pragmatical" French gentleman, and two more Italians considered *"Theorists"* by the Frenchman. In true Grandisonian fashion, "Mr. Lowther suggested an alteration in their method, but in so easy and gentle a manner, as if he doubted not, but *such* was their intention when the state of the wounds would admit of that method of treatment, that the gentlemen came readily into it." Clementina benefits from English medicine as well. The *Spectator* had written that "melancholy is a kind of Demon that haunts our Island. . . ." and Richardson noted to Frances Grainger that "Nervous Maladies are in one particular English Bulldogs or Mastiffs, which you please: When once they seize, they never quit their Hold." Grandison, confident in the English method of treating nervous disorders, carries with him to Italy the opinion of several doctors concerning the best remedy for Clementina. Richardson himself received treatment through the mail from his friend Dr. George Cheyne, author of *The English Malady.* The letters between the two of them contain many descriptions of exotic cures. But Mr. Lowther and his colleagues are far different from the general impression one has of eighteenth-century physicians as depicted, for example, in *Spectator* 444 or in the remark in *Spectator* 21 that "When a Nation abounds in Physicians it grows thin of People."[11]

Considering Richardson's own poor opinion of the law and the dim view generally taken of the profession, the lawyers do not come off badly in *Grandison* either. Sir Charles is not anxious to become involved in costly and lengthy legal disputes in attempting to see justice done to the Mansfields. But we meet three lawyers, and all three seem reasonable and honest. Sir John Lambton in the Mansfield case and Blagrave, an attorney for the O-Haras, are both willing to settle matters without litigation. Our last view of Eusebius Sylvester, the lawyer for the Danby estate, finds him with "tears in his honest eyes," anxious to look into his own affairs to see what good he can do in imitation of Grandison. This Sylvester is certainly a different man from the lawyer who coincidentally had the same name, unknown to Richardson, and later took advantage of Richardson's generosity and goodwill.[12]

The characters representing the military are not so favorably treated. Richardson had earlier written to Lady Bradshaigh about the "savage spirit" in the *Iliad* and *Aeneid* that he thought promoted war throughout the ages. While the *Spectator* did not take a critical view of the military, probably because Steele was one of the authors, other writers considered soldiers ambitious and lovers of false glory. Thomas Fuller urged that a good soldier should detest dueling, while Denis Grenville maintained that in order for a soldier to be truly valiant, he must also be virtuous. In the novel, Captain Anderson, Charlotte Grandison's first love, is shown to be an opportunist and illiterate, too, while Major O-Hara and his relation Salmonet seem comical in their officiousness. Clementina's brother, the General, is immovable in his opinion and combative in his behavior, a man who would take stern measures with his sister and who is ungracious to Grandison. Sir Charles had an uncle who was in the military, and a military career was suggested to him; he served as a volunteer once, but after seeing his father nearly killed in a duel, he resolved against a soldier's life. The depraved tutor recommended by Grandison's uncle was a former officer forced to leave the military because of battle wounds. Besides his unpleasant experiences with military men, Grandison argues against the military because a soldier is not his own man: "a slave to the will of *his* superiors in command, as he is almost *obliged* to be a tyrant to those under him." And a woman who marries a soldier can rarely expect him at home. Sir Charles does offer to help the eldest Oldham boy launch a military career; but he lectures him on what to aim for and avoid "to qualify himself for a man of true honour; and spoke very handsomely of such gentlemen of the army as are real gentlemen." As in his portrayals of the medical and legal professions, Richardson maintains a balanced approach; goodness is not confined to or excluded from any calling.[13]

The gentleman was urged to have a good clergyman in his household, and the clergy are indeed prominent in *Grandison*. Early in the novel we meet "the most horrible-looking Clergyman" Harriet has ever seen, Pollexfen's choice to officiate at his attempted marriage to Harriet following her abduction. At the other extreme is Dr. Bartlett, "learned, prudent, humble," exhibiting a combination of reserve and politeness that "shewed that the fine Gentleman and the Clergyman were not separated" in him. Richardson does not attack the practices of a lax clergy as Henry Fielding does. His clergy are good but tend to remain in the background; we may recall Dr. Lewen in *Clarissa*, who was reluctant to become involved in a family dispute just when Clarissa expected him to help. Dr. Bartlett is respected and consulted and aids Grandison in his many charitable works, but he is not one who is constantly providing advice at crucial moments in the story. Father Marescotti and the Bishop in Bologna are more involved in

Porretta concerns, even to the point of Father Marescotti's being caught spying by Grandison. Nevertheless, by the end of the story, Dr. Bartlett and the Italian priest have put aside differences and engage in long talks. Another reconciliation between two clergymen has been effected by Grandmother Shirley, who had brought together Mr. Milbourne, a dissenting minister, and Dr. Curtis of the established church. In line with the tolerance we have observed in Richardson's perspective in chapter 3, it would seem that arguments about theological fine points had no place in his personal or literary scheme. Lady Bradshaigh had urged Richardson to read Swift's sermon on the Trinity, which, incidentally, urges the believer not to worry about understanding all the minutiae of dogma. Richardson responded that he would give the sermon a reading:

> But, as I hinted in my last, I have no notion of men's attempting to explain a mystery. In short, I am afraid of raising doubts in my own mind, which I cannot, from nature of the subject, lay. All that concerns us to know for the conduct of life, in order to fill us with a blessed hope, is plain and easy.[14]

A final calling must be considered, that of business and trade. One, of course, cannot help recalling the glorious panegyric on merchants in *Spectator* 69:

> there are not more useful Members in a Commonwealth than Merchants. They knit Mankind together in a mutual Intercourse of good Offices, distribute the Gifts of Nature, find Work for the Poor, add Wealth to the Rich, and Magnificence to the Great.

Sir Charles echoes this in his conversation with the young Danbys when he notes that British merchants "are the most useful members of the community." Emily Jervois's late father had acquired his wealth "by his own industry," and Mrs. Beaumont tells Clementina that if Sir Charles had not been "born to a fortune, he would make one." But merchants had another function: to prop up the sagging fortunes of the nobility in exchange for a title. Charlotte playfully refers to this in her remark about going "into the city for a wife," when she hears of the admiration of the Danby ladies for Sir Charles. She also admits being unable to remember "the names of city-knights." Charlotte, too, takes a dim view of Everard Grandison's new wife, the widow of an honest, well-to-do wine merchant, who has rescued him from his debts. Everard "has presented her with a genealogical table of his ancestors, drawn up and blazoned by heraldry art," a gift that obviously appeals to her vanity. Sir Charles combines the best of the merchant and aristocratic worlds: the generous and helpful spirit, found also in Jervois and Danby and urged on the younger Danbys, as well as the consciousness of his own rank in the world.[15]

As we consider the callings depicted and fictionalized by Richardson, we see that in each case the emphasis is on the possibilities for doing good and on depicting good examples from various professions. Sir Charles's discussion with Dr. Bartlett on the need for learning in various ranks could be applied to each person's capacity for performing good works within the limitations of his vocation:

> I could be glad, that only such children of the poor, as shew a peculiar ingenuity, have any great pains taken with them in their *books*. Husbandry and labour are what are most wanting to be encouraged among the lower class of people. Providence has given to men different genius's and capacities, for different ends; and that all might become useful links of the same great chain. Let us apply those talents to Labour, those to Learning, those to Trade, to Mechanics, in their different branches, which point out the different pursuits, and then no person will be unuseful; on the contrary, every one may be eminent in some way or other.[16]

A corollary to the ideas expressed in this passage is that of relative duties. As Samuel Clarke observed, ". . . every person, in every station of life whatsoever, wherein the Providence of God thinks fit to place him, has always some *plain* and *certain Duty*, which 'tis his present proper Business to attend to." The idea of duty was strong in courtesy and conduct literature, ranging from James I's *Basilikon Doron*, which begins with a description of the young prince's duties to God, to William Darrell's enumeration of duties as a Christian and a neighbor, to William Gouge's *Of Domesticall Duties* (1622), which includes mutual duties of husbands and wives as well as the duties of children, parents, servants, and masters. Even Chesterfield discusses what he calls religious and moral duties, the first consisting in an observance of the commandments and the second in following the Golden Rule. And George Whitefield, whose emphasis was different from that of the established church, nevertheless acknowledged that while one could not depend on salvation by good works, there "is no Doubt but you are to do your Duty."[17]

Richard Allestree advises that the child's duty to the parent is to care for him in sickness, senility, and in poverty; and this applies "not only to the kind and virtuous, but even to the harshest and wickedest parent." Indeed, the child is obliged to conceal any infirmities of the parents, as Noah's sons did. Thomas Fuller makes the obligation binding, "Not onely if his father hath been a pelican, but though he hath been an estridge unto him, and neglected him in his youth."

Richardson himself echoes these sentiments in a letter to Frances Grainger, saying that if a parent's faults cannot be concealed, they should be made light of. And Harriet enjoins filial duty even if the parent is remiss in his duty. Richardson had voiced his concern to Lady Bradshaigh about the "stiffness," excessive reverence, and reserve that he felt existed between himself and his daughters. Nevertheless, he declared that the examples in literature must propose a higher ideal since theirs is an age in which "there is more Danger of Duty being *Under-* than *Over*-done."[18]

Sir Charles is confronted with unusual demands upon his filial duty. This is seen especially in his behavior after his father dies. In his treatment of Mrs. Oldham and Miss Obrien, his father's mistress and prospective paramour, he "was very desirous to conceal his father's frailty from the world." And even after those matters are settled fairly, quietly, and discreetly, he honors the memory of his father and declares "all my father's steps, in which I could tread, I did: and have chosen rather to build upon, than demolish his foundations." The funeral for his father is "decent, but not ostentatious," and the excess funds which would have been spent are presented to distressed housekeepers and poor tenant farmers. His monument inscription will instruct the living rather than praise the dead. After this, in accordance with his mother's deathbed request that he look after his sisters, he sees to it that Caroline and Charlotte receive what they are entitled to from their father's estate. Then he assists Caroline in pursuing her desire to marry Lord L., a worthy man in character and fortune. He extricates Charlotte from the clutches of the fortune-hunting Captain Anderson. Grandison extends the range of filial duty when he becomes "more than a father to his *uncle*." It was not denied that parents could have a corrupting influence on children, but it is rare to have the younger person expostulate with the older person in the conduct books. Richardson may have found a precedent for such behavior in Defoe's *Family Instructor,* where parents who have been remiss in religious instruction are subtly chastised by the perceptive questions of their children. Lord. W. had been antagonized by Sir Charles's father, and Sir Charles sets out to regain the good graces of his uncle, relieve him of the immoral and unpleasant affair with Mrs. Giffard, and even to court a wife for him in the person of Miss Mansfield. Grandison is Richardson's most important example of filial duty among the male characters, for none of the others is beset with quite the same dilemmas.[19]

Grandison was accused by some critics of negligence in not consulting his father about his courtship of Clementina. Lady Bradshaigh wrote to Richardson that several of her acquaintances wondered about this: "Tho' he was *sure* of his approbation, yet he was so strict in point of Duty that it is Thought not quite in character." Plumer in his *Candid Examination* makes the same point. Richardson's response to Lady Bradshaigh echoes Grandison's answer to Clementina's brother, the General: Grandison had no intention of addressing Clementina when first introduced to the family; but when he realized there was some hope of being accepted as a suitor, religion and country became impediments; and when those obstacles were overcome, he would have consulted his father. None of the conduct books deals with such a specific complication in courtship as Grandison's. Lady Bradshaigh had called his situation "difficult" and "delicate." Richardson explained his intention:

> And must a good man, in delicate cases, be judged by *general* example, and not be allowed to *give* one? . . . One of my great views in this piece is, for the sake of the Sex, to shew the Vincibility of that passion wch. indulged, occasions so many disgraces to it, and so much unhappiness in families; and shall not the hero of the story, when called upon, be made to give an Example of that Vincibility?[20]

In the other courtships in *Grandison*, however, the problem for the male characters is not one of failure to consult parents, but rather the obligation to find a spouse with an appropriate background. Gilbert Burnet's rule, representative of most courtesy writers, is the guide here:

> Gentlemen in their Marriages ought to consider a great many things more than Fortune, tho', generally speaking, that is the only thing sought for: A good Understanding, good Principles, and a good Temper, with a liberal Education, and acceptable Person, are the first things to be considered: And certainly Fortune ought to come after all these.

Lady D., making inquiries for her son, declares, "I look farther than to the *person* of woman: tho' my Lord will by no means have beauty left out in the qualifications of a wife. I look to the family to whom a lady owes her education and training-up. Quality, however, I stand not upon. A man of quality, you know, confers quality on his wife." Sir Rowland sets forth similar requirements: good character, religious education, familiarity with household matters, and last of all, fortune. Worthy Lord L., exasperated by a capricious Sir Thomas, vows to marry Caroline without a dowry. Sir Charles describes Miss Mansfield to Lord W., emphasizing her qualities of mind and management, as well as her good family, though sunk in its fortunes. Finally, Grandison himself has always stressed Harriet's attractive character before that of her person. And when the time comes for settlements to be made, he insists that the additional funds offered by the Selbys to make up for a "*supposed* deficiency" in Harriet's dowry be retained for the benefit of the Selby nieces.[21]

Fortune becomes more important in the case of young William Wilson and the Danbys. Their behavior tends to reflect the advice of Caleb Trenchfield to his apprentice son. He regards marriage as a business proposition that should be entertained only with sufficient financial support. Grandison assists the footman Wilson by collecting a purse for his intended, Miss Awberry. Wilson tells Grandison that now he will be able to join his sister's business since "he shall have something to carry into the stock," and he will be able to marry, too. Sir Charles enables the Danbys to enter the business world with more than "scanty beginnings." Learning that Miss Danby has had to forgo marriage to a merchant's son because she lacks a dowry, Grandison cautions that fathers cannot be blamed "who expect a fortune to be brought into their family, in some measure equivalent to the benefit the new-comer hopes to receive from it; especially in mercantile families. . . ."[22]

A final word must be said about a courtship that is being held in abeyance for reasons of prudence rather than monetary considerations. Young Beauchamp has asked Grandison for permission to court Emily, Grandison's ward; Emily seems to have an unspoken and unconscious regard for him. Her fortune is so large that it might be the primary attraction for some suitors; but money can be no object to a person of Beauchamp's wealth. Everyone would be pleased with the match. However, Grandison, as her guardian, asks Beauchamp to wait until Emily is older and in a position to show a preference to him: "I am not a friend to *very* early marriages." Thus, in matters of filial duty, Richardson introduces a full range of situations for the reader's consideration.[23]

Mutual duties between the husband and wife constitute another important topic in courtesy and conduct literature. One of the first marriages described is that of Grandison's parents, a reflection of what might have happened had Clarissa married Lovelace. As Harriet observes: "But who shall answer for the reformation of an habitual libertine, when a temptation offers?" Lady Grandison bears with Sir Thomas, devoting her time to her household and to the education of her children, much as the Marquis of Halifax would have advised his daughter. The Grandison marriage might be compared with that of Lord W. and Miss Mansfield. Their happiness, it is suggested, comes from a sense of gratefulness on both their parts: he to her for marrying a gouty, though reformed old rake, and she to him for accepting a woman from a family fallen on evil days. Grandison says that "she must consider her marriage with him, tho' as an act of condescension, yet partly as a preferment. Her tenderness will, by this means, be engaged; yet her dignity supported. . . ." To Miss Mansfield he counsels, "*Your* goodness will make *him* good. I dare say that he will engage your gratitude; and I defy a good mind to separate love from gratitude." Richardson did not believe reformed rakes made the best husbands. Lady Bradshaigh agreed that in general they might not, but grants that there might be exceptions if the woman could be convinced that the rake was "sincerely reclaimed." Her description of such a man closely mirrors Lord W.'s situation: "A rake, reformed by time, age, or infirmities, generally wants only the power of being what he was; but a sensible man, who reforms in the prime of his days, and apparently from laudable motives, may, I think, be esteemed worthy. . . ."[24]

On the other side of the coin, Richardson furnishes several examples of husbands who have difficulties with their wives. Mrs. O-Hara, Emily Jervois's mother, had not been a good wife to her first husband. Her second marriage hardly differs from the first until she and O-Hara convert to Methodism. Their improved conduct may also be due to monetary contributions from Emily's estate, encouraged by Sir Charles; Grandison advises Emily that O-Hara's dependence on his wife's annuity "may make it convenient to both, to live in a more creditable manner." Another troublesome wife is Lady Beauchamp. Sir Harry Beauchamp, a widower, has married a young women who had been repulsed by his son, unknown to the father. She takes revenge on young Beauchamp by marrying the father and seeing to it that the son remains abroad on a reduced allowance. Her reformation comes about through the good offices of Sir Charles, who adroitly convinces Lady Beauchamp to use her wifely influence to bring young Beauchamp home and thus to lay an obligation on Sir Harry, calling forth his gratitude. Such gratitude, coupled with Lady Beauchamp's sense of having bestowed a favor, leads to a reconciliation among husband, wife, and exiled son. A third example of a recalcitrant wife is seen in the marriage of Charlotte Grandison and Lord G. This marriage is difficult to begin with. Charlotte is aloof, willful, and wittier than Lord G., who is too solicitous, good-natured, and not a match for her raillery. Richardson suggests that the change must come from Charlotte rather than Lord G. And the change does come through a combination of influences: the regard others seem to have for Lord G., the subtle pressure of family members on Charlotte to be faithful to her marital duty, her gradual recognition of Lord G.'s good points, and the subsequent tempering of her raillery. Her eventual perception of the true esteem Lord G. has for her is a factor as well. Finally, Charlotte mellows through marriage and motherhood.[25]

Some readers wanted to see Sir Charles in the role of a parent. But Richardson responded that this had already been treated in *Pamela II*, and that Sir Charles's behavior toward children is demonstrated in a tender and cheerful regard for the children of Mrs. Oldham, Mrs. Reeves's little boy, Lady L.'s son, and Lady G.'s daughter. He further felt that a conversation on the education of children would have been forced and inappropriate coming from unmarried or newly married individuals. Richardson might have added that the reader can still see the results of certain kinds of parental conduct: Sir Charles and Lady L. are the children of a good mother, while Charlotte perhaps bears tinges of her father's whimsicalness. Harriet has been educated by a solicitous grandfather, and Emily will soon have the guidance of the family in Northamptonshire as its "second Harriet." On the other hand, Lady Betty Williams's daughter and some of her friends have embarked on imprudent marriages, leading Harriet to comment that Lady Betty reaped what she had sown.[26]

While Richardson may not have dwelt on the parental character, he does dwell at some length on the parental solicitude a master must have for his servant. Defoe had treated the problem of insubordinate servants in England in several of his works. Their moral behavior as well as their susceptibility to "eye service," working only when observed, appear to have been the bane of households. Sir Charles alludes to the fact that servants are better in Italy than in England. Conduct books accounted for part of the problem with English servants by pointing out that masters lacked orderly households, that they did not look out for the welfare of servants, and that sometimes they set a bad example. Both the *Spectator* and Darrell's Eusebius in *The Gentleman Instructed* recommend a fatherly demeanor toward servants, recognizing the difference in stations but exhibiting solicitude for their well-being.[27]

Grandison's own servants appear to be exemplary. They do not accept gratuities, they are attentive and respectful, and they are good. Lord W. inquires of Sir Charles how he manages to have such fine servants; his own "have been a continual plague." Grandison responds that he treats them as part of the family, sets a good example, and gently expostulates with them for faults. In addition, he demands sobriety and insists that they be kind to one another. We also learn that their spiritual welfare is attended to by Dr. Bartlett, who leads them in regular prayers. This was a practice highly recommended by the conduct-book writers. Grandison further elaborates on his notions of the master-servant relationship when he discusses with the Porrettas what he would expect from Italian Catholic servants in his household should he marry Clementina. Clementina may choose her own servants, but in the event of their misbehavior, Grandison would consider them as his own servants with the power of dismissal. Otherwise, independence on the part of servants might result in disputes between husband and wife. Richardson also provides an example of a good servant corrupted by a bad master. William Wilson, Harriet's footman, is employed by Bagenhall and Pollexfen, who force him to kidnap unwary young women for their own base designs. It is through Sir Charles's efforts that he is reformed and installed in an honest business; Grandison hopes that Wilson's example may influence other servants in the same predicament.[28]

Grandison's wedding day prompts him to celebrate it by presenting monetary gifts to the poor and distressed in the parish; he also gives a small purse to the little Floras who strewed the bridal path with flowers. These gestures, along with Grandison's serious sense of his duty to visit the sick, are reminders of some of the obvious ways of fulfilling one's duty to one's neighbor. Actually, the conduct books went quite far in their prescription for practical methods of doing good. Isaac Barrow observes that because a gentleman has more benefits, he also has more obligations, and therefore besides giving financial help he must expect to:

> direct and advise the ignorant, to comfort the afflicted, to reclaim the wicked, and encourage the good by his wisedom. It is his business to protect the weak, to rescue the oppressed, to ease those who grone under heavy burthens.

Naturally, this is a delicate task. "It requires a great deal of address," Archbishop John Tillotson cautions, "and gentle application so to manage the business of reproof, as not to irritate and exasperate the person whom we reprove, instead of curing him." Yet, in this respect as in others, Grandison comes right up to the mark. Harriet says,

> See him so delicate in his behavior and address to Miss Mansfield, and carry in your thoughts his gaiety and adroit management to Lady Beauchamp . . . and you will hardly think him the same man. . . . Yet *this* may be said in his behalf;—He but accommodates himself to the persons he has to deal with:—He can be a man of gay wit, when he pleases to *descend*, as indeed his sister Charlotte has often found, as she has given occasion for the exercise of that talent in him;—and that virtue, for its own sake, is his choice; since had he been a free-liver, he would have been a dangerous man.[29]

There are many characters in need of reclamation in *Sir Charles Grandison,* and his quietly forceful methods include techniques not mentioned in conventional courtesy works. Grandison is not uniformly successful. Nevertheless, he persists in his efforts as enjoined by such conduct-book writers as Richard Allestree: ". . .if all our wooings and intreatings of men to have mercy on their own souls will not work on them, yet be sure to continue still to exhort by thy example." Everard Grandison is one who seems impervious to Grandison's reproofs. He refuses to scale down his living expenses, to cease gambling, or to associate with more reputable friends. Several rescues by Sir Charles result in momentary good behavior, but then Everard returns to his old ways. Sir Hargrave and his friends claim they are reformed by Sir Charles's example, but they resume their libertine behavior on the Continent. Jeronymo della Porretta at first refuses to heed Sir Charles's advice to tread a straighter path, so Sir Charles forgoes his friendship until by accident he has occasion to rescue him. There may be hope for Jeronymo's reform, just as there is for that of Lord W.[30]

Sir Charles seems to have better luck reclaiming the female characters of the novel. Beginning with Mrs. Oldham, his father's mistress, Sir Charles distinguishes between the sin and the sinner. While his sisters are contemptuous and cold, Sir Charles recognizes Mrs. Oldham's good qualities and takes measures to ensure her continued good conduct. In the case of Mrs. Giffard, Lord W.'s mistress, Grandison is not afraid to use money to guarantee good behavior, a technique also used with the O-Haras. He is willing to underwrite annuity payments to Mrs. Giffard until Lord W. feels that he can cheerfully bring himself to pay the additional amount. But Grandison also tells her to "go and sin no more" and urges her to allot part of the annuity to provide young girls with dowries. Grandison also assures the good behavior of Miss Obrien through a contribution toward her dowry. In reconciling members of his own rank, money plays no part. This is evident in the harmony Grandison effects between Lady Beauchamp and her husband. And his efforts to bring the brash Olivia to her senses are confined to attempts to lead her into a recognition of how she has degraded herself by her actions. Grandison is not solely responsible for Charlotte's reformation, but his contribution is a similar attempt to underscore her marital duties.[31]

Gentlemen were also expected to aid and rescue those who had been exploited. Grandison exerts his influence to relieve the long-standing problems of the Mansfield family. He rescues Mr. Danby from murderers and later effects a posthumous reconciliation between

Danby and his partially disinherited niece and nephews. Danby had left Grandison a large legacy in gratitude for rescuing him and a small amount to the children of the brother who had attempted to have him murdered. Grandison's fairness and generosity dictate that the legacy really belongs to Danby's relatives, and he attempts to determine his own actions by what Mr. Danby would have done if his illness had not soured "a disposition that was naturally all benevolence." Grandison writes to Dr. Bartlett that "the *intention* of the bequeather, in doubtful cases, ought always to be considered," and he extends Danby's "generosity" to yet another family neglected by him in his will. Grandison considers the presumed good intention of an individual in several other cases. He pays his sister Caroline "the sum I think she would have been intitled to expect from my father's bounty, and the family circumstances, had life been lent him to settle his affairs, and make a will." Mrs. Oldham is allowed to keep Sir Thomas's presents to her: "Had he made a will, would they not have been yours?" And Emily is encouraged to increase her mother's annuity. Grandison advises the young girl that Mr. Jervois would have provided more for his ill-tempered wife if he had thought it might do some good; he thinks the money will now have the desired effect of ensuring good behavior. Grandison's action fulfills the obligation of duty to neighbor in a unique way. In several cases it has helped to reclaim a wayward soul, it reconciles the living with the dead, it enables the dead to continue to do good, and it provides an example for the beneficiaries. He admonishes the Danbys "to do good to your fellow-creatures." They in turn respond "that their hearts were opened by the example set them; and, they hoped, would never be shut."[32]

Grandison brings about reconciliation in another significant way, by refusing to engage in dueling. The courtesy and conduct books were, of course, unanimous in their abhorrence of this practice. William Ramesey wrote, ". . . not only Charity is thereby infringed, but all sobriety, meekness, patience, humility, forgiveness of Injuries, gratitude, and all other Virtues. . . ." Mary Delany observed to Richardson, "I think you have many difficulties to encounter for your *fine gentleman,* an epithet not often understood; as little known. And no part more difficult than to make him brave, and avoid duelling, that reigning curse." Grandison rejects challenges to duels by Pollexfen, Greville, the General, and the Count of Belvedere. However, he possesses great skill with the sword, so his enemies know that his refusal to fight is not owing to fear. Allestree advocated a similar approach. One should make one's life

so uniformly Christian, that it may be evident, 'tis Conscience, not Fear
that works with them. . . . To this may be added a chearful and free
exposing himself to all warrantable dangers, when any publick account of
hazard is offered; if he then shew himself daring, 'twill be apparent that
'tis not the fear of Death, but Sin, which locks up his Sword from private
Duels.

Grandison deflects challenges by repeated declarations of his principles; to Pollexfen and his friends he provides a dissertation on the
history of dueling as well as an account of his own experience. Sir
Charles also goes beyond refusing to duel, however, and converts
adversaries into friends. As Tillotson suggested, one should conquer
an enemy by "overcoming him in the noblest Manner, and walking
him *gently* till he be cool, and without Force effectually subduing him
to be our Friend." It should be added that Sir Charles is not afraid to
fight in self-defense, as seen when O-Hara and Salmonet draw upon
him in his own home. Nor is he slow to take up the defense of others,
as he does when he rescues Harriet and disarms Pollexfen. All in all,
Richardson seems to have captured in Grandison the right spirit of
bravery as contrasted with the rashness of more unreasonable minds.
Grandison's verbal response to a succession of challenges would have
received high marks from the conduct-book writers.[33]
   A final duty that must be considered as a legacy of courtesy and
conduct writers, is one's duty to God. Grandison, who assiduously
follows the required external observances of the Anglican church, is
opposed to a chamber marriage for Charlotte. He will not travel on
the Sabbath, he appears according to form at parish services the
Sunday after his wedding and later takes communion, and he insists
on having Lord and Lady L.'s infant christened at church. In all these
cases his main concern is to set a good example "to the lower orders
of people." At the same time, "without making an ostentatious
pretension to religion," he is "the very Christian in practice, that
these doctrines teach a man to be." Rather than engage in a polemical
discussion, he prefers to preach by action. Richardson once wrote
that "religion is the cheerfulest thing in the world," and Grandison
exhibits a suitably "chearful piety" in his demeanor whenever he
worships. Grandison also respects good men of every faith; in fact, he
asks Dr. Bartlett to dispense alms to the "industrious poor, of *all*
persuasions," and he will not debate religious questions in a foreign
country. The religious compromise proposed to the Italians to raise
his daughters as Catholics and his sons as Protestants drew more
unfriendly comments from Richardson's readers than it did from the
characters in the story. As a staunch Protestant, however, he will not

be swayed by the Italians to change his religion, even for the sake of appearance. At the same time, no religion is severely criticized in *Grandison.* Aunt Nell and the O-Haras have turned Methodist, and while this is not appealing to Charlotte, she does admire the zealousness of this sect and its missionary effort to reach "subterranean colliers, tinners, and the most profligate of men." If Clementina is an ardent Catholic, she is not superstitious, and Harriet fairmindedly notes that her "glorious Enthusiasm . . . rightly directed, has heretofore given the palm of martyrdom to Saints." What appears to be most important is that, regardless of one's formal profession, one must live up to its tenets. As the Protestant-turned-Catholic Bagenhall says of himself and the Jewish Merceda, "We have been both of us sad dogs" in respect to the practice of goodness.[34]

Another aspect of duty to God was preparation for death. Conduct-book writers warned that repentance must not be postponed even when hope was given for recovery from illness. One did not know when death was coming, and one might not be properly disposed. There are several deathbed scenes. Young Lorimer dies "in horror not to be described; begging for longer life, and promising reformation on that condition." Pollexfen finds repentance nearly impossible, while Sir Thomas Grandison intends to repent but "lived not to begin the promised *alteration.*" Sir Charles, on the other hand, who has warned Jeronymo, Clementina's brother, about the inability of a guilty life to soften "the agonies of the inevitable hour," does not himself fear death. Harriet remarks that "he can pity a dying friend, without saddening his own heart; for he lives the life of duty as he goes along, and fears not the inevitable lot!" Grandison's notions of an earthly life as preparation for an eternal one are expressed in private meditations that he has written.[35]

There is no doubt about the fact that Grandison is without a peer in his performance of the duties expected of him. Francis Plumer wrote in *A Candid Examination:*

Sir *Charles* himself is greatly good: *Pious, humane, generous,* and *brave.* He considers himself in the Circumstance every Man stands, to owe a Duty to God, his Neighbour and himself. We cannot form the Idea of a *Gentleman,* who is ignorant that there are certain Duties, which belong to him to perform in each of these Relations, *as a Man.* Sir *Charles* is very active in the Discharge of them all. . . . His Piety is a rational Piety. . . . He is *zealous in good Works;* seeks all Occasions of exercising the Benevolence of his enlarged Heart. He is virtuous and temperate in himself, makes all charitable Allowances for the Failings of others; and, like a true Christian, is ready to return Good for Evil.

At the same time, Richardson demonstrates that good men are subject to adversity. As Tillotson observes: "More especially good men are particularly liable to a great many evils and sufferings upon account of their piety and virtue." We are told that Grandison has been subject to temptations; and, of course, he experiences great distress in his relations with the Porretta family. Frequently he remarks that he has not provoked this situation through rashness or giving offense. His sisters attribute his difficulties to his "compassionate nature." But Reverend Philip Skelton's advice to Richardson seems sound, "Your good man will be out of nature, if he is not persecuted: nay, he will be no very good man, if the world do not give him this testimony."[36]

Richardson's good man did not satisfy everyone. Hester Mulso wrote, "The only objection I have to his book is, that I apprehend it will occasion the kingdom's being overrun with old maids. It will give the women an idea of perfection in a man which they never had before." Such an example would cause women to be more particular, the consequence of which "will be a single life to ninety-nine out of a hundred." Others had objected to Grandison's seeming perfection because he appeared to be an unrealistic model. Lady Bradshaigh, however, wrote to one of her correspondents that Richardson was setting a standard of "not what we *are,* but what we *ought* to be. . . . there is nothing recom̄ended . . . but what is preach'd by our most Eminent devines, and what is Com̄anded in Scripture as *duties,* by our *Saviour* himself." Richardson himself anticipated his readers' criticisms. To David Graham he wrote that a good character prompts readers to judge by their own standards so that "its very Perfections are made its Faults." To Lady Echlin he added:

A good Character is a Gauntlett thrown out, As some apprehend, it reflects upon themselves, they perhaps think they have a Right to be affronted. The Character of a mere Mortal cannot, ought not, to be quite perfect. It is sufficient if its Errors be not premeditated, wilful, and unrepented of.

Another writer, on the other hand, commended Richardson's portrayal of Grandison in such difficult circumstances so "that his Virtues may be more conspicuous." But Richardson had not intended his good man to be entirely without imperfection, "lest I should draw a *faultless monster.*" He added, "I would draw him as a mortal. He should have all the human passions to struggle with; and those he cannot conquer he shall endeavor to make subservient to the cause of virtue." Not surprisingly, Harriet is constantly trying to determine if Sir Charles has any faults. Yet he himself admits to having faults, particularly a passionate nature coupled with pride in his family's name. He sees the same weakness in Clementina's brother, the General, and hopes to take warning from his example. But whether the faults are real or assumed, Grandison is certainly not devoid of human warmth and emotion: he expresses anger, can become exasperated and ruffled. In the main, the assessment in the preface is accurate: Grandison is "the Example of a Man acting uniformly well thro' a Variety of trying Scenes. . . ." He is also an example of someone who has attained a high degree of perfection.[37]

There is no doubt about the fact that Sir Charles Grandison performs the duties expected of him in the midst of trials and difficulties. We might well ask at this point what kind of spirit or thought informs the fulfillment of those duties. Several explanations can be ruled out at once. Grandison faces calamities, but they are not attributed by the characters or author to what Samuel Clarke would call the "wise Disposition of the Providence of *God,* governing the World. . . ." Nor are his difficulties connected with spiritual warfare, what one writer would describe as Christians "sent into the World, as Soldiers into the Field, to fight against it, the Flesh, and the Devil. . . ." And while Grandison suffers because of his distresses, it is not suggested that his suffering should be accompanied by obedient submission to God's will, as suggested by Allestree. Rather, Richardson appears to be proposing another model of behavior: the benevolent man of feeling. R. S. Crane has examined the origins of this idea and has defined it in terms of four components: virtue as active and universal benevolence; benevolence motivated through feeling, compassion, and pity; benevolence as natural to man; benevolence rewarded by a feeling of self-approving joy.[38]

Sir Charles is the principal model of this ideal, though other characters are partially endowed with the requisite qualities. Lord W. is able to give a gift with grace, and Mr. Lowther has a "natural benevolence." Dr. Bartlett has a "natural kindness of heart," just as Charlotte has a "good heart." Many of the characters display feeling through tears. Sir Rowland exhibits the "visible emotions of a manly heart," while others express empathy for the distresses of their friends through tears. Tears are shed for Harriet when her friends think Sir Charles has married Clementina. Then, too, Harriet weeps for the distresses of Clementina. More tears are shed at the recognition of goodness: Mrs. Oldham, Lord W., and the Danbys all pay homage to Grandison's goodness in precisely this manner. Tears also serve as a source of relief for Harriet. But Grandison stands above it all. I have already discussed his effort to enrich all within his sphere: friends, enemies, people of every faith or no faith. And we are told that he delights in doing good. Tillotson explains that to "do good, is to be like God." In another sermon he affirms that "they that are advanced to a great height above others, may, like the heavenly bodies, dispense a general light and influence, and scatter happiness and blessings among all that are below them." It is within this context that characters refer to Sir Charles as an imitator of the Almighty, an instrument of Providence.[39]

Grandison's benevolence seems to be prompted by a feeling heart. His difficulties with the Porrettas are partially attributed to his compassion, and he admits to having great feeling for the misfortunes of others. Dr. Bartlett says to Harriet that a "heart that is able to partake of the distress of another, cannot wilfully give it." Grandison's feelings are nevertheless expressed in a reserved manner. When he is moved by his mother's picture, for example, he withdraws until he is composed. He also gives others the opportunity to collect themselves, as in the case of Mrs. Giffard and Lord W. At the same time, he rejoices in the improved behavior of Lady Beauchamp to her husband with eyes that "glisten with pleasure." Above all, Grandison's benevolence is portrayed as a natural kind of goodness. In a discussion with Lord W., he compares himself to his father:

> If I should happen to be more right than my father in some things, he might have the advantage of me in others; and in those I happen to do, that are generally thought laudable, what merit have I? Since all this time (directed by a natural bias) I am pursuing my own predominant passion; and that, perhaps, with as much ardor, and as little power to resist it, as my father had to restrain his.[40]

The final mark of the benevolent man of feeling is the personal satisfaction he receives from doing good. Tillotson describes it well:

> So that the benefits we do to others are not more welcome to them that receive them, than they are delightful to us that do them. . . . But the pleasure of doing good remains after a thing is done, the thoughts of it lie easy in our minds, and the reflection upon it afterwards does for ever minister joy and delight to us.

Grandison and other characters frequently remark that "goodness and beneficence brought with them their own rewards." This aspect of Grandison's character prompts Clementina to conclude that no reward, including her own hand in marriage, would be adequate to thank Grandison for rescuing her brother Jeronymo from assassins: "Who, that knows him, knows not that he can enjoy the reward in the action?" As we recall Richardson's three major works, we begin to see a pattern: Pamela's virtue is repaid with earthly benefits, Clarissa's goodness is recognized in heaven, and Sir Charles Grandison's benevolence is its own reward.[41]

How, then, may we describe Richardson's hero? In Sir Charles Grandison we find the truly complete gentleman, and this as regards formation, accomplishments, and the fulfillment of duty under circumstances far more complex than any found in previous conduct books. Containing sparks of Steele's Christian Hero and the benevolent man of feeling, he is also a "Man of TRUE HONOUR." Harriet attributes to him "the un-ostentatious merit of a *truly Good man.*" Perhaps the best description is to be found in another one of her reflections:

> After the Anderson, the Danby, the Lord W. affairs, he appeared to me in a much more shining light than an hero would have done, returning in a triumphal car covered with laurels, and dragging captive princes at its wheels. How much more glorious a character is that of *The Friend of Mankind,* than that of *The Conqueror of Nations!*[42]

NOTES

1. Samuel Richardson to Lady Echlin, 10 October 1754, Yale; W. Lee Ustick, "Changing Ideals of Aristocratic Character and Conduct in Seventeenth-Century England," *Modern Philology* 30 (November 1932): 147–66.

2. Peacham, *Compleat Gentleman,* 2–9; Patricia Ann Lee, "The Ideal of the English Gentleman in the Early Seventeenth Century" (Ph.D. diss., Columbia, 1966), 6; Katherine S. Van Eerde, "The Creation of the Baronetage in England," *Huntington Library Quarterly* 22 (August 1959): 313–22; on Sir Thomas see *SCG,* 1:329; on Sir Charles and nobility, 3:241; Panton, *Speculum Juventutis,* 25; [Grenville], *Counsel and Directions,* 106; on the Marchioness see *SCG,* 2:119; on Jeronymo 2:139 and 141; on Olivia 2:641; on Everard 3:348; on Pollexfen 2:431.

3. On Lovelace, see Richardson to Lady Bradshaigh, 15 December 1748, FC XI, f. 10; *Spectator,* ed. Bond, 1:448–49, no. 108; on Everard, see *SCG,* 3:4; on Bagenhall 1:170; on Lord W. 2:59; on Greville 1:25; on Sir Thomas 1:311 and 326; on Lord G.'s foibles, see 2:419; 3:237; 1:237; 2:417, 519, 436–37, and 656.

4. On Walden, see *SCG,* 1:46–48; Patrick Delany to Richardson, 20 December 1753, *Correspondence,* 4:82–84; on Lord D., see *SCG,* 1:214; on Sir Charles and learning see 3:245–46; on Sir Charles's education 2:136 and 3:288; on Sir Charles and dueling 1:263–66.

5. Francis Osborn, *Advice to a Son,* 6th ed. (Oxford: Tho. Robinson, 1658), 80; Gailhard, *Compleat Gentleman,* pt. 2, p. 7; on Creutzer see *SCG,* 1:385, 457, and 461.

6. On Harriet's views see *SCG,* 2:291 and 1:193; on Pollexfen 1:45; on Lord W.'s views 2:40; on Dr. Bartlett's views 2:325; Richardson, *Pamela II,* 435–36, Letter 101.

7. Gailhard, *Compleat Gentleman,* pt. 2, p. 44; on places visited see *SCG,* 1:456–62, 181, and 263; on cardinals 2:651; Gailhard, *Compleat Gentleman,* pt. 2, pp. 186–87; on the Porrettas see *SCG,* 2:156, 167, 187.

8. Henry Fielding, "An Essay on Conversation," in *Miscellanies,* ed. Henry Knight Miller (Middletown, Conn.: Wesleyan University Press, 1972), 123; Lord Chesterfield, *Letters of*

Philip Dormer Fourth Earl of Chesterfield to His Godson and Successor, ed. The Earl of Carnarvon (Oxford: Clarendon Press, 1890), Letter 199, 9 August 1768, pp. 262–63; [Darrell], *Gentleman Instructed,* pt. 1, pp. 7–8, suggests Chesterfield's notions; on Sir Charles's manner, see *SCG,* 3:92–93 and 1:146–47; on Sir Charles's appearance 1:181; on Sir Charles and Lady Beauchamp 2:274 and 279; Sir Charles and conversation 3:137; 1:450; 2:290; 3:184; 3:215; and 3:445–46; for conduct books on conversation see [Darrell], *Gentleman Instructed,* pt. 3, p. 534 and *Art of Complaisance* (London: John Starkey, 1673), chap. 6; Chesterfield, *Letters to Godson,* Letter 135, no. 7, n.d., pp. 177–78; E. Sprague Allen, "Chesterfield's Objection to Laughter," *Modern Language Notes* 38 (May 1923):279–87; Virgil B. Heltzel, "Chesterfield and the Anti-Laughter Tradition," *Modern Philology* 26 (August 1928): 73–90; *SCG,* 1:47–48 and 106–7.

9. *Art of Complaisance,* 33; Lord Chesterfield, *Letters to His Son,* ed. Oliver H. G. Leigh, 2 vols. (New York: The Chesterfield Press, 1917), 9 October 1746, 1:2; Fuller, B. D., *Holy State,* 164–65 misnumbered 194–95; *Spectator,* ed. Bond, 2:92–93, no. 150; Sir Matthew Hale, *Several Tracts* (London: W. Shrowsbery, 1684), 29; Jeremy Taylor, *The Rule and Exercise of Holy Living,* 10th ed. (London: Richard Royston, 1674), 102; on Pollexfen, see *SCG,* 1:45; on Everard 1:231; on Lord G. and Sir Walter 1:399 and 230; Grandison favored revival of the sumptuary laws, 3:124; Grandison opposed the foreign influence in dress, see 3:263–64; he also favored less ostentation during the king's progress, 3:268.

10. Obadiah Walker, *Of Education* (Oxon: At the Theater, 1673), pt. 1, pp. 69 and 110; Gailhard, *Compleat Gentleman,* pt. 2, p. 48; for Mrs. Shirley on dancing see *SCG,* 2:516–17; 3:262 and 215; on Sir Charles's dancing 3:93 and 2:323; on musicianship 2:374 and 345; on Sir Charles's other accomplishments 2:274 and 3:95; Richardson said, "Singing is a greater Promoter of Chearfulness than even Instrumental Music," Richardson to Sarah Chapone, 19 September 1753, FC XII, 2, f. 88v.

11. Lady Echlin to Richardson, 5 January 1758, *Correspondence,* 5:90; on Mr. Lowther see *SCG,* 2:451–52; *Spectator,* ed. Bond, 3:454, no. 387; Richardson to Frances Grainger, 28 September 1751, Yale MS Vault File; see also Richardson to Sarah Wescomb, 12 June 1754, *European Magazine* 54 (August 1808): 95; on nervous disorders see *SCG,* 2:313; *Cheyne,* 5–137; *Spectator,* ed. Bond, 1:90, no. 21.

12. Richardson expressed his low opinion of the law to Silvester, Richardson to Eusebius Silvester, 20 July 1756, FC XIV, 4, f. 25; William de Britaine expresses similar sentiments, *Human Prudence,* 11th ed. (London: Richard Sare, 1718), 140; on Sir John Lambton see *SCG,* 3:2–3; on Mr. Sylvester 1:455–56; 2:667 and 318; Richardson's complete correspondence with Eusebius Silvester is in the Forster Collection XIV, 4, ff. 1–28 and XV, 1, ff. 29–58.

13. Richardson to Lady Bradshaigh [late November 1749?], *Correspondence,* 4:287; [François Genard], *The School of Man, Translated from the French* (London: Lockyer Davis, 1753), 263; Fuller, B.D., *Holy State,* 122; [Grenville], *Counsel and Directions,* 170–72; on Anderson see *SCG,* 1:409; on O-Hara and Salmonet 2:67; on the General 3:312 and 2:248–52; on Sir Charles and the military 1:262–63 and 3:95; on Creutzer 1:319; Sir Charles's views of the military 1:414–15 and 2:306.

14. John Evelyn, *Memoires for my Grandson,* ed. Geoffrey Keynes (London: Nonesuch Press, 1926), 34; Bishop Gilbert Burnet, *Bishop Burnet's History of His Own Time. Vol. II.* (London: Joseph Downing and Henry Woodfall, 1734),655; on Pollexfen's clergyman see *SCG,* 1:154; on Dr. Bartlett 1:226 and 229; Richardson, *Clarissa,* 1:364, Letter 75 and 4:108, Letter 47; on Father Marescotti see *SCG,* 2:577 and 3:410; on reconciliation of clergy 3:140; Richardson to Lady Bradshaigh, 2 June 1753, *Selected Letters,* 235.

15. *Spectator,* ed. Bond, 1:296, no. 69; for Sir Charles's comment see *SCG,* 1:455; on Jervois 2:21; on Sir Charles 2:169; Charlotte on merchants 2:322–23; on city wives 1:331; on Everard's wife 3:113, 267, and 348.

16. Sir Charles on ranks *SCG,* 2:477–78.

17. Samuel Clarke, Sermon 3, "Every Man is principally to regard his own proper Duty," *Sermons,* 7th ed., 11 vols. (London: J. and P. Knapton, 1749), 7:35; [Darrell], *Gentleman Instructed;* William Gouge, *Of Domesticall Duties,* 3d ed. (London: Edward Brewster, 1634); Chesterfield, *Letters to Godson,* Letter 108, n.d., p. 142 and Letter 129, no. 1, 31 October 1765, p. 165; George Whitefield, "The Necessity of the Righteousness of Christ. A Farewell Sermon Presented at Morefields, June 3, 1739," *Discourses on the following Subjects* (London: Charles Whitefield, 1739), 14.

18. [Allestree], *Whole Duty,* 182–83, 179; Fuller, B.D., *Holy State,* 15–16; Richardson to Frances Grainger, 1 February 1749/50, Pierpont Morgan Library; for Harriet on filial duty see *SCG,* 1:315, 321, and 333; Richardson to Lady Bradshaigh, 12 July 1757, FC XI, f. 209–10v.

19. On Sir Charles and Mrs. Oldham, see *SCG,* 1:366; on Miss Obrien 1:376; Sir Charles on his father 3:124 and 2:39–40; Sir Thomas's funeral 1:361; Sir Charles and Lord W. 2:38; [Allestree], *Whole Duty,* 189; on Lord W. see *SCG,* 1:350.

20. [Allestree], *Whole Duty,* 182; Lady Bradshaigh to Richardson, 27 September 1754, FC XI, f. 129; [Plumer?], *Candid Examination,* 45–46; Richardson to Lady Bradshaigh, 30 May 1754, *Selected Letters,* 309; Lady Bradshaigh to Richardson, 1 November in 27 November 1753, FC XI, f. 45–46v; Richardson to Lady Bradshaigh, 14 February 1754, *Selected Letters,* 285.

21. Burnet, *History,* 2:652; for Lady D.'s requirements see *SCG,* 1:214; Sir Rowland 1:31; on Lord L. 1:328 and 331; on Miss Mansfield 2:266; Sir Charles on Harriet 3:36–37.

22. On Wilson, *SCG,* 1:391–92; on the Danbys 2:60 and 1:453–54.

23. On Emily, *SCG,* 2:550–51; 3:347 and 442–44.

24. On Sir Thomas see *SCG,* 1:353; [Halifax], *Lady's New-years Gift,* 25, 59, and 35; on Lord W. and Miss Mansfield *SCG,* 2:90 and 271; Lady Bradshaigh to Richardson, [17 November 1748?], *Correspondence,* 4:196–97.

25. On Mrs. O-Hara see *SCG,* 3:22 and 116–17; 2:75; on Lady Beauchamp 1:463 and 2:272–85; on Charlotte 3:348; 2:544 and 514; and 3:402–4.

26. Julia[n Bere] to Richardson, 14 March 1754, FC XV, 4, f. 20–1; Richardson to Thomas Edwards, 5 April 1754, *Selected Letters,* 299; Samuel Richardson, "Copy of a Letter to a Lady, who was solicitous for an additional volume to the History of Sir Charles Grandison," in *SCG,* 3:469–70.

27. [Daniel Defoe], *The Great Law of Subordination* (London: S. Harding et al., 1724); [Defoe], *Religious Courtship,* Appendix, pt. 3; Thomas Seaton, *The Conduct of Servants in Great Families* (London: Tim. Goodwin, 1720), 81–82; on Italian servants, see *SCG,* 2:237; *Spectator,* ed. Bond, 1:439–40, no. 106; [Darrell], *Gentleman Instructed,* pt. 3, p. 506.

28. On Sir Charles's servants see *SCG,* 3:40; 2:654 and 32; 1:229; 2:353–54; and 3:279; [Allestree], *Whole Duty,* 202–5; [Darrell], *Gentleman Instructed,* pt. 1, p. 87; Evelyn, *Memoires,* 16; for Sir Charles on Clementina's servants see *SCG,* 2:531–32; on Wilson 1:122, 160, 169 and 170–76.

29. On Sir Charles's wedding gift see *SCG,* 3:240 and 232; on visiting the sick 3:461; Isaac Barrow, *Of Industry,* 2d ed. (London: Brab Aylmer, 1712), 135–37; John Tillotson, Sermon 42, "Against evil-speaking," *Works,* 3:192; on Sir Charles's techniques see *SCG,* 2:272.

30. [Allestree], *Whole Duty,* 222.

31. On Mrs. Oldham see *SCG,* 1:364–76; on Mrs. Giffard see 2:51 and 55; on Miss Obrien 1:377; on Olivia 2:640–44.

32. Robert South, Sermon 49, "If it be possible, as much as lieth in you, live peaceably with all men. Romans xii.18," *Sermons Preached Upon Several Occasions,* 7 vols. (Oxford: Clarendon Press, 1823), 7:93; on the Danbys see *SCG,* 1:447–56; Sir Charles on intention of bequeather 2:479; 1:383 and 371–72; and 2:75.

33. [William Ramesey], *The Gentlemans Companion* (London: Rowland Reynolds, 1672), 83; Panton, *Speculum Juventutis,* bks. 6 and 7; Osborn, *Advice,* 139; Mary Delany to Richardson, 15 June 1751, *Correspondence,* 4:42; [Richard Allestree], *The Gentleman's Calling*

(London: Robert Pawlet, 1676), 143–44; John Tillotson, *Maxims and Discourses Moral and Divine*, ed. Laurence Echard (London: J. Tonson, 1719), 66; Sir Charles on dueling *SCG*, 1:205–6 and 254–67; 3:71–72; and 2:250; Sir Charles on self-defense 2:67 and 1:140–41.

34. On Charlotte's wedding see *SCG*, 2:327; on christening 3:265–66; Sir Charles as a Christian 1:440; 2:379 and 575; on cheerful piety see Richardson to Lady Bradshaigh [late November 1749?], *Selected Letters*, 135; echoed in *Spectator*, ed. Bond, 4:251–54, no. 494; on Sir Charles's demeanor see *SCG*, 3:84; on Sir Charles's charity 2:12; on religion abroad 2:155; on the compromise see Lady Bradshaigh to Richardson, 21 May 1754, FC XI, f. 99; Richardson to Lady Bradshaigh, 9 July 1754, FC XI, f. 110v; Sarah Chapone to Richardson, 10 December 1753, FC XIII, 1, 94v; [CP?] to [Miss G?], 23 January 1754, FC XV, 3, f. 27v; Anonymous to Richardson, 26 January 1754, FC XV, 3, f. 32; Anonymous to Richardson, n.d., FC XV, 3, f. 57; Richardson to Cox Macro, 22 March 1754, FC XV, 4, f. 23–23v; Samuel Richardson, "Answer to a Letter from a Friend, Who had Objected to Sir Charles Grandison's Offer to allow his Daughters by Lady Clementina, had his Marriage with her taken Effect, to be educated Roman Catholics, March 25, 1754," FC Richardsoniana, ff. 5–8; on changing religion see *SCG*, 2:528 and 530; on Methodists 3:22; for Harriet on Clementina see 2:573 and 577; 3:351; on Bagenhall 1:266 and 254.

35. Taylor, *Holy Living*, 277; Jeremy Taylor, *The Rule and Exercises of Holy Dying* (London: Richard Royston, 1674); [Allestree], *Whole Duty*, 79; [John Dunton], *The Hazard of a Death-Bed-Repentance* (London: n.p., 1708); on Lorimer see *SCG*, 1:461; on Pollexfen 3:142–43 and 461–62; on Sir Thomas's temporary resolution 1:323; on Sir Thomas's death 1:356; on Jeronymo 2:140; on Sir Charles and death 1:440 and 3:266; Sir Charles's "Reflexions" 3:292–93.

36. [Plumer?], *Candid Examination*, 7–8; Tillotson, Sermon 68, "Good men Strangers and sojourners upon earth," *Works*, 5:172; on Sir Charles's temptations see *SCG*, 2:492; on Sir Charles's distresses 2:196, 557, 559, and 598; 3:68; Philip Skelton to Richardson, 10 May 1751, *Correspondence*, 5:210.

37. Hester Mulso Chapone to Elizabeth Carter, 11 February [?], Johnson, ed., *Bluestocking Letters*, 175; Lady Bradshaigh to Richardson, 11 December 1753, FC XI, f. 57; Richardson to David Graham, 3 May 1750, *Selected Letters*, 157; Richardson to Lady Echlin, 10 October 1754, Yale; [CP?] to [Miss G?], 3 February 1754, FC XV, 3, ff. 30v–31; Anne Donnellan to Richardson, 25 September 1750, *Correspondence*, 4:32–33; Richardson to Lady Bradshaigh, 8 February 1754, *Selected Letters*, 280; on "faultless monster" see Richardson to Hester Mulso, 11 July 1751, *Correspondence*, 3:168–70; Richardson to Hester Mulso, 27 July 1751, *Correspondence*, 3:172; on Sir Charles's faults see *SCG*, 1:183, 373, and 394–95; 2:83, 89, and 113; Sir Charles as passionate 1:206 and 438; 2:63, 157, 633, and 641; on Sir Charles's pride 1:378, 380, and 384; 2:57, 223, 458, 472, and 643; 3:46 and 125; on Sir Charles's distresses 2:286, 180, 206, 597, and 633; Sir Charles's anger 3:70 and 2:470; preface, 1:4.

38. Clarke, Sermon 10, "The Shortness and Vanity of Humane Life." *Sermons*, 6:152; [Woodward], *Reformation of Manners*, 94; [Allestree], *Whole Duty*, 21; R. S. Crane, "Suggestions Toward a Genealogy of the 'Man of Feeling,'" *English Literary History* 1 (December 1934): 205–30; recently, Crane's point of view has been attacked by Donald Greene, who finds even earlier dates for the antecedents of the man of feeling; see "Latitudinarianism and Sensibility: The Genealogy of the 'Man of Feeling' Reconsidered," *Modern Philology* 75 (November 1977): 159–83.

39. On Lord W. see *SCG*, 2:342; on Mr. Lowther 2:628; on Dr. Bartlett 2:388; on Charlotte see 2:442; on Sir Rowland 1:92; on tears 2:538, 540, and 128; 1:310–11, 372, 380 and 455; Harriet relieved by tears 2:304; Sir Charles's doing good 1:131 and 2:61; Tillotson, Sermon 158, "Of doing good," *Works*, 9:20; this is echoed in Peacham, *Gentleman Instructed*, 18–19; Tillotson, Sermon 212, "Of diligence in our general and particular calling," *Works*, 11:65; Sir Charles imitates God, *SCG*, 2:307; 3:241; 2:611 and 285.

40. On a feeling heart see *SCG*, 2:45 and 258; Sir Charles not a Stoic 1:414; Sir Charles's reserve 1:369; Mrs. Giffard 2:49; Lord W. 2:55; Lady Beauchamp 2:655; doing good is natural 2:40.

41. Tillotson, Sermon 18, "The example of Jesus in doing good," *Works*, 1:427–28; on the reward of doing good see *SCG*, 2:665 and 667; 1:456; and 2:566; Clementina's comment, *SCG*, 2:566.

42. Preface, *SCG*, 1:4; Harriet on Sir Charles 3:462 and 2:70.

5

THE LADIES' CALLING

SAMUEL Richardson, describing Harriet Byron to Thomas Edwards, wrote,

> I designed her to have a livelier Turn than Clarissa, and something to be Defective in, in the way of Vivacity, in order, were I to proceed, to rein her in, when the good Man appeared, as she is to be but the Second Character: But not to be in the least wanting, as to Purity of Manners: No vile Accommodation to the Times! She should not have my good Man, if she was in the least indelicate in her Morals.

Richardson had already defined the "Whole Duty of a Woman" in *Clarissa* and the two parts of *Pamela*. In *Grandison*, by contrast, his focus is on the good man, and as all the other characters revolve around or reflect Sir Charles, it is the portrait of one man's conduct that is naturally the most complete. Nevertheless, Richardson has not ignored themes central to the conduct of women. His treatment of these issues and his own special emphases form the subject of this chapter.[1]

Traditional courtesy and conduct books guided the behavior of ladies in several ways. Castiglione devoted the third section of the *Courtier* to women. Other authors such as Allestree in *The Whole Duty of Man* felt that the application of their ideas fell equally to both sexes. Allestree did, however, write a companion volume to *The Gentleman's Calling* titled *The Ladies Calling*. Darrell added a supplementary section to his *Gentleman Instructed*. These separate volumes or supplements generally covered the same ground as the gentleman's edition, with special emphasis on the duties, accomplishments, and attitudes considered appropriate for women. Steele's *The Ladies Library* (1714), whose contents were gleaned from many sources, lists the following topics: employment, wit and delicacy, recreations, dress, chastity, modesty, meekness, charity, envy, detraction, censure and reproof, ignorance, and pride. *The Young Ladies*

Conduct (1722), attributed to John Essex, and James Fordyce's *Sermons to Young Women* (1766, 3d ed.) concentrate on similar matters and also suggest subjects suitable for academic study. To cite still another example, the concept of reciprocal duties between parents and children, husbands and wives, mistresses and servants governs William Gouge's *Of Domesticall Duties* (1622). Finally, practical household matters were discussed in domestic household manuals, which contained recipes, medical remedies, gardening secrets, and even tricks in the art of angling. What Richardson has done for the ladies in his story of a good man is to interweave a smaller conduct book into the larger fabric so that the woman's duties, accomplishments, and behavior complement those of the main figure.[2]

The courtesy and conduct books encouraged education for women. James Bland wrote that it was only "ill Custom" that seems to have prevented women from engaging in study. Wetenhall Wilkes declared, along with other writers, that learning could help a woman distinguish between good and evil. Some writers would express reservations about how much a woman should exhibit her learning, but this was really no bar to learning itself. As Elizabeth Joceline wrote, "But where Learning and Wisdom meet in a vertuously disposed Woman, she is the fittest Closet for all Goodness. She is like a well-balanced Ship, that may bear *all* her Sail." Richardson was fortunate in his own female acquaintances. He confided to Stinstra:

> we in England may glory in numbers of women of genius. I in particular may—I could introduce you, Sir, to such a circle of my own acquaintance!—No man has been so honoured by the fine spirits of the sex as I have been. I verily think, that the women of the politest regions are not to vie with ours. And the taste and numbers are every day increasing, though in an age of such general dissipation.

He was acquainted with Elizabeth Carter, the classical scholar, of whom Dr. Johnson once said she "could make a pudding as well as translate Epictetus." Hester Mulso Chapone was the author of a very practical conduct book of her own, *Letters on the Improvement of the Mind* (1773), while Catherine Talbot, a corrector of *Sir Charles Grandison*, composed *Reflections on the Seven Days of the Week* (1770). Talbot knew the Continental literature and parts of her daily journal are recorded in French. Richardson told Lady Bradshaigh that he was "no enemy to the distaff; but the woman who writes a book, breaks not thereby the rank she holds in the world." He encouraged such female writers as Charlotte Lennox and Sarah Fielding, as well as the more modest work of the unknown author of the

Magdalen House penitents' stories and Mrs. Sarah Chapone's *Remarks on Mrs. Muilman's Letter To the Right Honourable The Earl of Chesterfield* (1750). He also offered assistance to Anna Meades and her *The History of Sir William Harrington* (1771). Mrs. Chapone tried to interest Richardson in another project intended to publicize the accomplishments of learned women from Britain's past. George Ballard's *Memoirs of the Lives of Several Ladies* (1752) assembles one hundred and thirty biographies ranging from Mrs. Astell and Mrs. Rowe to Elizabeth I and Mary queen of Scots, and according to Mrs. Chapone, Ballard hoped to demonstrate that learning and piety are not incompatible in a woman.[3]

Richardson had corresponded at length on the subject of education for women. To Lady Bradshaigh and Frances Grainger he emphasized the role of "intellectual, as well as domestic, companions to men of the best sense!" But he spoke against both male and female pedants and against those women who would neglect "Family Management and Oeconomy." Mentioning Clarissa's view on the subject, he adds that somebody must attend to household affairs: "Shall it be left to Servants? Who shall direct and inspect those Servants?" Lady Bradshaigh owned that she did "not approve of great learning in women. . . . No farther would I have them to advance, than to what would enable them to write and converse with ease and propriety, and make themselves useful in every stage of life. I hate to hear Latin out of a woman's mouth. There is something in it, to me, masculine. . . ." Richardson countered her arguments briskly, citing Elizabeth Carter as "an example, that women may be trusted with Latin and even Greek, and yet not think themselves above their domestic duties." He further added that he did not think that "because a man is superficial, a woman must be so too, for fear she should meet with a husband to whom she may have superior understanding." In another letter he humorously suggested, "Would it not be very pretty for parents on both sides to make it the first subject of their inquiries, whether the girl, as a recommendation, were a greater fool, or more ignorant, than the young fellow; and if not, that they should reject her, for the booby's sake?"[4]

On the whole, Richardson's position as expressed in his correspondence is echoed in *Sir Charles Grandison*. Harriet Byron is consistently acclaimed for her beauties of mind as well as person. Even the libertine Greville admits conversion from having "considered all intellectual attainments as either useless or impertinent in women. . . . A wife, a learned lady, I considered as a very unnatural character." Harriet had been educated by her grandfather to be an English scholar as well as a student of the Bible. Hence her familiarity with the

Moderns rather than the Ancients when the pedant Walden engages her in debate. She possesses the facility in French and Italian recommended by the conduct-book writers, and, most important, her learning does not seem to have interfered with her skill in the domestic arts. Charlotte Grandison's father gave her a "modern education" consisting of history, geography, music, French, and Italian, and her maid confides to Harriet that she is not only a "reading lady" but also knows how to manage everything from a "private family-dinner, to a sumptuous entertainment." Her penchant for raillery does not hide a lively gracefulness acquired, Harriet notes, without the benefit of foreign travel. Miss Stevens and Miss Clements, young ladies Harriet has met at Lady Betty Williams's, are also "reading ladies"; Miss Stevens "takes no pride in shewing it," while Miss Clements has not "suffered her pen to run away with her needle; nor her reading to interfere with that housewifry which the best judges hold so indispensable in the character of a good woman." Mr. Reeves, Harriet's cousin, sums up Richardson's balanced view on the question of learning; it should not get in the way of a knowledge of manners and good breeding in the case of men, nor in the way of a woman's being agreeable or behaving better.[5]

Jeronymo della Porretta has spoken to Grandison "with contempt of the generality of the Italian women, for their illiterateness." However, the Marchioness della Porretta and her daughter-in-law, the General's new wife, have been schooled in France, something the Bishop perceives as tending to soften "the Italian reserve." Clementina has had the benefit of a good education at home, one that surpasses that "ever allowed or sought after by the Italian Ladies." One of her tutors, of course, is Grandison himself, who is engaged in teaching English. The Count of Belvedere admires "intellectual improvements" in a woman, and he thus appears all the more anxious to marry Clementina on account of her superior background. Clementina's education had made her extremely dutiful, but there is also the faint hint that she may have been spoiled. Grandison writes that she "was not easily diverted from any thing she took strongly into her head; and they never had accustomed her to contradiction." Lady Bradshaigh had suggested this might be the case, and Richardson agreed. Little else is said about the Italian ladies' education except for the fact that Lady Olivia "surpassed every-body" in her harpsichord playing; unfortunately, she must be castigated by Sir Charles for not living a life befitting the superior advantages she has received. Admittedly, Richardson seems to depict exceptional Italians, but this is certainly in line with his balanced viewpoint, which tends to avoid stereotypes. As Grandison notes of the Porrettas, "in Italy, as well as in other countries, there are persons of honour, of goodness, of generosity; and who are above reserve, vindictiveness, jealousy, and those other bad passions by which some persons mark indiscriminately a whole nation."[6]

Another part of the education of the young woman was an exposure to public entertainments. Sir Charles Grandison, as Emily's guardian, presents a brief program to Dr. Bartlett for his ward's introduction into public life. He admits that he does not like that kind of life and that Emily would be better without knowledge of it. But as he has said with regard to matters of dress and taste, "I think we should conform something to the taste of the times in which we live." So Emily, in the company of the Grandison sisters and Sir Charles, attends these events, and the exposure, in turn, enables her to place such amusements in their proper perspective: "A boundary is set to her imagination; and that by her own choice; for she thinks lightly of them. . . ." Harriet herself comes to a different view of the public entertainments. After her abduction from a masquerade, not only she but Lady Betty acknowledge the dangers of such diversions, Lady Betty vowing "never again" to go to a masquerade. Besides, Harriet has met the Grandisons, "a family that had no need to look out of itself for entertainments." Her reflection at the conclusion of her London visit is a wise one:

> Is it, Lucy, that I have more experience and discernment now, or less charity and good-nature, than when I first came to town? for then I thought well, in the main, of Lady Betty Williams. But tho' she is a good-natur'd, obliging woman; she is so immersed in the love of public diversions! . . . how learned should I have been in all the gaieties of the modern life; what a fine Lady, possibly; had I not been carried into more rational . . . scenes; and had I followed the lead of this Lady, as she (kindly, as to her intention) had designed I should![7]

Good conversation certainly plays a prominent role in *Grandison*. The conduct-book writers had cautioned women against being too forward in conversation. One should not be overanxious to gain "wide Applause"; like the music of the spheres, a woman's tongue should be "sweet and charming, but not to be heard at distance." John Essex, on the other hand, urged ladies not to be timorous in conversation. Harriet is at first reluctant to engage in public debate with Walden; her dilemma is that of the woman with "some little genius" who will be thought affected, whether she conceals her abilities or allows others to draw her into discussion. But in another episode, Mrs. Shirley encourages women to contribute to conversations and suggests that the subject matter be raised above such commonplaces as the weather. Participants would thus have an opportunity to improve themselves in a relatively painless way. *Grandison* is replete with examples of conversations for the benefit of those in Northamptonshire as well as the reader. We read about family senates, congresses, assemblies, and canvassings. Charlotte is "tried" before her family for her behavior with Captain Anderson, and Harriet's wedding date is determined by a Northamptonshire family tribunal. The same tribunal decides that Harriet should not worry any more about notions of "divided or second-placed Love." Several instructive conversations are reported verbatim; Harriet records "a very agreeable conversation" that runs the gamut from masquerades, to judging other people, to love and courtship, to marriages between people of unequal years. Emily's future conduct toward her mother is discussed in a family senate, while the Italians engage in endless debates and deliberations about what course of action to take with Clementina. When the Italians and English gather together at the end of the story, Harriet confides that their conversations are not about "trifling subjects."[8]

Besides providing instruction in debatable matters of conduct, the discussions in *Grandison* go beyond normal conduct-book fare in that they also afford the reader an opportunity of observing conversational technique in practice. Grandmother Shirley is skilled in conversation. During one discussion, Harriet observes that Grandison at first intended only to listen, but that Mrs. Shirley "drew him in," a technique in which Sir Charles himself excels. Harriet, exhibiting a different kind of ability, maintains the desired complaisance in conversation by tactfully avoiding awkward questions or by deflecting them through her own perceptive queries. When, for instance, the family discusses the merits of Sir Walter Watkyns and Lord G., she admits that she "did not care to give an opinion, that might either *hurt* or *humour* my Charlotte." And rather than answer Lady L.'s pointed question about whether Charlotte is bound by her promise to Captain Anderson, she instead asks Charlotte what Sir Charles calls a "very proper question." In much the same way, when consulted about Charlotte's behavior toward Lord G., Harriet judiciously gives her the benefit of the doubt. When Lady D. commends Harriet for her tact during a visit of Lord D. to the Reeves's, Harriet writes:

> Had I been silent, when my Lord directed his discourse to me, or answer'd only No, or Yes, the Countess would have thought me very vain; and, that I ascribed to myself the consequence she so generously

gave me, with respect to my Lord. I therefore behaved and answered unaffectedly; but avoided such a promptness of speech, as would have looked like making pretensions to knowledge and opinion, though some of my Lord's questions were apparently design'd to engage me into freedom of discourse.

Charlotte's raillery, on the other hand, exceeds the limit set by conduct writers. While most writers recognize the positive attributes of raillery, and while Charlotte's observations impart a light, humorous, and often incisive touch to a conversation, there is a less pleasant side to consider. Particularly when her comments are made at the expense of Lord G., we are led to believe that her wit is perhaps something other than the "delicious sawce" described by the author of the *Art of Complaisance*. Obadiah Walker said that there was "no greater enemy to Peace and Charity" than raillery at the expense of others, and Grandison's rebukes of Charlotte make this clear.[9]

Little attention is paid in *Grandison* to other accomplishments considered suitable for women. Sir Charles's mother had been skilled in needlework and shellwork; but the latter was an afterthought on Richardson's part. Lady Bradshaigh had complained about Charlotte's rather derogatory comment on Lord G.'s shell collection. Richardson had obviously forgotten that Lady Bradshaigh had presented the Richardsons with a sample of her own shellwork, and he tried to rectify the oversight by attributing the skill to Sir Charles's mother. Emily can translate an Italian sonnet into English prose, while Harriet and the Grandison sisters are musical and can dance.[10]

Matters of taste and dress for women are also treated only in passing in *Sir Charles Grandison*. The excessive attention paid by women to dress had been ridiculed both in conduct books and the *Spectator*. We know Sir Charles follows the fashion to avoid singularity; but Harriet desires more modest and simple attire for herself. She is embarrassed by the gaudiness of her masquerade costume. When the time approaches to order her wedding apparel from London, she entreats Charlotte not to send anything displaying too much glare; rich dresses are not necessary to demonstrate the family's status: "Simplicity only can be elegance."[11]

Richardson's greatest interest does not, however, appear to lie in such specifics of female upbringing. Rather, his attention centers on the matter of courtship. With four daughters of his own, this may not be surprising. As he confessed to Thomas Edwards, his daughters were good girls, but "neither rich enough, nor handsome enough, to attract lovers. How should I rejoice to see my eldest happily married!" Several courtships had simmered beneath the roof at North

End; indeed, the famous drawing by Susanna Highmore of Richardson reading *Grandison* to a group of his young friends indicates that some of his listeners eventually married each other. Hester Mulso was among those who met her future husband, John Chapone, at North End. As for Richardson himself, he courted two wives, and many unrecorded courtships must have been discussed by the regular stream of visitors to his home. One of his correspondents, Mary Granville Pendarves Delany, had had colorful though unfortunate experiences with men. At the age of seventeen she was forced to marry an ill-natured, sickly man of sixty. Her plight also included resisting two seducers and rejecting Lord Baltimore because he proposed at the opera. Eventually, she married an Irish clergyman, Patrick Delany. Yet it is experiences such as these that may have caused her to regret that daughters were not taught "to aim at a higher reward than even that of a good husband. . . . It sometimes happens that husbands are not obtained; then how great the mortification, not to obtain that which we were taught to think the highest part of felicity." Naturally, one cannot ascertain the exact degree to which stories such as Mrs. Delany's may have influenced Richardson's thinking and work. Nevertheless, we know that Richardson had definite ideas about courtship and marriage. Besides giving form to traditional issues, he felt there were misconceptions that needed to be exposed and corrected.[12]

The concept of reciprocal duties between parents and children in regard to courtship and marriage figures as prominently in *Grandison* as it does in conduct literature. The Marquis of Halifax advised his daughter that young women were seldom allowed to choose their husbands, as parents were generally the best guides in these matters. Adam Petrie agreed, although he urged parents not to force their children to marry. Filial obedience in matters of choosing a marriage partner was thus an enduring topic of discussion and one that prompted a spirited debate between Richardson and such correspondents as Frances Grainger, Hester Mulso, and Sarah Chapone. To Miss Grainger he affirmed that he did "not love a Tyrant-Parent." To Mrs. Chapone he added that parents did not have the right to command children to marry against their feelings. But he disagreed with Hester Mulso, who would demand duty from the child only if the parent were kind. Richardson argued that the child should see the parent's faults, learn from them, but conceal them from the world. At the same time, a child was obligated to obey parents for "Conscience's Sake" and to realize that "in all reciprocal Duties, the Non-Performance of the Duty on one Part, is not an excuse for the Failure of the other."[13]

In *Grandison,* issues tend to become more complex than usual. Sir Charles's sisters relate the story of Caroline's difficulty with their father's objections to the addresses of the worthy Lord L. Harriet repeats Richardson's arguments when asked by the sisters if their father's prohibition against writing to Lord L. and their brother was not unnatural: "Ought you not to have done *your* duty, whether your father did *his,* or not?" Caroline remains respectful in spite of the merciless railing of her father and eventually, of course, she becomes Lady L. Thus, as Harriet notes, she is "rewarded for her patient duty." Charlotte Grandison is an instructive instance of a woman who momentarily transfers her filial duty to Captain Anderson, making him "my father, my guardian, my brother" when she promises not to marry without his consent while he remains single. Then, too, Richardson presents the case of Sir Charles's mother, who took the advice of her relatives before settling on Sir Thomas. But Lady L. intimates "that they consented, *because* it was her choice. . . ." and not because they thought the match was a prudent one. Lady Grandison had been attracted by Sir Thomas's person and poetry; but his lack of judgment ultimately made their married life very difficult.[14]

Clementina's dilemma in terms of filial duty is somewhat different from that of the Grandison sisters and their mother. Grandison says of her that "Gratitude, piety, sincerity, and every duty of the social life, are constitutional virtues in this Lady. No disturbance of mind can weaken, much less efface them." Her superior duties to God rather than her duty to her parents militate against marriage to Grandison. But a problem arises when, anxious to take the veil, she cites duty to God as a ground for refusing marriage to Count Belvedere. This runs counter to the wish of her parents and deceased grandfathers, who have stipulated that if she should ever decide to enter a convent, the legacy intended for her would go to her cousin Laurana. Clementina is not unduly concerned about such mundane matters, but Grandison, along with her parents, argues that filial duty is itself an article of religion:

> May it not be justly said, that to obey your parents, is to serve God? Would the generous, the noble-minded Clementina della Porretta, *narrow,* as I may say, her piety, by limiting it . . . when she could, at least, *equally* serve God, and benefit her own soul, by obeying her parents, by fulfilling the will of her deceased grandfathers, and by obliging all her other near and dear relations?

Sir Charles also contends along traditional Latitudinarian Protestant lines that if Clementina cloisters herself she will limit her potential for doing good.[15]

Significantly, Richardson enlarges the conventional discussion of filial duty in matters of marriage to include the dilemma of the independent woman, the young lady who did not have to consult parents about her marriage partner. Richardson wrote to Mrs. Sarah Chapone that he had given Hester Mulso innumerable reasons and case histories "to shew that Women are safest when dependent." He questions whether widows "at any Age, make so good Bargains for themselves, as Parents and Guardians make for their Children or Wards?" A wealthy widow, he argues further, is fair game for fortune hunters and is thus "safest in her own keeping." Harriet, an orphan reared by close relatives, has been left to her own discretion in the choice of a marriage partner. On the one hand, Mrs. Shirley and Mrs. Selby are not afraid to advise her. They are the ones from whom Lady D., in her son's behalf, and Sir Charles request approval to court Harriet. On the other hand, they leave the decision entirely up to her, and she admits that such freedom is not an easy burden to bear: "those young women are happiest, whose friends take all the trouble of this sort upon *them;* only consulting their daughters inclinations as preliminaries are adjusting." Harriet's prudence and discretion as an independent woman are sharply contrasted with the behavior of Lady Olivia, a lady "made too soon her own mistress." Willing to give up religion and virtue, she flees from Italy to England in an attempt to ensnare Grandison. Harriet reflects that if Olivia had had parents, she would not have had a fortune and hence "would have shone, as she is well qualified to do, in a dependent state, in Italy, and made some worthy man and herself happy."[16]

Another commonly held idea Richardson hoped to refute was the romantic notion of love; this topic was again characteristically Richardsonian. To Lady Bradshaigh he confided that some of his female readers had "notions of ideal Love, that never can be carried into practice." The source of these romantic notions, according to Richardson and other conduct-book writers, was romances. Abbé D'Ancourt cautioned that "both the fictitious and the marvellous leave false Notions and Images upon the Mind," and Allestree in *The Ladies Calling* echoed this sentiment. Grandmother Shirley admits having read romances as a young woman, and this "unnatural kind of writing" gave the youthful Henrietta "very high ideas of first impressions; of eternal constancy; of Love raised to a pitch of idolatry." Thus, when a perfectly acceptable Mr. Shirley was proposed, she objected that she had no strong feelings for him; she also worried that after marriage she might meet "the very one, the kindred soul, who must irresistably claim my whole heart." Her prudent friend Mrs. Eggleton answered the first objection by counseling that "Esteem, heightened by Gratitude, and enforced by Duty" would "soon ripen into Love." This is an objection that Charlotte Grandison, too, eventually overcomes. As for the second objection, Mrs. Eggleton reminded Henrietta that contrary to the depictions of "poets and romance-writers" our passions should be "our servants, not our masters," and we have it in our power to control them.[17]

Richardson also pleads for common sense in a related matter. Mary Delany and Lady Bradshaigh both agreed that Harriet should not have owned her love for Sir Charles to Sir Rowland, to Lady D., to her relations, and to the Grandison sisters. Richardson argues that he is trying to set a new example. Sir Charles admires Harriet for her frankness and asks why women are "ashamed of owning a laudable passion? Surely there is nothing shameful in *discreet* Love." Harriet is aware of a woman's fear of appearing either too forward or too reserved. She sees insincerity in the custom that would urge reserve and permit "tricks" to find out the man's heart first. It is also suggested that if Clementina had not been so secretive about her regard for Grandison, her reason might not have been "overturned." Harriet's candor is equally evident in her frank regard for Clementina. Lady Echlin thought there was " 'too much parade and compliment' " in Harriet's " 'unbounded profession of friendship for that lady.' " But again, Richardson defends his unique example. He wished to show "an instance of female magnanimity" contrary to the usual examples portrayed in literature:

> Poets have made ungovernable Passion, Jealousy, Rage, Fury, to be the Consequences of a Rivalship in a Woman's Bosom. I wanted to shew that Meekness, Patience, Magnanimity, might have Place there, and govern the whole Conduct of a Woman ardently in Love, + even? + when she had no Hopes of succeeding.[18]

Richardson also wanted to underscore a position he had taken in *Clarissa* against the proposition "that a reformed Rake makes the best Husband." He observed to Hester Mulso that good women professed to admire goodness, but they were ultimately seduced by the flattery of "encroaching Men." The conduct-book writers cautioned women against succumbing to flattery, what Harriet calls "the vice of men." Thus, Halifax wrote, "as *strong perfumes* are seldom used but when they are necessary to smother an unwelcome *scent;* so *Excess of good words,* leave room to believe they are strewed to cover something which is to gain admittance under a Disguise. . . ." Harriet has been taught about "the vile enterprizes of men" by her grandmother's "frightful stories." But she admits, too, that had she not been acquainted with such libertines as Greville, Fenwick, and Pollexfen, she might have been deluded by the compliments of Everard Grandison. There "is a great dearth of good men," she notes, and Sir Charles regrets that a "wretched effeminacy seems to prevail" among men. He adds that women, too, appear to have little regard for marriage; consequently, their attitude does not discourage "free-livers." Charlotte wishes Miss Mansfield and Lord W. well, but says that she "never was fond of matches between sober young women, and battered old rakes." Lord W.'s case, however, is the only one countenanced in *Grandison*, and it is suggested that he is not a "habitual libertine," unlike his brother-in-law, Sir Thomas Grandison. When Harriet learns of Sir Thomas's poor behavior to his wife, his sister, and his daughters, she declares that men such as these are self-centered; anyone who thinks they make good husbands is speaking "against general experience." It is presumptuous to think they can be reclaimed, and a young woman would be well advised to remain single rather than throw in her lot with such a person. Grandison would add that the "sprightly airs" admired before marriage by a woman will either vanish or be "carried abroad. The disagreeable will be brought home." And if such a man reforms, his guilt may make him unsociable.[19]

Richardson continues his discussion of reciprocal duties as they apply to the marital state. When Sir Charles's mother finds that her husband is a spendthrift and cannot be brought to mend his ways, she takes measures to maintain the family's reputation. Harriet exclaims, "Who will say, that mothers may not be the *most* useful persons in the family, when they do their duty, and their husbands are defective in theirs?" Richardson had written to Mrs. Chapone, "But surely, Madam, the Faults of an Husband will not excuse the Faults of a Wife; when the Duty is reciprocal, the Failure of one Side, gives a Merit to the Performance of the other." Just so, Charlotte's marriage is a variation on this very theme of reciprocal marital duties. Lord G.'s "fault" is that he is "too fond" of Charlotte and thus overly tolerant of her subtle ridicule of his innocent foibles. Charlotte, for her part, is remiss because she has not acknowledged Lord G.'s good points. Eventually, under the gentle tutelage of the ladies at Selby House, she mends her ways. Richardson provides a number of undeveloped examples of other marriages. Among the happy couples, we see Lord and Lady L., the Reeveses, and the Selbys. The Marchioness della Porretta and her husband have been married for a long time, and before the family's encounter with Grandison, theirs apparently was a harmonious match. By the same token, the wife of the General is a goodhearted, well-educated woman, but we do not see how she manages her volatile spouse. Nor do we see how Lady W. or Everard's new wife handles a formerly wayward husband.[20]

Several instructive conversations among the characters focus directly upon marital cases. One of these involves the example of a fifteen-year-old girl forced to marry when she was "indifferent to the man" and "had formed no right notions of the state." Another case is that of a married woman who was susceptible to flattery and consequently thought she could be happier with the flatterers than with her own husband. Lady L. mentions the case of a nobleman who rails against matrimony, but "who makes a very indifferent husband to an obliging wife." Grandison agrees that there are many marriages like this but adds that adversity can teach "modesty, humility, and compassion." On another occasion, Lord L. raises the question of marriages of unequal years. He recalls a woman who at twenty married a man over fifty, hoping his early death would leave her a rich widow. But her husband lived twenty more years; now she is engaged to a young man of twenty-two. Sir Charles observes that retribution "will frequently take its course. . . . Thirty years hence, the now young man will perhaps fall into the error of his predecessor, if he outlives the wife he is going to take, and be punished in the same way." One way of summarizing Richardson's ideas of the foundations for matrimonial felicity can be found in a conversation among Harriet, Charlotte, and Lady L., who have been discussing the household arrangements of Lord and Lady L. Charlotte observes that the two are "*tender* of disobliging, and so *studious* of obliging each other." "Delicate observances," says Harriet, are the keys to marital harmony, whether performed from fear, a sense of duty, or from genuine affection.[21]

Smooth management of household affairs certainly contributes to domestic tranquillity, and conduct literature underscored this. *Spectator* 15, for example, describes Aurelia and her husband, whose family "abound with good Sense. . . . Their Family is under so regular an Oeconomy, in its Hours of Devotion and Repast, Employment and Diversion, that it looks like a little Common-Wealth within it self." Harriet reflects on the examples she has had and recalls that her grandfather had described families as "little communities." To be sure, there are many examples in *Grandison* of women who are skilled in family management: Sir Charles's mother, Mrs. Oldham, Lady L., Charlotte, the Mansfield sisters. Lady D., who could "manage a Machiavel" must fall into this category, too, and as Charlotte observes, Emily will have good teachers in Northamptonshire. Harriet, who is an early riser, as Richardson was, directs the Selby household in "a *succession* of *orderliness*." In fact,

Mrs. Curzon, the housekeeper at Grandison Hall, looks forward to her service under Harriet precisely because of this ability; it "was a pleasure . . . to receive commands from persons who knew when things were properly done." Harriet recalls that her grandmother had always said that to direct servants effectively, one must know something of the work to be done. She also follows the advice given by Halifax that "it may be more adviseable for you, to *gain the Servant* you find in a Family, than to tye your self too fast to those you carry into it." She tells Mrs. Curzon that only one servant will come with her; she will make no changes in the existing staff. Managing servants was actually no easy matter. Richardson once asked for a copy of Lady Bradshaigh's rules for women servants, which contained conventional advice: attend to prayers and church services, do not lie or grumble, dress plainly and neatly, save money rather than spend it on clothing, do not keep late hours with men, and above all, "have the fear of god before your Eyes." Both Harriet and Clementina must choose male servants, Harriet's choice being an unfortunate one, since William Wilson plays a prominent part in her abduction by Sir Hargrave. On the other hand, she and Mrs. Reeves are not entirely mistaken in their judgment of his character: Wilson proves to be Richardson's example for a good servant corrupted by a bad master who ultimately reforms. Among other servants of female characters, we are briefly introduced to Charlotte's Jenny and Emily's Anne. Camilla, Clementina's attendant in Italy, lends a harmless note of intrigue as she bears messages between the Porrettas and Grandison in disguise.[22]

Although children naturally represented the primary area of domestic duty, Richardson's intention was not to develop detailed guidelines in *Grandison;* he felt that he had dealt adequately with the subject in *Pamela II.* He does, however, allude to some of the issues of childrearing discussed in the conduct books. We may recall that Pamela wished to nurse her own child, a practice applauded by the authorities. But Mr. B. refused to permit it as a test of Pamela's obedience. Tillotson, incidentally, had allowed for "the interposition of the father's authority." Charlotte decides to nurse baby Harriet, unknown to Lord G.; his discovery is a joyful one for him and one of the most amusing parts of *Grandison.* Swaddling of infants was another debatable question, and the current thinking opposed it. Lady L.'s little boy has "the free exercise of his limbs." But Richardson seems more intent on showing what comes of proper as well as dubious childrearing practices without elaborating on specific methods. Harriet and the Grandisons, for example, may be contrasted with Lady Betty Williams's children. Lady Betty is not evil or unpleasant, but she devoted too much of her time to public entertainments. Harriet is especially troubled when she learns that Lady Betty sent her children abroad for an education. The relation between her and her daughter is one of friends or "Lovers," as Harriet says, rather than of parent and child. The consequences of such an upbringing are predictable: young Miss Williams elopes with a penniless ensign. Another acquaintance of Harriet's in her first days in London, Miss Cantillon, has also run off with an impoverished captain. These imprudent marriages are criticized implicitly in Grandmother Shirley's instructive comment to the single girls on Harriet's wedding day:

> "See . . . the Reward of Duty, Virtue, and Obedience! How unhappy must those Parents and Relations be, whose Daughters, unlike our Harriet, have disgraced themselves, and their families, by a shameful Choice."[23]

Perhaps because Richardson has concentrated on Sir Charles, we are given few opportunities to see the female characters engaging in duties to their neighbors, an obligation the conduct-book writers considered essential for women as well as for men. In *Pamela II* we are guided through one of Pamela's "benevolent weekly rounds," where we witness calls on the sick, infirm, and unfortunate of the neighborhood. Clarissa, too, had her worthy poor. But in *Grandison* there are no visitations of the sick or conspicuous examples of almsgiving. Harriet offers a contribution toward the little fund Grandison is collecting for the reformed Wilson, but Sir Charles discourages the gesture because it would seem inappropriate coming from the injured party. The Selbys give food to the poor, Grandmother Shirley has reconciled two clergymen, and Emily furnishes her mother and Mr. O-Hara with a chariot for their more convenient attendance at Methodist services. Harriet reproves and corrects Charlotte's behavior, certainly within the sphere of duty to one's neighbor. Nonetheless, these are singular instances of charitable behavior. What *Grandison* does emphasize is the duty and potential for female characters to exercise their benevolence. Sir Charles urges both Clementina and Olivia to use their abilities and their means to do good. Harriet, too, intimates that with an enlarged fortune her powers to help others would be increased.[24]

Another idea that Richardson allows to remain somewhat undeveloped is that of duty to God on the part of the female characters. Clementina, of course, claims her superior duty to God as her reason for refusing Grandison. Her approach to her faith is considered zealous and enthusiastic, yet without the customary superstition that English Protestants often associated with Catholics. Grandison's sisters are not depicted as particularly fervent or regular in public worship services, though their admiration for Sir Charles's cheerful practices is evident. As a matter of fact, Grandison must encourage a church wedding for Charlotte as well as a church christening for the child of Lord and Lady L. Charlotte takes a doubtful, though appreciative, view of the Methodists, who have converted Aunt Nell and Mrs. O-Hara. She also reveres Grandmother Shirley for her "habitual piety," something that has obviously influenced Harriet. Harriet's approach to religion is not extreme, but she does feel the obligation to go to church to thank the Almighty for her deliverance from Sir Hargrave. We learn, too, that she prays daily for the restoration of Clementina's health. Dr. Bartlett is consulted periodically about religious matters. But some of their sessions must involve secular learning; Harriet writes that she is "stealing from this good man a little improvement in my geography. . . ." It is from Dr. Bartlett that she learns that Sir Charles's admiration for her "is founded upon her piety, and upon the amiable qualities of her mind." Regarding death, Richardson depicts two contrasting female deathbed scenes. Lady Grandison's last moments afford an example of an individual properly disposed for her final hour. On the other hand, Laurana, Clementina's jealous and vindictive cousin, commits suicide. Grandison, as one would expect, is disturbed by such self-destruction and reflects "how ill was such a soul as Laurana's prepared to rush into Eternity."[25]

In line with Richardson's advice on courtship and marital life, Harriet observes that fewer people are marrying and accounts for this by the "luxury of the age." Her concern is an old one. One tract, *Marriage Promoted* (1690), warning that the neglect of marriage was threatening the life of the nation, proposed a special tax on those who rejected wedlock, the proceeds to be applied to dowries for young women. *Spectator* 526 worried, too, about the perilous condition of marriage. Sir Charles, who would have everyone marry, provides the portions of a number of women to this end. But recognizing the difficulty of single women, he and Dr. Bartlett also propose a scheme of Protestant nunneries, something similar to the educational academy that Defoe had proposed for unmarried women. Grandison's plan would offer an alternative for women of limited means who did not choose to gain a living by needlework or entering domestic service. No vows would be taken; the society would be supported by benefactors, by the fruits of the women's labors, and by any fortune a woman might bring with her. Lady Mary Wortley Montagu applauded the idea. Grandison also suggests another kind of institution, "An Hospital for Female Penitents," which might prevent fallen young women from embarking on a career of prostitution. The author himself supported London's Magdalen House, which opened in 1758, and he discussed it with Lady Bradshaigh and Lady Echlin. He also helped Lady Barbara Montagu's anonymous friend publish the true histories of some of the penitents.[26]

Richardson draws a few examples of women who have chosen the single life and who, at the same time, are neither misfits nor eccentrics. Mrs. Beaumont, an English Protestant who has lived in Italy for many years, was deprived of her rightful fortune by an uncle. But she and Mrs. Eggleton, Grandmother Shirley's friend, are not enemies to marriage; indeed, they appear to be promoters of the state. Harriet goes as far as to chastise Charlotte for poking fun at old maids such as Aunt Nell. Though Aunt Nell has her foibles, she and Lord G.'s more reserved Aunt Gertrude do not seem to fit the description of old maids in Steele's *Ladies Library:*

> If the superannuated *Virgins* would behave themselves with Gravity and Reservedness, addict themselves to the strictest Virtue and Piety, they would give the World some Cause to believe, 'twas not their *Necessity* but their *Choice,* which first kept them unmarry'd.

And Lady Gertrude provides several good reasons for a woman's choosing the single life, though she thinks women are best off in the married state. Then, too, the single life of widowhood is indirectly advocated. Lady Beauchamp, Everard Grandison's wife, and Mrs. O-Hara are all remarried widows. While Lady Beauchamp and Mrs. O-Hara are reformed by the novel's end, and Everard and his wine merchant's wife may succeed in matrimony, all three of the marriages have inauspicious beginnings, reflecting the generally negative view of remarriage found in conduct books. As one of them puts it, "Marriage is so great an adventure, that one seems enough for the whole life." Sir Charles himself remarks that he would not marry a widow. Widows ideally were to lead pious and charitable lives. Grandmother Shirley is a credit to her widowed state and to old age. As a kind of female Nestor, she has made her old age valuable to others and, as the *Tatler* recommended, turned her "experience to the entertainment and advantage of mankind." Lady D. rounds out Richardson's portrait of unmarried widows; an energetic forthright woman, she nevertheless recognizes that two people may have equally good methods. She assures Harriet that as a mother-in-law she will only give advice when asked and will not expect it to be taken.[27]

Reviewing Richardson's version of *The Ladies Calling* it may well be asked what kind of conduct book has been written for the distaff side? Without question, the main focus of *Sir Charles Grandison* is the portrayal of the good man, a rather different task from the one the author set for himself in *Pamela* and *Clarissa*. Nevertheless, a full range of female characters serves as an active complement to his central theme, enabling Richardson to consider both traditional conduct-book issues as well as those matters which were of particular concern to him. His female characters obviously had a special place in his heart. Early in the writing of *Grandison* Richardson confided to Lady Bradshaigh that "a good woman is my favourite character; . . . I can do twenty agreeable things for her, none of which would appear in a striking light in a man."[28] We may fairly conclude that Richardson did all of his "twenty agreeable things" for the distaff side and more.

NOTES

1. Samuel Richardson to Thomas Edwards, 13 February 1750/51, Pierpont Morgan Library; Richardson to Frances Grainger, 28 February 1750, British Library 33964, f. 365.

2. [Darrell], *A Supplement To the First Part of the Gentleman Instructed; With a Word to the Ladies* (London: n.p., 1716), bound with *Gentleman Instructed;* see also [Defoe], *The Family Instructor,* vol. 1, 16th ed. (1766), vol. 2, 8th ed. (1766); [Defoe], *Religious Courtship,* [Steele], *Ladies Library; The Accomplish'd Ladies Delight,* 3d ed. (London: Benjamin Harris, 1683); *New and Excellent Experiments and Secrets In the Art of Angling* (London: n.p., 1677); Astraea Hill to Mrs. Richardson, 17 December 1740, FC XIII, 2, f. 31v.

3. James Bland, *An Essay in Praise of Women* (London: J. Roberts et al., 1733), 203; Wetenhall Wilkes, *An Essay on the Pleasures and Advantages of Female Literature* (London: T. Cooper and R. Caswell, 1741), 7; [Elizabeth Joceline], *The Mother's Legacy to Her Unborn Child* (London: Joseph Downing, 1724), xxxiv; Richardson to Johannes Stinstra, 20 March 1754, *Selected Letters,* 298; Samuel Johnson, *The Works of Samuel Johnson, LL.D.,* 15 vols. (London: J. Buckland et al., vols. 1–13, 1787, vol. 14, 1788; London: Elliot and Kay, vol. 15, 1789), 11:205; Journal of Catherine Talbot, British Library 46,690; Richardson to Lady Bradshaigh [April–October 1751?], *Correspondence,* 6:120; Richardson's correspondence with Lady Barbara Montagu is at Cornell; Richardson's correspondence with Anna Meades is at the British Library, Add. MS. 28,097; Sarah Chapone to Richardson, 24 November 1750, FC XII, 2, f. 17v–18; Richardson is listed among the subscribers of Ballard's book; see George Ballard, *Memoirs of Several Ladies of Great Britain* (Oxford: W. Jackson, 1752), xv.

4. Richardson to Lady Bradshaigh, [April–October 1751?], *Correspondence,* 6:122; on family management see Richardson to Frances Grainger, 6 August 1750, ff. 1–2. Hyde Collection; on women's learning see Lady Bradshaigh to Richardson, [28 December 1750?] *Correspondence,* 6:52–53; Lady Bradshaigh to Richardson, 9 February 1750, *Correspondence,* 6:70–71; Richardson to Lady Bradshaigh, [February–March 1751?], *Correspondence,* 6:78–79; Richardson to Lady Bradshaigh, [January 1751?], *Correspondence,* 6:58.

5. On Harriet see *SCG,* 1:216, 236, and 9; on Harriet's education 1:53; 2:294, 363, and 369; on Charlotte's education 1:179–80 and 193; on Stevens and Clements 1:21 and 102; Mr. Reeves's opinion 1:55 and 59; for Richardson on Reeves see Richardson to Patrick Delany, 22 December

1753, *Selected Letters*, 261–62; see also the discussion on education and the difference between the sexes in *SCG*, 3:242–51.

6. For Jeronymo on Italian women see *SCG*, 2:139; on the Porretta ladies 2:123 and 468; 3:62; on a spoiled Clementina 2:215; Richardson to Lady Bradshaigh, 30 May 1754, FC XI, f. 103; and Richardson to Lady Bradshaigh, 14 February 1754, *Selected Letters*, 288; on Olivia see *SCG*, 2:374 and 641; Sir Charles on Italy 2:123.

7. For Sir Charles's program see *SCG*, 2:8; for Harriet's views see 1:22; on masquerades 1:143 and 168; Harriet's reflections 2:407–8.

8. *Advice to the Fair* (London: J. Wilford, 1736), pt. 2, p. 10; [Richard Allestree], *The Ladies Calling* (Oxford: At the Theater, 1673), pt. 1, p. 7; [Darrell], *Supplement to Gentleman Instructed*, 156; [John Essex], *The Young Ladies Conduct* (London: John Brotherton, 1722), viii; for Harriet on learning see *SCG*, 1:51–52; Mrs. Shirley on conversation 3:243–44; on Charlotte 1:414; on Harriet's "tribunal" 3:129–31; on divided love 3:19; a conversation 1:425–30; on Emily 2:71–77; other "congresses" 2:225, 333, 465, 529, and 3:61; Harriet on conversations 3:410.

9. On Sir Charles and Mrs. Shirley see *SCG*, 3:140; on Harriet's tact see 1:400 and 410; on Lady D. and Harriet 2:289–90; *Art of Complaisance*, 40; Walker, *Of Education*, 243; for others on raillery see Lord Chesterfield, *Letters to His Godson*, Letter 137, no. 9, n.d., p. 183 and [Chevalier Joachim Trotti de la Chétardie], *Instructions for a Young Nobleman* (London: R. Bentley and S. Magnes, 1683), 17–18; for Sir Charles's rebuke see *SCG*, 2:86.

10. On shellwork see *SCG*, 2:417; 3:277; Richardson to Lady Bradshaigh, 8 February 1754, FC XI, f. 67v; Richardson to Lady Bradshaigh, 8 April 1754, FC XI, f. 96: Catherine Talbot described the "indifferent Shells" that decorated Parson's Green, Catherine Talbot to [Mrs. A. Berkeley?], 9 October 1756, British Library 39311, f. 83b; on Emily see *SCG*, 1:431–32.

11. *Spectator*, ed. Bond, 4:27–30, no. 435; [Halifax], *Lady's New-years Gift*, 88; on Harriet's costume see *SCG*, 1:115; Harriet on dress 3:172–73.

12. On Richardson's daughters see Richardson to Thomas Edwards, 30 December 1754, *Correspondence*, 3:104; for Miss Highmore's drawing see Eaves and Kimpel, *Richardson*, plate 11, and on Mrs. Delany see 174–75; Mary Delany to Richardson, 16 August 1751, *Correspondence*, 4:44.

13. [Halifax], *Lady's New years Gift*, 25; Adam Petrie, *Rules of Good Deportment*, 41; for Richardson's discussion on parental authority with Mrs. Sarah Chapone see Sarah Chapone to Richardson, 22 February 1752, FC XII, 2, ff. 58–61; Richardson to Sarah Chapone, 2 March 1752, FC XII, 2, ff. 38–45; Sarah Chapone to Richardson, [March 1752?], FC XII, 2, ff. 47–57; on "Tyrant-Parent" see Richardson to Grainger, 1 February 1749/50, Pierpont Morgan Library; on commanding children to marry and on Hester Mulso's opinion see Richardson to Sarah Chapone, 18 April 1752, FC XII, 2, ff. 62–73; for Richardson's extended discussion with Hester Mulso see Mulso to Richardson, 12 October 1750, 10 November 1750, 3 January 1750/51, Hester Mulso Chapone, *Works*, 2:29–34, 37–85, 89–143; on parents' faults and reciprocal duties see Richardson to Grainger, 22 January 1749/50, Yale University; for Richardson's extended discussion with Frances Grainger see Richardson to Grainger, 20 December 1748, Pierpont Morgan Library; Richardson to Grainger, 5 December 1749, Hyde Collection; Richardson to Grainger, 21 December 1749, *Selected Letters*, 136–41; Richardson to Grainger, 28 February 1750, British Library 33964, ff. 365–66; Richardson to Grainger, 29 March 1750, *Selected Letters*, 150–57; Richardson to Grainger, 8 September 1750, Houghton Library, fMS Eng 870 (38); Harriet echoes Richardson in *SCG*, 1:315; on unnatural commands 1:321.

14. On Caroline *SCG*, 1:333; on duty to parents 1:352; on Caroline 1:334 and 342; on Charlotte 1:408–9; on Lady Grandison and Sir Thomas see 1:311.

15. On Clementina see *SCG*, 2:490; Clementina's position 2:564–67, 573, and 575; on Clementina's inheritance 3:429; 2:456, 129, and 534; Sir Charles's argument 2:619–21 and 3:431.

16. Richardson to Sarah Chapone, 2 March 1752, *Selected Letters*, 203; Richardson to Sarah Chapone, 18 April 1752, FC XII, 2, f. 67; for Mrs. Shirley on Harriet see *SCG; 3*:74; on Harriet's independence 3:103 and 1:11; Harriet on independence 1:64; on Olivia 2:371, 368–69 and 364–65; Lawrence Stone deals in detail with the greater freedom of choice in selecting marriage partners.

17. Richardson to Lady Bradshaigh, 14 February 1754, *Selected Letters*, 290–91; Abbé D'Ancourt, *The Lady's Preceptor* (London: B. Dod, 1743), 60; [Allestree], *Ladies Calling*, pt. 2, p. 10; for Charlotte on epic poets see *SCG*, 3:197–98; on Mrs. Shirley 3:398–99 and 401.

18. For Harriet's frankness see Mary Delany to Richardson, 14 December 1751, *Correspondence*, 4:52; Lady Bradshaigh to Richardson, 1 November in 27 November 1753, FC XI f. 45; Lady Bradshaigh to Richardson, 8 November in 27 November 1753, FC XI, f. 47; on Richardson's defense see Richardson to Lady Bradshaigh, 8 December 1753, *Selected Letters*, 251 and 257; Richardson to Lady Bradshaigh, 5 October 1753, *Selected Letters*, 244–45; for Sir Charles on frankness see *SCG*, 2:113 and 1:453; on Harriet's frankness 2:414; 3:355, 249, and 99; Harriet on reserve 1:423 and 2:1–2; on Clementina see Richardson to Isabella Sutton, 7 November 1751, *Correspondence*, 4:133; *SCG*, 2:320, 165, and 125–26; Lady Echlin to Richardson, 12 August 1754, *Correspondence*, 5:12; Richardson to Lady Echlin, 12 September 1754, *Correspondence*, 5:22–23; Richardson to Lady Echlin, 24 July 1754, State University of New York at Buffalo.

19. Richardson to Lady Bradshaigh, 26 October 1748, *Selected Letters*, 94; Richardson to Hester Mulso, 3 September 1751, *Selected Letters*, 189; Richardson to Lady Bradshaigh, 9 October 1754, FC XI, f. 132; for Harriet on flattery see *SCG*, 1:18; [Halifax], *Lady's New years Gift*, 112; other writers who echo this are D'Ancourt, *Lady's Preceptor*, 13; and [James Burgh], *Thoughts on Education* (London: G. Freer, 1747), 55–56; on Mrs. Shirley's stories see *SCG*, 1:177; for Harriet on Everard see 1:227–28; on the age, 2:348 and 10; Charlotte on rakes 2:441; on Sir Thomas 1:353; Harriet on reformed rakes 1:342 and 25–26; Sir Charles on rakes 1:429–30; it was suggested to Harriet by Mr. Reeves, who was impressed by Sir Hargrave's fortune, that she marry, reform him, and use his wealth to help "multitudes," 1:64.

20. For Harriet on Lady Grandison see *SCG*, 1:312; Richardson to Sarah Chapone, 2 March 1752, *Selected Letters*, 201; on Lord G. *SCG*, 2:413; Sir Charles on Charlotte 2:85; Charlotte on Lord G. 2:516 and 514; on Lord and Lady L. 2:349 and 98.

21. On marriage cases see *SCG*, 2:358; on marriage of unequal years 1:430; Harriet and Charlotte on marriage 1:244; 2:350; for Richardson's debates with Lady Bradshaigh on love and fear in marriage see *Correspondence*, 6:129–213.

22. *Spectator*, ed. Bond, 1:68, no. 15; on families see *SCG*, 1:25; on Mrs. Oldham 1:319; on Charlotte 1:180; on Miss Mansfield 2:267; on Lady D. 3:86; on Richardson as early riser see Richardson to Elizabeth Carter, 4 July 1753, Hyde Collection, f. 1; on Harriet's methods see *SCG*, 2:544 and 162; good Lady L., interestingly, is not an early riser; see 2:69; on Mrs. Curzon see 3:276; [Halifax], *Lady's New-years Gift*, 65 and 84; Richardson to Lady Bradshaigh, 2 September 1757, FC XI, f. 217; "Some Rules which are Expected to be observ'd by the Women Servants, and some advice, which it is hoped they will think their Interest to follow," 2 October 1757, FC XI, ff. 219–20v; Fuller, B.D., *Holy State*, 3; on Clementina's English servant see *SCG*, 3:325–26; on Wilson 1:97–98; Harriet on servants 1:23.

23. John Cleland, *Hropaideia* (Oxford: Joseph Barnes, 1607), 19; Gailhard, *Compleat Gentleman*, 7; Gouge, *Of Domesticall Duties*, 515–26; [Steele], Ladies Library, 2:187; Caleb Trenchfield, *A Cap of Gray Hairs for a Green Head* (London: A. Bettesworth, 1710), 133; Tillotson, Sermon 51, "Of the education of children," *Works*, 4:8; on Charlotte see *SCG*, 3:402–4; on swaddling see *Accomplish'd Lady's Delight*, 10th ed. (London: Daniel Pratt, 1719), 47; [William Cadogan], *An Essay upon Nursing* (London: J. Roberts, 1748), 9; on baby L., see *SCG*, 3:209 and 261; on Lady Betty and modern mothers 1:21–22; 2:553 and 408; on the elopements 3:13; Mrs. Shirley's remarks 3:227.

24. Richardson, *Pamela II*, 181–85, Letter 37; on Harriet's contribution see *SCG*, 1:295; on the Selbys 2:544; on Mrs. Shirley's reconciliation 3:140; on Emily 3:167–69; on reproving others see [Halifax], *Lady's New-years Gift*, 120–21 and Petrie, *Of Good Deportment*, 47; Harriet on increased duties *SCG*, 1:85 and 3:28.

25. Charlotte on Grandmother Shirley, *SCG*, 2:416; Harriet's prayers of thanksgiving, 1:194 and 199; on Harriet's praying for Clementina, 2:304, 404, and 555; Harriet and Dr. Bartlett, 1:440 and 2:77; Sir Charles on Harriet's piety, 2:326; Lady Grandison's death 1:315–18; on Laurana's suicide 3:446–47; Sir Charles on suicide 3:448.

26. For Harriet on fewer marriages see *SCG*, 1:231–32; *Marriage Promoted* (London: Richard Baldwin, 1690), 55–56; *Spectator*, ed. Bond, 4:382–85, no. 528; for Sir Charles on marriage, see *SCG*, 1:428; [Daniel Defoe], *An Essay upon Projects* (London: Tho. Cockerill, 1697), 282–87; Sir Charles on nunneries and on shelter for prostitutes *SCG*, 3:9 and 2:355–56; Lady Mary Wortley Montagu to Lady Bute, 20 October [1755], Lady Mary Wortley Montagu, *Complete Letters*, ed. Halsband, 3:97–98; on Richardson's support of Magdalen House see *SCG*, 2:676, n. 356; Sale, *Richardson*, 119–20; Eaves and Kimpel, *Richardson*, 463–65 and 561; Lady Echlin to Richardson, 13 December 1759, *Correspondence*, 5:97–98; Lady Bradshaigh to Richardson, 18 September 1759, FC XI, f. 253v; Lady Bradshaigh to Richardson, 2 December 1759, FC XI, ff. 255v–56v; Lady Bradshaigh to Richardson, 22 May 1759, FC XI, ff. 257–58v and Richardson to Lady Bradshaigh, 18 October 1759, FC XI, f. 261; the Lady Barbara Montagu correspondence is at Cornell.

27. On Mrs. Beaumont see *SCG*, 2:128; for Charlotte's comments see 2:417 and 444; for Charlotte chastised see 3:397 and 2:662; on Aunt Nell's foibles see 3:22, 115, and 198; for Lady Gertrude's views see 3:407–8; [Steele], *Ladies Library*, 2:41; on Aunt Nell's history see *SCG*, 1:342 and 346; [Allestree], *Ladies Calling*, pt. 2, p. 4 echoes Steele; Fuller, B.D., *Holy State*, chap. 10; Sir Thomas Overbury, *Sir Thomas Overbury His Wife* (London: Philip Cheturn, 1664), "A vertuous Widow" and "An ordinary Widow," n.p.; [Allestree], *Ladies Calling*, pt. 2, p. 80; George A. Aitken, ed. *The Tatler*, 4 vols. (London: Duckworth & Co., 1899), 3:102–3, no. 132; Sir Charles's view *SCG*, 2:43; on old age see 3:21, 182, 34, and 1:19.

28. Richardson to Lady Bradshaigh, 24 March [1751], *Selected Letters*, 180.

EPILOGUE

RICHARDSON'S exchange of opinion with those interested in a variety of alternative endings and sequels to *Grandison* is perhaps one final indication of how central was the theme of the conduct book. Numerous correspondents guaranteed the author a ready supply of literary advisers, and as work on his last novel progressed, they speculated on potential concluding episodes. To Thomas Edwards he wrote that he had "frighted Miss Mulso, Miss Highmore, Miss Prescott, &c. with allowing them to think I intended a tragical ending to Sir Charles." He is, in fact, known to have teased Lady Bradshaigh with the idea that Harriet might die in childbirth, having bequeathed her husband and her surviving child to Clementina: "I can draw, I fancy, a charming Child-bed Death." This would, of course, have added still another typical conduct-book situation to an already heavy roster. The Porrettas might even do the unthinkable and convert. Miss Grainger thought he might extend the range of conduct-book dilemmas by treating the "behaviour of ye survivor of a happy marriage . . . in either S^r. Charles or his Harriet." Later, after publication, it was suggested that he should write additional volumes and, as if momentarily interested, he insisted on some suggestions.[1]

Perhaps the need to choose between many intriguing alternatives in connection with ending and sequel was one of the things that weighed heavily on Richardson, for he declared at the time that he was "in a manner worn out." Edwards, however, felt that writing was essential to Richardson's well-being: "Your active mind must be employed." At the same time, Richardson insisted that he now wanted nothing more than to pay visits to his friends and devote himself to letter writing. When he assured Edwards that he could "see no Likelihood that I should recover Spirits enough to attempt resuming the Pen," he may have had in mind the dubious results of *Pamela II* or Defoe's remark that the writing of sequels was always risky. On the other hand, he may, in fact, have been exhausted. He had, after all, spent himself in a manner unprecedented during his lifetime.[2]

Just before the completion of *Grandison,* however, Richardson had

"

begun to abstract and collect the maxims and sentiments from his last work for the benefit of those who read only for the story—more interest in plot at the expense of underlying instruction was a problem that plagued him throughout his writing career. In a sense, the resulting *Collection of Moral Sentiments* brought Richardson full circle in his writing projects and back to the kinds of works he had first authored. He was obviously uncomfortable with a production so closely resembling the conventional conduct book: "It is a dry Performance, Dull Morality, and Sentences, some pertinent, some impertinent, divested of Story, and Amusement. . . ." His *Collection* was at best anticlimactic, since the scope of his work had gone far beyond earlier conduct-book writers to fictionalize a full range of human problems in a fresh and much more powerful way. *Sir Charles Grandison* was itself the culmination of the conduct-book tradition and the most "compleat" realization by far of Samuel Richardson's lifelong aim.[3]

NOTES

1. Richardson to Thomas Edwards, 21 August 1752, FC XII, 1, f. 58v; see also Richardson to Isabella Sutton, 24 July 1752, *Correspondence,* 4:137; Richardson to Lady Bradshaigh, 8 February 1754, *Selected Letters,* 276–77; Frances Grainger to Richardson, 23 May 1754, FC XV, 3, f. 46v; Richardson to Lady Bradshaigh, 9 July 1754, FC XI, f. 110v.

2. Richardson to Lady Bradshaigh, 9 July 1754, FC XI, f. 110v; Thomas Edwards to Richardson, 4 February 1755, FC XII, 1, f. 133; Richardson to Sarah Wescomb, 22 March 1754, *European Magazine* 54 (August 1808): 95; Richardson to Hester Mulso, 30 August 1756, *Correspondence,* 3:232; Richardson to Thomas Edwards, 23 February 1755, FC XII, 1, f. 134v; [Defoe], *The Family Instructor,* 2:preface.

3. Eaves and Kimpel, *Richardson,* 420–21; Richardson to Thomas Edwards, [August 1755?], FC XII, 1, 145v; Richardson to Benjamin Kennicott, 26 November 1754, Yale MS Vault file.

BIBLIOGRAPHY

I. PRIMARY SOURCES

1. Richardson's Works

(Date in parentheses after title indicates first publication.)

[Richardson, Samuel]. *Aesop's Fables. With Instructive Morals and Reflections, Abstracted from all Party Considerations, Adapted To All Capacities; And design'd to promote Religion, Morality, and Universal Benevolence. Containing Two Hundred and Forty Fables with a Cut Engraved on Copper to each Fable. And the Life of Aesop prefixed, By Mr. Richardson* (1740). London: J. F. and C. Rivington et al., n.d.

[Richardson, Samuel]. *The Apprentice's Vade Mecum: Or, Young Man's Pocket Companion. In Three Parts* (1734). London: J. Roberts, 1734.

[Richardson, Samuel]. *A Collection Of the Moral and Instructive Sentiments, Maxims, Cautions, and Reflexions, Contained in the Histories of Pamela, Clarissa, and Sir Charles Grandison. Digested under Proper Heads, With References to the Volume, and Page, both in Octavo and Twelves, in the respective Histories. To which are subjoined, Two Letters from the Editor of those Works: The one, in Answer to a Lady who was solicitous for an additional Volume to the History of Sir Charles Grandison. The other, in Reply to a Gentleman, who had objected to Sir Charles's offer'd Compromise in the Article of Religion, had he married a Roman Catholic Lady* (1755). London: S. Richardson, 1755.

[Richardson, Samuel]. "Rambler No. 97." In *The Yale Edition of the Works of Samuel Johnson*. Edited by W. J. Bate and Albrecht B. Strauss. New Haven: Yale University Press, 1969, 4:153–59.

Richardson, Samuel. *Clarissa Or, The History of a Young Lady* (1748). 4 vols. Edited by John Butt. New York: Everyman's Library, 1976.

———. *Clarissa: Preface, Hints of Prefaces, and Postscript*. Edited by R. F. Brissenden. Los Angeles: Augustan Reprint Society No. 103, 1964.

———. *Familiar Letters on Important Occasions* (1741). Edited by Brian W. Downs. London: George Routledge and Sons, Ltd., 1928.

———. "History of Mrs. Beaumont, A Fragment. In a Letter from Dr. Bartlett to Miss Byron." In *The Correspondence of Samuel Richardson*. Edited by Anna Laetitia Barbauld, 5:301–48. 1804, reprint. New York: AMS Press, Inc., 1966.

————. *The History of Sir Charles Grandison* (1754). Edited by Jocelyn Harris. 3 vols. London: Oxford University Press, 1972.

————. *The History of Sir Charles Grandison, Abridged from the Works of Samuel Richardson, Esq. Author of Pamela and Clarissa.* 11th ed. Philadelphia: Mathew Carey, 1794.

————. *The History of Sir Charles Grandison: A New and Abridged Edition.* Edited by Mary Howitt. London: George Routledge and Sons, [1873].

————. *Letters from Sir Charles Grandison Selected with a Biographical Introduction and Connecting Notes.* Edited by George Saintsbury. 2 vols. London: George Allen, 1895.

————. *Meditations Collected from the Sacred Books; And Adapted to the Different Stages of a Deep Distress; Gloriously surmounted by Patience, Piety, and Resignation. Being those mentioned in the History of Clarissa as drawn up by her for her own Use. To Each of which is prefixed, A Short Historical Account, Connecting it with the Story.* London: J. Osborn, Andr. Millar, J. and J. Rivington, and James Leake, 1750.

————. *Pamela, or, Virtue Rewarded* (1740). Edited by T. C. Duncan Eaves and Ben D. Kimpel. Boston: Houghton Mifflin Company, 1971.

————. *Pamela.* Introduction by M. Kinkead-Weekes. 2 vols. New York: Everyman's Library, 1974.

————. "Private Thoughts on Mr. Ditcher's Proposal and Address. Transcribed from my Pocket Almanack 1757. And thence tore out, and destroy'd, after what follows, was transcribed from it." In Joseph W. Reed, Jr., "A New Samuel Richardson Manuscript." *The Yale University Library Gazette* 42 (April 1968): 215–31.

2. Manuscript Collections

Gemeentelijke Archief Dienst, Amsterdam
  Johannes Stinstra
Universiteits-Bibliotheek van Amsterdam
  Henry Home, Lord Kames
Bath Municipal Libraries and Victoria Art Gallery
  Dr. William Oliver Letter
University of Pennsylvania, Philadelphia
  Benjamin Kennicott
Pierpont Morgan Library, New York
  Lady Echlin
  Thomas Edwards
  Frances Grainger
  Samuel Johnson
  Benjamin Kennicott
  Charlotte Lennox

Samuel Lobb
Jean André de Luc
Thomas Sheridan
Mary Watts
Edward Young
Princeton University, Robert H. Taylor Collection
Elizabeth Carter
Colley Cibber
Lady Echlin
Samuel Johnson
Samuel Lobb
Elizabeth Pennington
Frances Sheridan
Rice University, Fondren Library, Houston, Texas
Anne Richardson
Royal National Hospital for Rheumatic Diseases, Bath, England
Ralph Allen
President of Governors of Bath Hospital
Wellesley College
Edward Young
Wisbech and Fenland Museum, Wisbech, Cambridgeshire, England
Robert Dodsley
Lady Barbara Montagu
Yale University, Beinecke Rare Book and Manuscript Library
Lady Echlin
Christian F. Gellert–Speck Collection
Frances Grainger
Benjamin Kennicott
Catherine Lintot
Mr. Mills
Lady Barbara Montagu–Osborn Collection
Joseph Spence–Osborn Collection
Mary Watts
Edward Young–Tinker Collection
Henry W. and Albert A. Berg Collection of the New York Public Library
Elizabeth Carter
Dr. George Cheyne
Colley Cibber
Lady Echlin
Ethelinda, Charlotte, and Henrietta
Sarah Wescomb
Edward Young
Bodleian Library, Oxford
Thomas Edwards Correspondence
Boston Public Library
Lady Echlin
David Garrick

British Library, London
  Mark Akenside
  Thomas Birch
  Alexis Claude Clairaut
  John Duncombe
  Lady Echlin
  Alexander Gordon
  Frances Grainger
  Aaron Hill
  Cox Macro
  Anna Meades
  Society for the Encouragement of Learning
  John Ward
Brown University, Providence, Rhode Island
  Thomas Edwards
State University of New York at Buffalo, The Poetry/Rare Books Collection
  Elizabeth Carter
  Lady Echlin
Columbia University, New York
  Peter Peckard
Cornell University, Ithaca, New York
  Lady Barbara Montagu
Mrs. A. Cory-Wright
  Samuel Lobb
  William Lobb
University of Edinburgh
  Dr. George Cheyne
Forster Collection, Victoria and Albert Museum, London
  Lady Dorothy Bradshaigh
  Mrs. Sarah Chapone
  Thomas Edwards
  Aaron Hill
  Urania Johnson
  Miss Righton
  Sarah Wescomb Scudamore
  Eusebius Silvester
  Other miscellaneous correspondence
Freies Deutsches Hochstift, Frankfurt am Main
  Meta Klopstock
Harvard University, Houghton Library
  Elizabeth Carter
  Lady Echlin
  Frances Grainer
  Susanna Highmore
  Urania Johnson
  Charlotte Lennox

Lady Barbara Montagu
John Rivington
Sarah Scott
Frances Sheridan
Thomas Sheridan
Edward Young
Haverford College, Haverford, Pennsylvania
Sarah Wescomb Scudamore
Historical Society of Pennsylvania, Philadelphia
Frances Grainger
Benjamin Kennicott
Frances Sheridan
Tobias Smollett
Edward Young
Huntington Library, San Marino, California
Charles Chauncey
Samuel Johnson
Sarah Wescomb
Hyde Collection, Somerville, New Jersey
Isaac Hawkins Brown
Elizabeth Carter
Lady Echlin
Thomas Edwards
Sarah Fielding
Frances Grainger
Samuel Johnson
Jean André de Luc
Lady Barbara Montagu
Elizabeth Pennington
Psalmanazar
John Rivington
John Swinton
Thomas Wilson
Indiana University, Bloomington
Lady Echlin
William Warbuton
University of Iowa, Iowa City
Mark Hildesley
University of Leeds, Brotherton Library
Susanna Highmore
Deutsches Buch- und Schrift-museum, Leipzig
Erasmus Reich
Universitätsbibliothek, "Sammlung Clodius," Leipzig
Meta Klopstock
Liverpool Public Library
Alexis Claude Clairaut

Maine Historical Society
  Meta Klopstock
National Library of Ireland, Dublin
  Patrick Delany
National Library of Scotland, Edinburgh
  Hester Mulso
  Edward Young
New-York Historical Society, New York
  Thomas and Frances Sheridan
New York University, Fales Collection
  Lady Echlin
Northamptonshire Record Office, Delapré Abbey, Northampton, England
  Sir John Dryden, Seventh Baronet.

3. Published Correspondence

Richardson, Samuel. *The Correspondence of Samuel Richardson, Author of Pamela, Clarissa, and Sir Charles Grandison. Selected from the Original Manuscripts, Bequeathed by Him to His Family. To which are prefixed, A Biographical Account of That Author, and Observations on His Writings.* Edited by Anna Laetitia Barbauld. 6 vols. 1804; reprint, New York: AMS Press, Inc., 1966.

————. *The Richardson-Stinstra Correspondence and Stinstra's Prefaces to Clarissa.* Edited by William D. Slattery. Carbondale: Southern Illinois University Press, 1969.

————. *Selected Letters of Samuel Richardson.* Edited by John Carroll. Oxford: Clarendon Press, 1964.

With Elizabeth Carter, *Monthly Magazine* 33 (1812): 533–43.

With Dr. George Cheyne, "The Letters of Doctor George Cheyne to Samuel Richardson (1733–1743)." Edited by Charles F. Mullett. *The University of Missouri Studies* 18 (1943): 5–137.

With Joseph Highmore, *Gentleman's Magazine* 87 (1817): pt. 2, p. 210.

With Susanna Highmore, *Gentleman's Magazine* 86 (1816): pt. 1, pp. 506–8.

With Charlotte Lennox, *Harvard Library Bulletin* 18 (October 1970): 334–44; 19 (January 1971): 36–60; 19 (April 1971): 165–86; 19 (October 1971): 416–35.

With Tobias Smollett, *Monthly Magazine* 68 (1819): 326–28.

With Sarah Wescomb, *European Magazine and London Review* 53 (1808): 370–72 and 429; 54 (1808): 10–13, 94–98, and 190–92; 55 (1809): 101–4.

With Edward Young, *Monthly Magazine* 36 (1813): 418–23; 37 (1814): 138–42, 326–30; 38 (1814): 429–34; 39 (1815): 230–33; 40 (1815): 134–37; 41 (1816): 230–34; 42 (1816): 39–41, 331–35; 43 (1817): 327–29; 44 (1817): 327–30; 45 (1818): 238–39; 46 (1818): 43–45; 47 (1819): 134–37.

4. Courtesy and Conduct Literature

(Date in parentheses after title indicates first publication.)

The Accomplish'd Ladies Delight in Preserving, Physick, Beautifying, and Cookery. 3d ed. enlarged. London: Benjamin Harris, 1683.

The Accomplish'd Lady's Delight, in Preserving, Physick, Beautifying, Cookery, Gardening. 10th ed. inlarged. London: Daniel Pratt, 1719.

Advice to the Fair: An Epistolary Essay, in Three Parts: On Dress, Converse, and Marriage: Address'd to a Sister. London: J. Wilford, 1736.

The Agreeable Companion; Or, An Universal Medley of Wit and Good-Humour. London: W. Bickerton, 1745.

Ainsworth, Robert. *The Most Natural and Easy Way of Institution, By Making a Domestic Education Less Chargeable to Parents, and More Easy and Beneficial to Children* (1698). 2d ed. London: E. Currell and J. Wilford, 1736.

[Allestree, Richard]. *Art of Contentment, By the Author of The Whole Duty Of Man, &c.* (1675). Oxford: At the Theater, 1719.

[Allestree, Richard]. *The Causes of the Decay of Christian Piety. Or an Impartial Survey Of the Ruines of Christian Religion, Undermin'd by Unchristian Practice. Written by the Author of The Whole Duty of Man* (1667). London: Robert Pawlett, 1677.

[Allestree, Richard]. *The Gentleman's Calling. Written by the Author of the Whole Duty of Man* (1660). London: Robert Pawlet, 1676.

[Allestree, Richard]. *The Government of the Tongue By the Author of The Whole Duty of Man, &c.* (1674). 3d impression. Oxford: At the Theater, 1675.

[Allestree, Richard]. *The Ladies Calling. In Two Parts. By the Author of the Whole Duty of Man, The Causes of the Decay of Christian Piety, and the Gentlemans Calling.* Oxford: At the Theater, 1673.

[Allestree, Richard]. *The Whole Duty of Man, Laid down In a Plain and Familiar Way for the Use of All, but especially the Meanest Reader. Divided into XVII Chapters. One whereof being read every Lord's Day, the Whole may be read over Thrice in the Year. Necessary for all Families. With Private Devotions for several Occasions* (1658). London: John Eyre, 1741.

Ancourt, Abbé D'. *The Lady's Preceptor. Or, A Letter to a Young Lady of Distinction upon Politeness. Taken from the French of the Abbé D'Ancourt, And Adapted to the Religion, Customs, and Manners of the English Nation. By a Gentleman of Cambridge.* London: J. Watts, 1743.

Argyle, Archibald [Campbell], Late Marquis of. *Instructions to a Son.* Printed at Edinborough and reprinted at London: D. Trench, 1661.

Armstrong, John, M.D. *The Art of Preserving Health: A Poem. In Four Books* (1744). 2d ed. London: A. Miller, 1745.

The Art of Complaisance or the Means to oblige in Conversation. London: John Starkey, 1673.

[Astell, Mary]. *An Essay In Defence of the Female Sex. In which are inserted the Characters of A Pedant, A Squire, A Beau, A vertuoso, A Poetaster, A City-Critick, &c. In a Letter to a Lady. Written by a Lady.* London: A. Roper and E. Wilkinson, 1696.

[Astell, Mary]. *Some Reflections upon Marriage. With Additions* (1700). 4th ed. London: William Parker, 1730.

Aurelius, Antoninus [Marcus]. *The Emperor Marcus Antoninus His Conversation With Himself. Together With the Preliminary Discourse of the Learned Gataker. As also, The Emperor's Life, Written by Monsieur D'acier, and Supported by the Authorities Collected by Dr. Stanhope. To which is added the Mythological Picture of Cebes the Theban, &c. Translated into English from the Respective Originals, by Jeremy Collier, M.A.* London: Richard Sare, 1701.

The Babees Book, . . . The Booke of Demeanor, The Boke of Curtasye, Seager's Schoole of Vertue, . . . and some Forewords on Education in Early England (ca. 1475). Edited by Frederick J. Furnivall. London: N. Trubner and Co. for the Early English Text Society, no 32, 1868.

[Baldwin, William]. *A Treatise of Morall Philosophie: Wherein is Contained the worthy sayings of Philosophers Emperours, Kings, and Orators: their lives and answers: of what linage they came: and of what Countrey they were: Whose worthy Sentences. notable Precepts, Counsels, and Parables, doe hereafter follow. First gathered & set forth by William Bauldwin, and now the Ninth time since inlarged by Thomas Palfreyman, Gentleman* (1547). London: William Stansby, n.d.

[Barnard, John]. *A Present for an Apprentice: Or, A Sure Guide, to Gain Both Esteem and Estate; with Rules for His Conduct to His Master and in the World. By a Late Lord Mayor of London* (1740). Glasgow: R. Urie, 1760.

Barrow, Isaac. *Of Industry, in Four Discourses: In General. In our General Calling, as Christians. In our Particular Calling, as Gentleman. In our particular calling, as Scholars* (1693). 2d ed. London: Brab. Aylmer, 1712.

Baxter, Richard. *The Catechizing of Families: A Teacher of Householders How to Teach their Housholds. Useful also to School-Masters and Tutors of Youth. For those that are past the common small Chatechisms, and would grow to a more rooted Faith. and to the fuller understanding of all that is commonly needful to a safe, holy, comfortable and profitable Life.* London: T. Parkhurst and B. Simmons, 1683.

[Bayly, Lewis]. *The Practice of Pietie.* (1613; 3d ed.). Last corrected edition. Amsterdam: Jo. Stafford, 1649.

Bland, James, *An Essay in Praise of Women: Or, A Looking-glass for Ladies to see their Perfections in.* London: J. Roberts et al., 1733.

Blount, Sir Tho. [mas] Pope. *Essays On Several Subjects* (1691). London: Richard Bently, 1692.

[Bramston, James]. *The Man of Taste, Occasion'd by an Epistle Of Mr. Pope's On that Subject. By the Author of the Art of Politicks.* Dublin: George Faulkner, 1733.

[Brathwait, Richard]. *Ar't asleepe Husband? A Boulster Lecture; Stored With all variety of witty jeasts, merry Tales, and other pleasant passages; Extracted, From the choicest flowers of Philosophy, Poesy, antient and moderne History. Illustrated with Examples of incomparable constancy, in the excellent History of Philocles and Doriclea. By Philogenes Panedonius.* London:R. B., 1640.

Brathwait, Richard. *The English Gentleman and English Gentlewoman, Both In one Volume couched, the 3ᵈ Edition revised, corrected & enlarged; with A Ladies Love Lecture, And a Supplement Lately annexed, and Entitled The Turtles Triumph* (1630). London: John Dawson, 1641.

Britaine, William de. *Human Prudence. Or, the Art By which a Man may Raise Himself and his Fortune to Grandeur. Corrected and very much Enlarged* (1680). 11th ed. London: Richard Sare, 1717.

Brown, Thomas. *A Legacy for the Ladies. Or, Characters of the Women. By the late Ingenious Mr. Thomas Brown, With a Comical View of London and Westminster: Or, The Merry Quack; wherein Physick is Rectified for both the Beaus and Ladies. In Two Parts. The First Part by Mr. Tho. Brown: The Second Part by Mr. Edw. Ward, Author of the London-Spy, &c. To which is prefixt, The Character of Mr. Tho. Brown, and his Writings, Written by Dr. Drake.* London: S. Briscoe, 1705.

[Burgh, James]. *Thoughts on Education, Tending chiefly To recommend to the Attention of the Public, some Particulars relating to that Subject; which are not generally considered with the Regard their Importance deserves. By the Author of Britain's Remembrancer.* London: G. Freer, 1747.

[Burnaby, Charles]. *The Ladies Visiting-Day. A Comedy. As it was Acted at The Theatre in Lincolns-Inn-Fields, By His Majesties Servants. With the Addition of a New Scene. By the Author of The Reformed Wife.* London: Peter Buck and Geo. Strahan, 1701.

Burnet, Bishop Gilbert. *Bishop Burnet's History of His Own Time. Vol. I. From the Restoration of King Charles II. To the Settlement of King William and Queen Mary at the Revolution: To which is prefix'd A Summary Recapitulation of Affairs in Church and State from King James I. to the Restoration in the Year 1660.* London: Thomas Ward, 1724.

————. *Bishop Burnet's History of His Own Time. Vol. II. From the Revolution to the Conclusion of the Treaty of Peace at Utrecht, in the Reign of Queen Anne. To Which is added, The Author's Life, by the Editor.* London: Joseph Downing and Henry Woodfall, 1734.

[Cadogan, William]. *An Essay upon Nursing, and the Management of Children, From their Birth to Three Years of Age. By a Physician. In a Letter to
one of the Governors of the Foundling Hospital. Published by Order of the
General Committee for transacting the Affairs of the said Hospital.*
London: J. Roberts, 1748.

Casa, Monsignor Giovanni de la. *Galateo: Or, A Treatise on Politeness and
Delicacy of Manners. Addressed to a Young Nobleman. From the Italian of
Monsig. Giovanni de la Casa, Archbishop of Benevento.* London: J.
Dodsley, 1774.

Castiglione, Baldassare, Count. *The Courtier of Count Baldessar Castilio,
devided into four Bookes. Verie necessarie and profitable for young Gentlemen and Gentlewomen abiding in Court, Pallace, or Place, done into
English by Thomas Hobby* (1528). London: John Wolfe, 1588.

Cibber, C[olley]. *The Lady's Lecture, A Theatrical Dialogue, between Sir
Charles Easy and his Mariageable Daughter. Being an Attempt to engage
Obedience by Filial Liberty: And to give the Maiden Conduct of Virtue,
Chearfulness.* London: W. Lewis, 1748.

Cleland, John. *Hropaideia, Or The Institution of a Young Noble Man.*
Oxford: Joseph Barnes, 1607.

[Collier, Jane]. *An Essay on the Art of ingeniously Tormenting; with Proper
Rules for The Exercise of that Pleasant Art. Humbly addressed, In the First
Part, To the Master, Husband, &c. In the Second Part, To the Wife, Friend,
&c. With some General Instructions for Plaguing all your Acquaintance.*
London: A Millar, 1753.

Confucius. *The Morals of Confucius A Chinese Philosopher, Who flourished
above Five Hundred Years before the coming of our Lord and Saviour
Jesus Christ. Being one of the most choicest Pieces of Learning remaining of
that Nation.* London: Randal Taylor, 1691.

[Constable, John]. *The Conversation of Gentlemen Considered In most of
the Ways, that make their mutual Company Agreeable, or Disagreeable.
In Six Dialogues.* London: J. Hoyles, 1738.

[Courtin, Antoine de]. *The Rules of Civility; Or Certain Ways of Deport-
ment observed amongst all persons of Quality upon several Occasions.
Newly revised and much Enlarged* (1671). London: J. Martyn and J.
Starkey, 1678.

[Coventry, Francis]. *The History of Pompey the Little: or, the Life and
Adventures of a Lap-Dog.* London: M. Cooper, 1751.

[Crouch, Nathaniel]. *Female Excellency, or the Ladies Glory. Illustrated In
the worthy Lives and memorable Actions of Nine Famous Women, who
have been renowned either for Virtue or Valour in the several Ages of the
world; namely, I. Deborah the Prophetess. II. The Valient Judith. III.
Queen Esther. IV. The Virtuous Susanna. V. The Chast Lucretia. VI.
Voadicia Queen of Brittain. VII. Mariamne wife to King Herod. VIII.
Clotilda Queen of France. IX. Andegona Princess of Spain. The whole*

adorned with Poems and the Picture of each Lady. By R.B. London: Nath. Crouch, 1688.

[Darrell, William]. *The Gentleman Instructed, In the Conduct of a Virtuous and Happy Life. In Three Parts. Written for the Instruction of a Young Nobleman. To which is added, A Word to the Ladies, by way of Supplement to the First Part* (1704). 6th ed. London: E. Smith, 1716.

[Defoe, Daniel]. *An Account of the Progress of the Reformation of Manners, In England, Scotland, and Ireland, and other Parts of Europe and America. With Reasons and Directions for our Engaging in this Glorious Work. In a Letter to a Friend. To which is added, Her Majesty's Proclamation for the Encouragement of Piety and Virtue, and for the Preventing and Punishing of Vice, Prophaneness, and Immorality.* 11th ed. London: J. Downing, 1702.

[Defoe, Daniel]. *The Compleat Mendicant: or, Unhappy Beggar.* London: E. Harris, 1699.

[Defoe, Daniel]. *The Complete English Tradesman, in Familiar Letters; Directing him in all the several Parts and Progressions of Trade.* London: Charles Rivington, 1726.

[Defoe, Daniel]. *Conjugal Lewdness; or, Matrimonial Whoredom.* London: T. Warner, 1727.

[Defoe, Daniel]. *An Essay upon Projects.* London: Tho. Cockerill, 1697.

[Defoe, Daniel]. *Every-Body's Business, is No-Body's Business; or Private Abuses, Publick Grievances: Exemplified In the Pride, Insolence, and Exorbitant Wages of our Women-Servants, Footmen, &c.* London: W. Meadows, 1725.

[Defoe, Daniel]. *The Family Instructor. In Three Parts. I. Relating to Fathers and Children. II. To Masters and Servants. III. To Husbands and Wives. Vol. I* (1715). 16th ed. London: H. Woodfall et al., 1766.

[Defoe, Daniel]. *The Family Instructor. In Two Parts. I. Relating to Family Breaches, and their obstructing Religious Duties. II. To the Great Mistake of mixing the Passions in the Managing and Correcting of Children. With A great Variety of Cases, relating to setting Ill Examples to Children and Servants. Vol. II* (1718). 8th ed. London: H. Woodfall et al., 1766.

[Defoe, Daniel]. *Good Advice to the Ladies: Shewing, That as the World goes, and is like to go, the best way for them is to keep Unmarried. By the Author of the True Born Englishman.* London: n.p., 1702.

[Defoe, Daniel]. *The Great Law of Subordination consider'd; Or, The Insolence and Unsufferable Behaviour of Servants in England duly enquir'd into. Illustrated With a great Variety of Examples, Historical Cases, and Remarkable Stories of the Behaviour of some particular Servants, suited to all the several Arguments made use of, as they go on. In Ten Familiar Letters.* London: S. Harding et al., 1724.

[Defoe, Daniel]. *A Lay-Man's Creed, Very Short for the Benefit of the Poor Reader.* London: J. Clark, 1713.

[Defoe, Daniel]. *The Meditations of Daniel Defoe.* Edited by George Harris Healey. N.p.: The Cummington Press, 1946.

[Defoe, Daniel]. *New Discoveries of the Dangers of Popery.* London: James Roberts, 1714.

[Defoe, Daniel]. *A New Family Instructor: Containing, A Brief and Clear Defence of the Christian Religion in General, Against the Errors of the Atheists, Jews, Deists and Sceptics: And of the Protestant Religion in Particular, Against the Superstitions of the Church of Rome. In familiar Discourses between a Father and his Children. In Two Parts* (1727). London: C. Rivington and T. Warner, 1732.

[Defoe, Daniel]. *Reformation of Manners, A Satyr.* N.p., 1702.

[Defoe, Daniel]. *Religious Courtship: Being Historical Discourses on the Necessity of Marrying Religious Husbands and Wives only. As Also Of Husbands and Wives being of the same Opinions in Religion with one another. With an Appendix Of the Necessity of taking none but Religious Servants, and a Proposal for the better managing of Servants.* London: E. Matthews et al., 1722.

[Defoe, Daniel]. *The True-Born Englishman. A Satyr.* N.p., 1700.

[Delany, Patrick]. *Reflections Upon Polygamy, and the Encouragement given to that Practice in the Scriptures of the Old Testament by Phileleutherus Dubliniensis.* London: J. Roberts, 1737.

[Deslandes, André]. *The Art of Being Easy at all Times, and In all Places. Written chiefly for the Use of a Lady of Quality. Made English from the French Original by Edward Combe, A.B. of Merton Coll. Oxon.* London: C. Rivington, 1724.

[Dodsley, Robert] *The Oeconomy of Human Life. Translated from an Indian Manuscript, written by an ancient Bramin. To which is prefixed An Account of the Manner in which the said Manuscript was discovered. In a Letter from an English Gentleman, now residing in China, to the Earl of ****.* London: M. Cooper, 1750.

[Dorrington, Theophilus]. *The Excellent Woman Described by her True Characters And their Opposites. Being a Just and Instructive Representation of the Vertues and Vices of the Sex. And Illustrated with the most Remarkable Instances in Ancient and Modern History. Part II. Done out of French, by T.D.* (1692). London: John Wyat, 1695.

[Dunton, John]. *The Athenian Gazette: or Casuistical Mercury, Resolving all the most Nice and Curious Questions Proposed by the Ingenious: From Tues. March 17th, to Saturday May 30th, 1691. The First Volume, Treating on the Several Subjects mentioned in the Contents at the Beginning of the Book.* London: John Dunton, 1691.

[Dunton, John]. *The Hazard of a Death-Bed-Repentance, Fairly Argued, From the late Remorse of W— late D— of D— With serious Reflections On his Adulterous Life. . . . Also, the Dying Remonstrance of other Persons of Quality. . . . The Whole resolving that Nice Question, How far a Death-*

Bed-Repentance is possible to be sincere? . . . To which is added, Conjugal Perjury, or an Essay upon Whoredom; Address'd to the Husbands of Quality that keep Misses. London: n.p., 1708.

Elyot, Thomas. *The Boke Named the Governour devised by Sir Thomas Elyot knyght* (1531). London: n.p., 1546.

The English Theophrastus: or, the Manners of the Age. Being the Modern Characters of the Court, the Town, and the City (1702). 3d ed. London: William Turner and John Chantry, 1708.

[Esprit, Jacques]. *The Falshood of Human Virtue. A Moral Essay. Done out of French.* London: Timothy Child, 1691.

Esprit, Jacques. *Discourses on the Deceitfulness of Humane Virtues. By Monsieur Esprit, of the French Academy at Paris. Done out of French by William Beauvoir, A.M. And Chaplain to His Grace James, Duke of Ormond. To which is Added, The Duke de la Rochefoucaut's Moral Reflections.* London: And. Bell, R. Smith, and J. Round, 1706.

[Essex, John]. *The Young Ladies Conduct: Or, Rules for Education, Under several Heads; With Instructions upon Dress, both before and after Marriage. And Advice to Young Wives.* London: John Brotherton, 1722.

Evelyn, John. *Memoires for my Grand-son* (1704). Edited by Geoffrey Keynes. Oxford: Nonesuch Press in Bloomsbury, 1926.

————. *Publick Employment and an Active Life with All Its Appanages, Such as Fame, Command, Riches, Conversation, &c. Prefer'd to Solitude. By J.E. Esq: S.R.S.* London: H. Herringman, 1667.

A Father's Advice to his Son: Laying down many Things which have a Tendency to direct and fix the Mind in Matters of the greatest Importance. A Book very useful for all young Persons. London: J. Roberts, 1736.

Fénelon, François de Salignac de la Mothe. *Instructions for the Education of a Daughter, By the Author of Telemachus. To which is added A small Tract of Instructions for the Conduct of young Ladies of the highest Rank. With Suitable Devotions Annexed. Done into English, and revised by Dr. George Hicks.* (1707). Edinburgh: James Reid, 1750.

The Fine Ladys Airs: or, an Equipage of Lovers. A Comedy. As it is Acted at the Theatre-Royal in Drury-Lane. Written by the Author of the Yeoman of Kent. London: Bernard Lintott, n.d.

Fordyce, James. *The Temple of Virtue. A Dream. Published from an original Manuscript.* London: T. Field, 1757.

[Forrester, James]. *The Polite Philosopher: Or, An Essay on that Art which Makes a Man Happy in Himself, and Agreeable to Others* (1734). 2d ed. with amendments and additions. London: E. Nutt and A. Dodd, 1736.

[Foxton, Thomas]. *Serino: Or, the Character of a Fine Gentleman; With Reference to Rerigion [sic], Learning, and the Conduct of Life. In which are inserted Five Poems. . . .* (1721). 2d ed. London: E. Curll, 1723.

Fuller, Thomas, B.D. *The Holy State.* Cambridge: John Williams, 1642.

Fuller, Thomas, M.D. *Introductio ad Prudentiam: or, Directions, Counsels, and Cautions, Tending to Prudent Management of Affairs in Common Life. Vol. I. To which is added An Appendix, concerning Sincerity and Deceit* (1726–1727). 3d ed. London: W. Innys, 1743.

———. *Introductio ad Prudentiam: Or, Directions, Counsels, and Cautions, Tending to Prudent Management of Affairs in Common Life. Vol. II. To which is added An Appendix, concerning Sincerity and Deceit.* 2d ed. (1726–1727). London: W. Innys and R. Manby, 1740.

Gailhard, J[ean]. *The Compleat Gentleman: Or Directions For the Education of Youth As to their Breeding at Home and Travelling Abroad. In Two Treatises. By J. Gailhard Gent. Who hath been Tutor Abroad to Several of the Nobility and Gentry.* London: John Starkey, 1678.

[Gauden, John]. *Discourse of Auxiliary Beauty. Or Artificiall Hansomenesse. In point of Conscience Between Two Ladies.* London: R. Royston, 1656.

[Genard, François]. *The School of Man. Translated from the French. To which is prefixed, A Key to the Satyrical Characters Interspersed in this Work* (1752). London: Lockyer Davis, 1753.

[Genard, François]. *The School of Woman: Or, Memoirs of Constantia. Address'd to the Duchess of *****. By the Author of the School of Man, A Moral Work: Suppressed at Paris, by Order of the King of France. Translated from the French.* London: J. Robinson, 1753.

Gordon, James. *The Character of a Generous Prince Drawn from the great Lines of Heroick Fortitude. From which By the Rule of Contraries, may be Delineated the Effigies of a Prodigious Tyrant. The Vertues of the Former, and the Vices of the Latter, being fully Represented; by a Pleasant variety of Examples, from Ancient and Modern History. By a Hearty Well-wisher of Her Majesties Government, and the Church of Eng.* London: Edw. Evets, 1703.

Gouge, William. *Of Domesticall Duties, Eight Treatises. . . .* (1622). 3d ed. London: Edward Brewster, 1634.

Gracian, Balthazar. *The Art of Prudence: Or, a Companion for a Man of Sense. Written Originally in Spanish by that Celebrated Author Balthazar Gracian; now made English from the best Edition of the Original, and Illustrated with the Sieur Amelot de la Houssaies Notes, By Mr. Savage* (1702). 3d ed. corrected. London: D. Browne et al., 1714.

Gratian, Baltasar. *The Complete Gentleman: Or a Description Of the several Qualifications, Both Natural and Acquired, That are necessary to form a Great Man. Written originally in Spanish, by Baltasar Gratian, And now Translated into English by T. Saldkeld.* London: T. Osborne, 1730.

Gregory, Dr. [John]. *A Father's Legacy to His Daughters* (1774). New York: T. and J. Swords, 1812.

[Grenville, Denis]. *Counsel and Directions Divine and Moral: in Plain and Familiar Letters of Advice from a Divine of the Church of England to A*

Young Gentleman, his Nephew, Soon after his Admission into a College in Oxford. London: Robert Clavell, 1685.

Hale, Sir Matthew. *Several Tracts Written by Sr Matthew Hale, Kt Sometime Lord Chief Justice of England: viz. I. A Discourse of Religion of Three Heads. . . . II. A Treatise touching Provision for the Poor. III. A Letter to his Children, Advising them how to behave themselves in their Speech. IV. A Letter to one of his Sons, after his Recovery from the Small-Pox* (Pt. II, 1683). London: W. Shrowsbery, 1684.

[Halifax, George Savile, Marquis of]. *The Lady's New-years Gift: or, Advice to a Daughter, Under these following Heads: Viz. Religion, Husband, House and Family. Servants, Behaviour and Conversation, Friendship, Censure, Vanity and Affectation, Pride. Diversions, Dancing* (1688). 2d ed. corrected. London: Matt. Gillyflower and James Partridge, 1688.

Hawkins, Francis. *Youth's Behaviour, Or Decency in Conversation Amongst Men. Composed in French by Grave Persons, for the use and benefit of their Youth. Now newly turned into English, By Francis Hawkins. Nephew to Sr Thomas Hawkins, Translator of Caussin's Holy Court. With the addition of Twenty six new Precepts, written by a grave Author, which are marked thus (*) and some more Additions. The Eighth Impression. Where-unto is added much Enlargement of three very usefull and profitable Alphabeticall Tables: the third Table having many hard words added, not untill this year 1663. Printed. Last of all is added, The first Entrance of a Youth in the University. All which new Additions may be sold by themselves* (1636). London: W. Lee, 1663.

[Haywood, Eliza]. *A Present for a Servant-Maid: Or, the Sure Means of gaining Love and Esteem.* London: T. Gardner, 1743.

[Haywood, Eliza]. *A Present for Women Addicted to Drinking. Adapted to All the different Stations of Life, from a Lady of Quality to a Common Servant.* London: W. Owen, 1750.

[Head, R.]. *The Canting Academy, or, the Devils Cabinet Opened; Wherein is Shewn The Mysterious and Villanous Practices of that wicked Crew, commonly known by the names of Hectors, Trapanners, Gilts, &c. . . .* London: Mat. Derw, 1673.

Huarte, John. *Examen de Ingenios. The Examination of mens Wits. In Which, By Discovering the varietie of natures, is shewed for what profession each one is apt, and how far he shall profit therein. By Iohn Huarte. Translated out of the Spanish tongue by M. Camillo Camilli. Englished out of his Italian by R. C. Esquire* (1594). London: Thomas Adams, 1616.

[James I]. *Basilikon Doron. Or His Maiesties Instructions to His Dearest Sonne, Henrie the Prince* (1599). London: John Norton, 1603.

[Joceline, Elizabeth]. *The Mother's Legacy to Her Unborn Child* (1624). London: Joseph Downing, 1724.

[Jones, Er]asmus. *The Man of Manners: Or, Plebeian Polish'd. Being Plain and Familiar Rules for a Modest and Genteel Behaviour, on most of the ordinary Occasions of Life. Whereby the many Vanities, Weaknesses and Impertinences incident to Human Nature, (which expose Persons to Contempt and Ridicule) may be easily avoided. Written chiefly for the Use and Benefit of Persons of Mean Births and Education, who have unaccountably plung'd themselves into Wealth and Power* (1735?). London: J. Roberts, [1737].

Kempis, Thomas à. *Of the Imitation of Christ. Three, both for wisedome, and godlines, most excellent bokes, made 170. yeeres since by one Thomas of Kempis, and for the worthiness thereof oft since translated out of Latine into sundrie languages by diuers godlie and learned men. Now newlie corrected, translated, and with most ample textes, and sentences of holie Scripture illustrated by Thomas Rogers.* London: Companie of Stationers, 1609.

[Kenrick, William]. *The Whole Duty of Woman. By a Lady. Written at the Desire of a Noble Lord.* London: R. Baldwin, 1753.

Kirke, William. *Mr. [Robert] Nelson's Companion for the Festivals and Fasts of the Church of England, Made more Useful, and Instructive, By reducing each Solemnity into a Practical Discourse. To which is prefix'd Some Account of Mr. Nelson's Life and Writings, with a true Copy of his last Will and Testament.* London: A. Bettesworth and E. Curll, 1715.

The Ladies' Diary: or Woman's Almanack, For the Year of our Lord 1762. Being the Second after Fissextile or Leap-Year. Containing New Improvements in Arts and Sciences, And many Entertaining Particulars; Adapted for the Use and Diversion of the Fair-Sex. Being the Fifty-Ninth Almanack Publish'd of this Kind. N.p.: Company of Stationers, 1762.

Lambert, Anna Thérèse. *The Marchioness De Lambert's Letters to Her Son and Daughter, On True Education, &c. &c. &c. Translated by Mr. Rowell.* London: M. Cooper, 1749.

Lancaster, Nathaniel. *The Plan of an Essay upon Delicacy with a Specimen of the Work. In Two Dialogues.* London: R. Dodsley, 1748.

Lassels, Richard. *The Voyage of Italy: Or, a Compleat Journey through Italy. In Two Parts. With the Characters of the People, and the Description of the Chief Towns, Churches, Monasteries, Tombs, Libraries, Palaces, Villa's, Gardens, Pictures, Statues, and Antiquities. As Also, Of the Interest, Government, Riches, Force, &c. of all the Princes. With Instructions concerning Travel. By Richard Lassels, Gent. who Travelled through Italy Five times, as Tutor to several of the English Nobility and Gentry* (1670). London: Charles Shortgrave, 1686.

Laurence, Edward. *The Duty of a Steward to his Lord, Represented under Several Plain and Distinct Articles; wherein may be seen the Indirect Practices of several Stewards, tending to Lessen, and the several Methods likely to Improve their Lords Estates. To which is added an Appendix, Shewing The Way to Plenty, Proposed to the Farmers; wherein are laid down general Rules and Directions for the Management and Improvement of a Farm. Both Design'd originally for the Use of the Several Stewards and Tenants of His Grace the Duke of Buckingham, and Now Improv'd and publish'd for the general Use and Interest of All the Nobility and Gentry throughout England.* London: John Shuckburgh, 1727.

Law, William. *A Serious Call to a Devout and Holy Life. Adapted to the State and Condition of All Orders of Christians* (1728). London: William Innys, 1729.

L'Estrange, Sir Roger. *Fables of Aesop And other Eminent Mythologists: With Morals and Reflections* (1692). 8th ed. corrected. London: A. Bettesworth et al., 1738.

L'Estrange, R[oger]. *Seneca's Morals By way of Abstract. Of Benefits, Part I* (1678). 3d ed. London: Ch. Brome, 1685.

L'Estrange, Ro[ger]. *Tully's Offices. In Three Books. Turned out of Latin into English. By Ro. L'Estrange* (1680). 3d ed. corrected. London: Charles Brome, 1684.

[Locke, John]. *Some Thoughts Concerning Education.* London: A. & J. Churchill, 1693.

[Lyttleton, George Lyttleton, 1st Baron]. *Advice to a Lady.* London: Lawton Gilliver, 1733.

Mackenzie, Sir George. *A Moral Essay, preferring Solitude to Publick Employment, And all it's Appanages; such as Fame, Command, Riches, Pleasures, Conversation, &c.* (1665). London: H. Sawbridge, 1685.

————. *Moral Gallantry. A Discourse, wherein The Author endeavours to prove, that Point of Honour (abstracting from all other tyes) obliges Men to be Virtuous. And that there is nothing so mean (or unworthy of a Gentleman) as Vice* (1667). Edinburgh and reprinted in London: J. Streater, 1669.

Markham, G[ervase]. *The English House-Wife, Containing The inward and outward Vertues which ought to be in a Compleat Woman. As her Skill in Physick, Chirurgery. . . . Ordering of great Feasts . . . and all other things belonging to an Houshold. A Work generally approved, and now the Eighth time much Augmented, Purged, and made more profitable and necessary for all men and the general good of this Nation* (1615). 8th ed. London: George Sawbridge, 1675.

Marriage Promoted. In a Discourse Of its Ancient and Modern Practice, Both under Heathen and Christian Common-Wealths. Together with their Laws and Encouragements for its Observance. And how far the like may be Practicable and Commodious in the Preservation of these Kingdoms. By a Person of Quality. London: Richard Baldwin, 1690.

[Morris, Corbyn]. *An Essay Towards Fixing the True Standards of Wit, Humour, Raillery, Satire, and Ridicule. To which is Added, an Analysis Of the Characters of an Humorist, Sir John Falstaff, Sir Roger De Coverly, and Don Quixote. Inscribed to the Right Honorable Robert Earl of Orford. By the Author of a Letter from a By-Stander.* London: J. Roberts and W. Bickerton, 1744.

[Moxon, Joseph]. *The Genteel House-keeper's Pastime, or the Mode of Carving at Table Represented in a Pack of playing-Cards. By which, together with the Instructions in this Book, any ordinary Capacity may easily learn how to cut up or carve (in Mode) all the most usual Dishes of Fish, Flesh, Fowl, and Bak'd Meats; and how to make the several Services of the same at the Table: With the several Sawces and Garnishes proper to each Dish of Meat. Set forth by several of the best Masters in the Faculty of Carving, and publish'd for publick Use* (1693?). London: J. Lenthall, 1717.

Nelson, James, Apothecary. *An Essay on the Government of Children, Under Three General Heads: Viz. Health, Manners and Education* (1753). 2d ed. London: M. Cooper, 1756.

Nelson, Robert. *An Address to Persons of Quality and Estate. To which is added, A Representation of the several Ways and Methods of doing Good, with some Reflections upon the Necessity and Excellency of Christian Beneficence* (1715). Dublin: Peter Wilson, 1752.

[Nencomb, Thomas]. *The Manners of the Age: In Thirteen Moral Satires. Written With a Design to expose the Vicious and Irregular Conduct of Both Sexes, in the various Pursuits of Life.* London: Jer. Batley, 1733.

New and Excellent Experiments and Secrets In the Art of Angling: Being Directions for the whole Art. London: n.p., 1677.

Newcastle, Margaret Cavendish, Duchess of. *Orations of Divers Sorts, Accommodated to Divers Places. Written By the Thrice Noble, Illustrious, and Excellent Princess, The Duchess of Newcastle* (1662?). 2d ed. London: A. Maxwell, 1668.

[Norris, John]. *Effigies Amoris. In English: or the Picture of Love Unveil'd* 2d ed. corrected. London: James Good, 1701.

Norris, John. *A Collection of Miscellanies: Consisting of Poems, Essays, Discourses and Letters, Occasionally Written* (1687). 2d ed. corrected. London: J. Crosley and Samuel Manship, 1692.

————. *Letters Concerning the Love of God, Between the Author of the Proposal to the Ladies and Mr. John Norris: Wherein his late Discourse, shewing That it ought to be intire and exclusive of all other Loves, is further cleared and justified.* London: Samuel Manship and Richard Wilkin, 1695.

————. *Of Religious Discourse in Common Conversation. In Three Parts.* Dublin: n.p., 1702.

————.*The Theory and Regulation of Love. A Moral Essay. In Two Parts. To which are added Letters Philosophical and Moral between the Author and Dr Henry More.* Oxford: Hen. Clements, 1688.

Nourse, Tim. *Campania Foelix. Or, A Discourse of the Benefits and Improvements of Husbandry: Containing Directions for all manner of Tillage, Pasturage, and Plantation; As also for the making of Cyder and*

Perry. With some Considerations upon I. Justice of the peace, and Inferior Officers. II. On Inns and Alehouses. III. On Servants and Labourers. IV. On the Poor. To which are Added, Two Essays: I. Of a Country-House. II. Of the Fuel of London. London: Tho. Bennet, 1700.

————. *A Discourse upon the Nature and Faculties of Man, in Several Essayes: With some Considerations Upon the Occurances of Humane Life.* London: Jacob Tonson, 1686.

[Ortique, Pierre d']. *The Art of Pleasing in Conversation: In French and English. Written by the famous Cardinal Richelieu* (1691). London: A. Bettesworth and F. Clay, 1722.

Osborn, Francis. *Advice to a Son. Or Directions For your better Conduct, Through the various and most important Encounters of this Life. Under these Generall Heads. I. Studies, &c. II. Love and Marriage. III. Travell. IV. Government. V. Religion. Conclusion* (1656). 6th ed. Oxford: Tho. Robinson, 1658.

Overbury, Sir Thomas. *Sir Thomas Overbury His Wife. With Additions of New Characters, and many other Witty Conceits never before Printed* (1614). 17th imp. London: Philip Chetwin, 1664.

Panton, Capt. Edw. Patrophilus. *Speculum Juventutis: Or, a True Mirror where Errors in Breeding Noble and Generous Youth, with the Miseries and Mischiefs that usually attend it, are clearly made manifest; as likewise Remedies for every growing Evil. Portray'd to the Life in the Legend of Sisaras and Vallinda* (1671). London: Charles Smith and Thomas Burrell, 1671.

Parker, Samuel. *Sylva. Familiar Letters Upon Occasional Subjects.* London: J. Nutt, 1701.

Peacham, Henry. *The Compleat Gentleman: Fashioning Him absolute in the most Necessary and Commendable Qualities, concerning Mind, or Body, that may be required in a Person of Honor. To which is added the Gentlemans Exercise or, An Exquisite practise, as well for drawing all manner of Beasts, as for making Colours, to be used in Painting, Limming, &c.* (1622). 3d imp. London: Richard Thrale, 1661.

[Penton, Stephen]. *The Guardian's Instruction, or, the Gentleman's Romance: Written for the Diversion and Service of the Gentry.* London: Simon Miller, 1688.

[Penton, Stephen]. *New Instructions to the Guardian: Shewing That the last Remedy to Prevent the Ruin, Advance the Interest, and Recover the Honour of this Nation is, I. A more Serious and Strict Education of the Nobility and Gentry. II. To breed up all their younger Sons to some Calling and Employment. III. More of them to Holy Orders. With A Method of Institution from Three Years of Age, to Twenty-One* (1694). London: Walter Kettilby, 1694.

Petrie, Adam. *Rules of Good Deportment or of Good Breeding For the Use of Youth.* Edinburgh: n.p., 1720.

Pineau-Duclos, Charles. *Memoirs Illustrating the Manners of the Present Age. Wherein are Contained The remarkable Incidents in the Life of a Young Nobleman. By Monsieur Du Clos, Historiographer to the French King, and Member of the Royal Academy at Paris. Translated from the French by a Gentleman*. 2 vols. London: J. Whiston et al., [1755].

Primaudaye, Peter de la. *The French Academie, wherein is discoursed the institution of Maners, and whatsoever els concerneth the good and happie life of all estates and callings, by precepts of doctrine, and examples of the lives of ancient Sages and famous men: . . . translated into English by T. B.* (1586). 3d ed. London: Geor. Bishop, 1594.

[Ramesey, William]. *The Gentleman's Companion: or, a Character of True Nobility and Gentility: In the way of Essay. By A Person of Quality. Written at first for his own Private Use, and now Published for the Benefit of all*. London: Rowland Reynolds, 1672.

Religious and Christian Advice to A daughter. Written by a Lady. London: R. Robinson, 1714.

Rochefoucauld, de la. *Moral Reflections and Maxims, Written by the late Duke de la Rochefoucauld. Newly made English from the Paris Edition.* London: And. Bell, R. Smith, and J. Round, 1706.

[Sacy, Louis de]. *A Discourse of Friendship. In Three Books. Translated from the French.* London: Booksellers of London and Westminster, 1707.

Seaton, Thomas. *The Conduct of Servants in Great Families. Consisting of Dissertations upon several Passages of the Holy Scriptures, relating to the Office of a Servant: With Ejaculations upon the Subject-Matter of Each Discourse. To these are annex'd, A Persuasive to a Constant Attendance at the Devotions of the Family, and at the Holy Communion: And an Earnest Exhortation to refrain from Swearing, Cursing, and Drunkenness: Each of which Subjects are distinctly treated in several Chapters. To which are added, Some Directions to Regulate the Private Devotions of Servants; with Prayers and Hymns for that Purpose. The Whole is composed for the Especial Use of Noblemen and Gentlemen's Servants.* London: Tim. Goodwin, 1720.

Selden, John. *Table-Talk Being the Discourses of John Selden, Esq; or His Sense of various Matters of Weight and high Consequence; Relating especially to Religion and State* (1689). 3d ed. London: Jacob Tonson and Awnsham and John Churchill, 1716.

Southern, A. C., ed. *An Elizabethan Recusant House comprising The Life of the Lady Magdalen Viscountess Montague (1538–1608)*. London: Sand and Co., 1954.

Sowter, John. *The Way to be Wise and Wealthy: Or, the Excellency of Industry and Frugality, As the due and regular Exercise thereof is the necessary Means of procuring the Happiness of This Life, and preparing for that of a Better. Recommended in particular to Gentleman, Scholar, Soldier, Trader, Sailor, Artificer, Husbandman. With A short Preface, perswad-*

ing all Protestants to lay aside Party-Prejudices, and to Unite and Love one another. London: Philip Bishop and William Taylor, 1716.

[Spence, Joseph]. ("Sir Harry Beaumont"). *Moralities: or, Essays, Letters, Fables; and Translations*. London: R. Dodsley, 1753.

Stanhope, Philip Dormer, Fourth Earl of Chesterfield. *Letters of Philip Dormer Fourth Earl of Chesterfield to His Godson and Successor*. Edited by The Earl of Carnarvon. Oxford: Clarendon Press, 1890.

———. *Letters to His Son on the Art of Becoming a Man of the World and a Gentleman*. 2 vols. New York: The Chesterfield Press, 1917.

———. *Letters Written By the Late Right Honourable Philip Dormer Stanhope, Earl of Chesterfield, to His Son, Philip Stanhope, Esq; Late Envoy Extraordinary at the Court of Dresden. Together with Several Other Pieces On Various Subjects. Published by Mrs. Eugenia Stanhope, From the Originals Now in Her Possession* (1774). 2 vols. 4th ed. revised and corrected. London: J. Dodsley, 1774.

[Steele, Richard]. *The Ladies Library. Written by a Lady. Published by Mr. Steele*. 3 vols. London: Jacob Tonson, 1714.

Swift, Jonathan. *A Proposal for Correcting the English Tongue. Polite Conversation, Etc.* Edited by Herbert Davis. Oxford: Shakespeare Head Press, 1957.

Talbot, Catherine. *Essays on Various Subjects in Prose and Verse; Together with Reflections on the Seven Days of the Week* (1772 and 1770). 2 vols. Dublin: Thomas Ewing, 1773.

Taylor, Jeremy. *Contemplations of the State of Man in this Life, and in That which is to come*. London: John Kidgell, 1684.

———. *The Rule and Exercises of Holy Dying. In which are described The Means and Instruments of preparing our selves and others respectively for a blessed Death; and the Remedies against the Evils and Temptations proper to the state of Sickness: Together with Prayers and Acts of Vertue to be used by Sick and Dying persons, or by others standing in their attendance. To which are added Rules for the Visitation of the Sick, and offices proper for that Ministery* (1651). London: Richard Royston, 1674.

———. *The Rule and Exercises of Holy Living. In which are described The Means and Instruments of obtaining every Vertue, and the Remedies against every Vice, and Considerations serving to the resisting all Temptations. Together with Prayers Containing The whole duty of a Christian, and the parts of Devotion fitted to all Occasions, and furnished for all Necessities* (1650). 10th ed. London: Richard Royston, 1674.

[Toussaint, François Vincent]. *Manners. Translated from the French*. N.p., 1749.

Trenchfield, Caleb. *A Cap of Gray Hairs for a Green Head: Or, the Father's Counsel to His Son, An Apprentice in London. Containing wholesome Instructions for the Management of a Mans whole Life. The Fifth Edition*.

With Additions of Precepts adapted to each Chapter (1671). London: A. Bettesworth, 1710.

Trotti de la Chétardie, Joachim. *Instructions for a Young Nobleman.* London: R. Bentley and S. Magnes, 1683.

Walker, Obadiah. *Of Education Especially of Young Gentlemen. In Two Parts.* Oxon.: At the Theater, 1673.

[Ward, Edward]. *The City Madam and the Country Maid: Or, Opposite Characters of a Virtuous Housewifely Damsel, and a Mechanick's Town-Bred Daughter. By the Author of The Pleasures of a Single Life, &c.* London: John Nutt, 1702.

[Waterland, Daniel]. *Advice to a Young Student. With a Method of Study for the Four First Years.* London: John Crownfield, 1730.

Watts, Thomas. *An Essay on the Proper Method For Forming the Man of Business: In a Letter, &c.* London: George Strahan et al., 1716.

Wilkes, Wetenhall. *An Essay on the Pleasures and Advantages of Female Literature. To this are subjoin'd, A Prosaic Essay on Poetry, taken from the Criticisms of several eminent Authors; The Chace, a Poem, and three Poetic Landscapes.* London: T. Cooper and R. Caswell, 1741.

W[instanley], W[illiam]. *The New Help to Discourse. Or Wit and Mirth, Intermixed With more serious Matters; Consisting of Pleasant, Philosophical, Physical, Historical, Moral, and Political Questoins [sic] and Answers: With Proverbs, Epitaphs, Epigrams, Riddles, Poesies, Rules for Behaviour &c. With several Wonders, and Varieties, particularly, A Concise History of all the Kings of England, from the No Man Conquest, down to King George. Together with Directions for the true Knowledge of several Matters concerning Astronomy, Holy. Days, and Husbandry, in a plain Method. By W. W. Gent. The Eighth Edition with many new Additions* (1669?). London: Peter Parker, 1721.

[Woodward, Josiah]. *An Account of the Societies for Reformation of Manners, in London and Westminster, And other Parts of the Kingdom. With a Persuasive to Persons of all Ranks, to be Zealous and Diligent in Promoting the Execution of the Laws against Prophaneness and Debauchery, For the Effecting A National Reformation* (1696). London: B. Aylmer, 1699.

Wotton, Henry. *An Essay on the Education of Children, in the First Rudiments of Learning. Together With A Narrative, William Wotton, a Child six Years of Age, had attained unto, upon the Improvement of those Rudiments, in the Latin, Greek, and Hebrew Tongues* (written 1672). London: T. Waller, 1753.

5. Letters, Memoirs, Journals, Travel Accounts

[Addison, Joseph]. *Remarks on Several Parts of Italy, &c. In the Years 1701, 1702, 1703* (1705). 2d ed. London: J. Tonson, 1718.

Angeloni, Battista. [John Shebbeare]. *Letters on the English Nation Translated from the Original Italian.* 2 vols. London: n.p., 1755.

Austen, Jane. *Jane Austen Letters 1796–1817.* Edited by R. W. Chapman. London: Oxford University Press, 1955.

————. *Jane Austen's Letters to her Sister Cassandra and Others.* Edited by R. W. Chapman. Vol. 2. 1811–17. Oxford: Clarendon Press, 1933.

Austen-Leigh, James Edward. *Memoir of Jane Austen.* Edited by R. W. Chapman. Oxford: Clarendon Press, 1951.

Baretti, Joseph. *An Account of the Manners and Customs of Italy: with Observations on the Mistakes of Some Travellers, with Regard to that Country* 2 vols. London: T. Davies, L. Davis and C. Rymers, 1768.

————. *An Appendix to the Account of Italy, In answer to Samuel Sharp, Esq.* London: T. Davies, L. Davis, C. Reymer, 1768.

Carter, Elizabeth. *Memoirs of the Life of Mrs. Elizabeth Carter, with A New Edition of Her Poems, Including some which have never appeared before; To which are added, some Miscellaneous Essays in Prose, Together with Her Notes on the Bible, and Answers to Objections Concerning the Christian Religion. By the Rev. Montagu Pennington, M.A.* (1807). 2 vols. 2d ed. London: F. C. and J. Rivington, 1808.

————. *A Series of Letters between Mrs. Elizabeth Carter and Miss Catherine Talbot, From the Year 1741 to 1770. To which are added, Letters from Mrs. Elizabeth Carter to Mrs. Vesey, Between the Years 1713 and 1787; Published from the Original Manuscripts in the Possession of the Rev. Montagu Pennington, M.A.* 4 vols. London: F. C. and J. Rivington, 1809.

Chapone, Hester Mulso. *The Works of Mrs. Chapone: Now First Collected. Containing I. Letters on the Improvement of the Mind. II. Miscellanies. III. Correspondence with Mr. Richardson. IV. Letters to Miss Carter. V. Fugitive Pieces. To which is Prefixed, an Account of her Life and Character, Drawn Up by Her Own Family.* 4 vols. London: John Murray, 1807.

A Collection of Voyages and Travels, Some now first Printed from Original Manuscripts. Others Translated out of Foreign Languages, and now first Publish'd in English. To which are Added some Few that have formerly appear'd in English, but do now for their Excellency and Scarceness deserve to be Reprinted. In Four Volumes. With a General Preface, giving an Account of the Progress of Navigation, from its first Beginning to the Perfection it is now in, &c. The Whole Illustrated with a great Number of Useful Maps, and Cuts, all engraven on Copper. London: Awnsham and John Churchill, 1704.

[Defoe, Daniel]. *A Tour Through the Whole Island of Great Britain. Divided into Circuits or Journies. . . . Originally begun by the celebrated Daniel DeFoe, continued by the late Mr. Richardson, Author of Clarissa, and brought down to the present Time by a Gentleman of Eminence in the Literary World* (1724–1727). 7th ed. 4 vols. London: J. and F. Rivington, 1769.

Delany, Mary. *The Autobiography and Correspondence of Mary Granville, Mrs. Delany.* Edited by Lady Llanover. 3 vols. London: Richard Bentley, 1861.

Eliot, George. *The George Eliot Letters.* Edited by Gordon S. Haight. 9 vols. New Haven: Yale University Press, 1954–78.

Franklin, Benjamin.*Autobiography of Benjamin Franklin.* Edited by John Bigelow. Garden City, New York: Doubleday Dolphin Books, n.d.

Johnson, R. Brimley, ed. *Bluestocking Letters.* London: John Lane, The Bodley Head Ltd., 1926.

Montagu, Lady Mary Wortley. *The Complete Letters of Lady Mary Wortley Montagu.* Edited by Robert Halsband. 3 vols. Oxford: Clarendon Press, 1967.

Perry, Charles. *A View of the Levant: Particularly of Constantinople, Syria, Egypt, and Greece. In Which Their Antiquities, Government, Politics, Maxims, Manners, and Customs, (with many other Circumstances and Contingencies) are attempted to be Described and Treated on. In Four Parts (1743).* London: T. Woodward, C. Davis, J. Shuckburgh, 1743.

Piozzi, Hester Lynch. *Observations and Reflections Made in the Course of a Journey Through France, Italy, and Germany.* 2 vols. London: A. Strahan and T. Cadell, 1789.

Pushkin, Alexander. *The Letters of Alexander Pushkin.* Translated by J. Thomas Shaw. 3 vols. in 1. Madison: University of Wisconsin Press, 1967.

Roe, Sir Thomas. *The Negotiations of Sir Thomas Roe, In His Embassy to the Ottoman Porte, from the Year 1621 to 1628 Inclusive: Containing a great Variety of curious and important Matters, relating not only to the Affairs of the Turkish Empire, but also to those of the Other States of Europe, in that Period: His Correspondences with the most illustrious Persons, for Dignity or Character; as with the Queen of Bohemia, Bethlem Gabor Prince of Transylvania, and other Potentates of different Nations, &c. And many useful and instructive Particulars, as well in relation to Trade and Commerce, as to Subjects of Literature; as Antient Manuscripts, Coins, Inscriptions, and other Antiquities. Now first published from the Originals.* London: G. Strahan et al., 1740.

Sharp, Samuel. *A View of the Customs, Manners, Drama, &c. of Italy, As They are Described in the Frusta Letteraria; and in The Account of Italy in English, Written by Mr. Baretti; compared with the Letters from Italy, Written by Mr. Sharp.* London: W. Nicoll, 1768.

Saussure, Monsieur César de. *A Foreign View of England in the Reigns of George I. & George II.* Translated by Madame Van Muyden. New York: E. P. Dutton and Company, 1902.

Talbot, Catherine. *Journal of Catherine Talbot.* British Library 46,690.

Trollope, Thomas Adolphus. *What I Remember.* New York: Harper & Brothers, 1888.

6. *Sermons, Tracts, Periodical Literature*

Clarke, Samuel. *Sermons. Containing Sermons on several Subjects, published from the Author's Manuscript. By John Clarke, D. D. Dean of Sarum. And Eighteen Sermons on several Occasions, published by the Author.* 7th ed. 11 vols. London: J. and P. Knapton, 1749.

[Delany, Patrick]. *Fifteen Sermons Upon Social Duties. By the Author of the Life of David.* London: J. Rivington, 1744.

[Delany, Patrick]. *Twenty Sermons Upon Social Duties and Their Opposite Vices. By the Author of the Life of David. To which is added, An Essay Towards Evidencing the Divine Originals of Tythes, Which the Author considers as a Species of Social Duties.* London: J. and J. Rivington, 1750.

Fleetwood, William. *The Relative Duties of Parents and Children, Husbands and Wives, Masters and Servants, Consider'd in Sixteen Sermons: With Three more upon the Case of Self-Murther.* London: Charles Harper, 1705.

Fordyce, James. *Sermons to Young Women: In Two Volumes. A new Ed. corrected and enlarged* (1765). Boston: John Mein, 1767.

Simon, Irene, ed. *Three Restoration Divines: Barrow, South, Tillotson.* 2 vols. Paris: Société d'Edition "Les Belles Lettres," 1967.

South, Robert. *Sermons Preached Upon Several Occasions.* 7 vols. Oxford: Clarendon Press, 1823.

The Spectator. Edited by Donald F. Bond. 5 vols. Oxford: Clarendon Press, 1965.

Steele, Richard. *Tracts and Pamphlets by Richard Steele.* Edited by Rae Blanchard. Baltimore: Johns Hopkins University Press, 1944.

The Tatler. Edited by George A. Aitken. 4 vols. London: Duckworth & Co., 1899.

Tillotson, John. *Maxims and Discourses Moral and Divine: Taken from the Works of Arch-Bishop Tillotson, And Methodized and Connected.* Edited by Laurence Echard. London: J. Tonson, 1719.

———. *The Works Of the Most Reverend John Tillotson, Lord Archbishop of Canterbury. In Twelve Volumes. Containing Two Hundred and Fifty Four Sermons and Discourses on Several Occasions: Together with the Rule of Faith; Prayers Composed by him for his own Use; A Discourse to his Servants before the Sacrament; And a Form of Prayer, Composed by him, for the Use of King William.* London: C. Hitch et al., 1757.

Wesley, John. *Wesley's Standard Sermons.* Edited by Edward H. Sugden. 3d ed. London: The Epworth Press, 1951.

Whitefield, George. *Discourses On the following Subjects, Viz. . . . To Which is added, Prayers on several Occasions.* London: Charles Whitefield, 1739.

———. *Eighteen Sermons. Taken verbatim in Short-Hand, and faithfully*

Transcribed by Joseph Gurney. Revised by Andrew Gifford. London: Joseph Gurney, 1771.

7. Miscellaneous Primary Sources

Austen, Jane. *The Novels of Jane Austen.* Edited by R. W. Chapman. 3d ed. 5 vols. London: Oxford University Press, 1933.

———. *Jane Austen's 'Sir Charles Grandison.'* Edited by Brian Southam. Oxford: Clarendon Press, 1980.

Ballard, George. *Memoirs of Several Ladies of Great Britain, Who have been celebrated for their writings or skill in the learned languages and sciences.* Oxford: W. Jackson, 1752.

Barnett, George L., ed. *Eighteenth-Century British Novelists on the Novel.* New York: Appleton-Century-Crofts, 1968.

Boyce, Benjamin ed. *Prefaces to Fiction.* Los Angeles: Augustan Reprint Society No. 32, 1952.

Bysshe, Edward. *The Art of English Poetry, Vol. the III^d. and IVth. Which, with the two former Vols, make a compleat Common-Place-Book of English Poetry: Containing The most natural, instructive, diverting and sublime Thoughts.* London: W. Taylor, 1718.

———. *The Art of English Poetry: Containing I. Rules for making Verses. II. A Dictionary of Rhymes. III. A Collection of the most Natural, Agreeable, and Sublime Thoughts, viz. Allusions, Similes, Descriptions and Characters, of Persons and Things; that are to be found in the best English Poets.* 2d ed. corrected and improved. London: Sam. Buckley, 1705.

[Campbell, Alexander?]. *Critical Remarks on Sir Charles Grandison, Clarissa and Pamela. Enquiring, Whether they have a tendency to corrupt or improve the Public Taste and Morals. In a Letter to the Author. By a Lover of Virtue.* London: J. Dowse, 1754.

[Chapone, Sarah]. *Remarks on Mrs. Muilman's Letter To the Right Honourable The Earl of Chesterfield. In a Letter to Mrs. Muilman. By a Lady.* London: William Owen and James Leake, 1750.

Cheyne, Dr. George. *The English Malady. Or, A Treatise of Nervous Diseases of all Kinds, as Spleen, Vapours, Lowness of Spirits, Hypochondriacal, and Hysterial Distempers, &c. In Three Parts. Part I. Of the Nature and Cause of Nervous Distempers. II. Of the Cure of Nervous Distempers. III. Variety of Cases that illustrate and confirm the Method of Cure. With the Author's own Case at large.* London: G. Strahan and Bath: J. Leake, 1733.

———. "The true Man of Pleasure." *Gentleman's Magazine* 5 (1735): 122–23.

A Defence of the Character of a Noble Lord, from the Scandalous Aspersions Contained in a Malicious Apology. In a Letter to the supposed Authors. London: W. Webb, jun., 1748.

Gally, Henry. *A Critical Essay on Characteristic-Writings (1725)*. Edited by Alexander H. Chorney. Los Angeles: Augustan Reprint Society No. 33, 1952.

Hartley, David. *Observations on Man, His Frame, His Duty, and His Expectations. In Two Parts*. London: Charles Hitch and Stephen Austen, and Bath: James Leake and Wm. Frederick, 1749.

Johnson, Samuel. *The Works of Samuel Johnson, LL.D.* 15 vols. London: J. Buckland et al., vols. 1–13, 1787, vol. 14, 1788; London: Elliot and Kay, vol. 15, 1789.

Lee, Nathaniel. *The Rival Queens*. Edited by P. F. Vernon. Lincoln: University of Nebraska Press, 1970.

Lillo, George. *The London Merchant; Or, The History of George Barnwell*. In *Plays of the Restoration and Eighteenth Century as they were acted at the Theatres-Royal by Their Majesties' Servants*. Edited by Dougald MacMillan and Howard Mumford Jones. New York: Henry Holt & Co., 1931.

[Lussan, Marguerite de]. *The Life and Heroic Actions of Balbe Berton, Chevalier de Grillon. Translated from the French by a Lady, And revised by Mr. Richardson, Author of Clarissa, Grandison, &c.* 2 vols. London: H. Woodgate and S. Brooks, [1760].

McBurney, William H. *Four Before Richardson: Selected English Novels, 1720–1727*. Lincoln: University of Nebraska Press, 1963.

Meades, Anna. *The History of Sir William Harrington*. 4 vols. 1771; reprint, New York: Garland Publishing Co., Inc., 1974.

[Muilman, Mrs. Teresia Constantia Phillips]. *An Apology for the Conduct of Mrs. T. C. Phillips; More Particularly, That Part of it which relates to her Marriage with an eminent Dutch Merchant. To which is now first added, Mrs. Phillips's Letter to the Earl of Chesterfield.* 3 vols. London: G. Smith, 1761.

[Muilman, Mrs. Teresia Constantia Phillips]. *A Counter-Apology: Or, Genuine Confession. Being a Caution to the Fair Sex in general. Containing the Secret History, Amours, and Intrigues, of M— P—, a famous British Courtezan; who underwent various Scenes of Life, and Changes of Fortune, both at Home and Abroad. Written by herself, and published at her Desire. Number I.* London: R. Young, 1749.

Otway, Thomas. *The Orphan: Or, the Unhappy Marriage. A Tragedy* (1680). London: W. Feales, 1735.

———. *Venice Preserved* (1682). Edited by Malcolm Kelsall. Lincoln: University of Nebraska Press, 1969.

The Parallel; Or, Pilkington and Phillips Compared. Being Remarks upon the Memoirs of those two celebrated Writers. By an Oxford Scholar. London: M. Cooper, 1748.

The Paths of Virtue delineated; Or, the History in Miniature Of the Celebrated Pamela, Clarissa Harlowe, and Sir Charles Grandison, Familiarized and Adapted To the Capacities of Youth. London: R. Baldwin, 1756.

Philips, Ambrose. *The Distrest Mother* (1712). In *The London Stage; A Collection of the Most Reputed Tragedies, Comedies, Operas, Melo-Dramas, Farces, and Interludes. Accurately printed from Acting Copies, as Performed At the Theatres Royal, and Carefully Collated and Revised.* Vol. 4. London: Sherwood & Co., [1827].

[Plumer, Francis?]. *A Candid Examination of the History of Sir Charles Grandison. In a Letter to a Lady of Distinction. Published by Permission.* London: Dodsley, 1754.

Principles of Virtue. Exemplified in many Quotations, with a Critical Review, and Remarks upon the Whole. London: J. Roberts, 1741.

Pushkin, Alexander. *Eugene Onegin.* Translated by Walter Arndt. New York: E.P. Dutton & Co., Inc. paperback, 1963.

Rowe, Nicholas. *The Fair Penitent* (1703). Edited by Malcolm Goldstein. Lincoln: University of Nebraska Press, 1969.

————. *The Tragedy of Jane Shore* (1714). Edited by Harry William Pedicord. Lincoln: University of Nebraska Press, 1974.

Williams, Ioan, ed. *Novel and Romance 1700–1800.* London: Routledge & Kegan Paul, 1970.

Würzbach, Natascha, ed. *The Novel in Letters: Epistolary Fiction in the Early English Novel 1678–1740.* London: Routledge and Kegan Paul, 1969.

Young, Edward. *Edward Young (1683–1765).* Edited by Brian Hepworth. Cheadle: Carcanet Press, 1975.

II. SECONDARY SOURCES

1. Criticism of Richardson's Works

Ball, Donald L. "*Pamela II:* A Primary Link in Richardson's Development as a Novelist." *Modern Philology* 66 (May 1968): 334–42.

————. *Samuel Richardson's Theory of Fiction.* The Hague: Mouton, 1971.

Barker, Gerard A. "Clarissa's 'Command of her Passions' ": Self-Censorship in the Third Edition." *Studies in English Literature* 10 (Summer 1970): 525–39.

————. "The Complacent Paragon: Exemplary Characterization in Richardson." *Studies in English Literature* 9 (Summer 1969): 503–19.

————. "Ferdinando Falkland's Fall: Grandison in Disarray." *Papers on Language and Literature* 16 (Fall 1980): 376–86.

————. "Form and Purpose in the Novels of Samuel Richardson." Ph.D. diss., Stanford University, 1961.

————. *Grandison's Heirs: The Paragon's Progress in the Late Eighteenth-Century English Novel.* Newark: University of Delaware Press, 1985.

Beasley, Jerry C. "Romance and the 'New' Novels of Richardson, Fielding, and Smollett." *Studies in English Literature* 16 (Summer 1976): 437–50.

Beer, Gillian. "Richardson, Milton, and the Status of Evil." *Review of English Studies,* n.s., 19 (August 1968): 261–70.

Bell, Michael Davitt. "Pamela's Wedding and the Marriage of the Lamb." *Philological Quarterly* 49 (January 1970): 100–112.

Benoist, Howard. "The Morality is the Message. A Study of Samuel Richardson's A Collection of the Moral and Instruction Sentiments, Maxims, Cautions, and Reflexions, Contained in the Histories of Pamela, Clarissa, and Sir Charles Grandison." Ph.D. diss., University of Pennsylvania, 1968.

Berggren, Noel David. "Grandisonian Depths: A Study of Richardson's Last Novel." Ph.D. diss., Yale, 1968.

Boas, Frederick S. *From Richardson to Pinero.* London: John Murray, 1936.

Brissenden, R. F. "Pamela." In *Twentieth Century Interpretations of Pamela,* edited by Rosemary Cowler, 50–56. Englewood Cliffs: Prentice-Hall, 1969.

Brophy, Elizabeth Bergen. *Samuel Richardson. The Triumph of Craft.* Knoxville: University of Tennessee Press, 1974.

Bullen, John Samuel. *Time and Space in the Novels of Samuel Richardson.* Logan: Utah State University Press, 1965.

Carroll, John. "Lovelace as Tragic Hero." *University of Toronto Quarterly* 42 (Fall 1972): 14–25.

————. "The Reasoning Imagination: A Study of Theme and Structure in the Novels of Samuel Richardson." Ph.d. diss., Harvard, 1960.

————. "Richardson on Pope and Swift." *University of Toronto Quarterly* 33 (October 1963): 19–29.

Carroll, John, ed. *Samuel Richardson.* Englewood Cliffs: Prentice-Hall, 1969.

Castle, Terry. *Clarissa's Ciphers.* Ithaca: Cornell University Press, 1982.

Connaughton, Michael E. "Richardson's Familiar Quotations: *Clarissa* and Bysshe's *Art of English Poetry.*" *Philological Quarterly* 60 (Spring 1981): 183–95.

Cowler, Rosemary, ed. *Twentieth Century Interpretations of Pamela.* Englewood Cliffs: Prentice-Hall, 1969.

Crabtree, Paul R. "Propriety, *Grandison,* and the Novel of Manners." *Modern Language Quarterly* 41 (June 1980): 151–61.

Crane, Ronald S. "A Note on Richardson's Relation to French Fiction." *Modern Philology* 16 (January 1919): 495–99.

————. "Richardson, Warburton and French Fiction." *Modern Language Review* 17 (January 1922): 17–23.

Daiches, David. "Samuel Richardson." In *Twentieth Century Interpretations of Pamela*, edited by Rosemary Cowler, 14–25. Englewood Cliffs: Prentice-Hall, 1969.

Dalziel, Margaret. "Richardson and Romance." *Journal of the Australasian Universities Language and Literature Association* 33 (May 1970): 5–24.

Denton, Ramona. "Anna Howe and Richardson's Ambivalent Artistry in *Clarissa*." *Philological Quarterly* 58 (Winter 1979): 53–62.

Dobson, Austin. *Samuel Richardson*. New York: The Macmillan Company, 1902.

Donovan, Robert A. "The Problem of Pamela, or, Virtue Unrewarded." *Studies in English Literature* 3 (Summer 1963): 377–95.

Doody, Margaret Anne. *A Natural Passion*. Oxford: Clarendon Press, 1964.

Dottin, Paul. *Samuel Richardson*. Paris: Librairie Académique, 1931.

Downs, Brian W. *Richardson*. London: George Routledge & Sons, Ltd., 1928.

Dussinger, John A. "Conscience and the Pattern of Christian Perfection in *Clarissa*." *PMLA* 81 (June 1966): 236–45.

———. "Richardson's 'Christian Vocation.'" *Papers on Language and Literature* 3 (Winter 1967): 3–19.

———. "Richardson's *Clarissa*: 'A Work of Tragic Species.'" Ph.D. diss., Princeton, 1964.

———. "Richardson's Tragic Muse." *Philological Quarterly* 46 (January 1967): 18–33.

Eagleton, Terry. *The Rape of Clarissa*. Oxford: Basil Blackwell, 1982.

Eaves, T. C. Duncan. "Graphic Illustration of the Novels of Samuel Richardson, 1740–1810." *Huntington Library Quarterly* 14 (Autumn 1951): 349–83.

Eaves, T. C. Duncan, and Ben D. Kimpel. "Cowper's 'An Ode on Reading Mr. Richardson's "History of Sir Charles Grandison."'" *Papers on Language and Literature* 2 (Winter 1966): 74–75.

———. "Richardsoniana." *Studies in Bibliography* 14 (1961): 232–34.

———. "Richardson's Connection with *Sir William Harrington*." *Papers on Language and Literature* 4 (Summer 1968): 276–87.

———. *Samuel Richardson*. Oxford: Clarendon Press, 1971.

———. "Samuel Richardson's London Houses." *Studies in Bibliography* 15 (1962): 135–48.

Farrell, William J. "The Style and the Action in *Clarissa*." *Studies in English Literature* 3 (Summer 1963): 365–75.

Flynn, Carol Houlihan. *Samuel Richardson: A Man of Letters*. Princeton: Princeton University Press, 1982.

Frail, Robert J. "The British Connection: The Abbé Prévost and the Translations of the Novels of Samuel Richardson." Ph.D. diss., Columbia, 1985.

Gillis, Christina Marsden. *The Paradox of Privacy: Epistolary Form in Clarissa.* Gainesville: University Presses of Florida, 1984.

Golden, Morris. *Richardson's Characters.* Ann Arbor: University of Michigan Press, 1963.

————. "Richardson's Repetitions." *PMLA* 82 (March 1967): 64–67.

Gorham, Maud Bassett. "The Tradition of Restoration Comedy in the Works of Richardson, Fielding and Smollett." 2 vols. Ph.D. diss., Radcliffe, 1910.

Hannaford, Richard Gordon. *Samuel Richardson: An Annotated Bibliography of Critical Studies.* New York and London: Garland Press, 1980.

Harris, Jocelyn. " 'All the impassioned, & most exceptionable parts of Richardson': Jane Austen's Juvenilia." In *The Interpretative Power: Essays on Literature in Honour of Margaret Dalziel,* edited by C. A. Gibson, 59–63. Dunedin, New Zealand: University of Otago, 1980.

————. "Anne Elliot, the Wife of Bath, and Other Friends." In *Jane Austen: New Perspectives,* edited by Janet Todd, 273–93. New York: Holmes & Meier Publishers, Inc., 1983.

————. " 'As if they had been living friends' " *Sir Charles Grandison* into *Mansfield Park,"* *Bulletin of Research in the Humanities* 83 (Autumn 1980): 360–504.

————. "Learning and Genius in *Sir Charles Grandison.*" In *Studies in the Eighteenth Century IV,* edited by R. F. Brissenden and J. C. Eade, 167–91. Canberra: Australian National University Press, 1979.

————. "Pride, Prejudice, and 'Grandison.' " Paper presented at the American Society for Eighteenth-Century Studies Meeting, Washington, D.C., 10 April 1981.

————. "The Reviser Observed: The Last Volume of *Sir Charles Grandison.*" *Studies in Bibliography* 29 (1979): 1–31.

————. "*Sir Charles Grandison* and the Little Senate: The Relation Between Samuel Richardson's Correspondence and His Last Novel." Ph.D. diss., University of London, 1968.

Hill, Christopher. "Clarissa Harlowe and Her Times." *Essays in Criticism* 5 (October 1955): 315–40.

Hilles, Frederick W. "The Plan of *Clarissa.*" *Philological Quarterly* 45 (January 1966): 236–48.

Hilson, J. C., and Rosalind Nicol. "Two Notes on 'Sir Charles Grandison.' " *Notes and Queries,* n.s., 22 (November 1975): 492–93.

Hornbeak, Katherine. "Richardson's Aesop." *Smith College Studies in Modern Languages* 19 (January 1938): 30–40.

————. "Richardson's *Familiar Letters* and the Domestic Conduct Books." *Smith College Studies in Modern Languages* 19 (January 1938): 1–29.

Hughes, Helen Sard. "English Epistolary Fiction Before Pamela." In *The*

Manly Anniversary Studies in Language and Literature, 156–69. Chicago: University of Chicago Press, 1923.

Hughes, Leo. "Theatrical Convention in Richardson: Some Observations on a Novelist's Technique." In *Restoration and Eighteenth-Century Literature*, edited by Carroll Camden, 239–50. Chicago: University of Chicago Press, 1963.

Jenkins, Owen. "Richardson's *Pamela* and Fielding's 'Vile Forgeries.'" *Philological Quarterly* 44 (April 1965): 200–210.

Kaplan, Fred. "'Our Short Story': The Narrative Devices of *Clarissa*." *Studies in English Literature* 11 (Summer 1971): 549–62.

Kearney, Anthony. "*Clarissa* and the Epistolary Form." *Essays in Criticism* 16 (January 1966): 44–56.

———. "Richardson's 'Pamela': the Aesthetic Case." *Review of English Literature* 7 (July 1966): 78–90.

Keast, William R. "The Two *Clarissas* in Johnson's *Dictionary*." *Studies in Philology* 54 (July 1957): 429–39.

Kermode, Frank. "Richardson and Fielding." In *Essays on the Eighteenth-Century Novel*, edited by Robert Donald Spector, 64–77. Bloomington: Indiana University Press, 1965.

Kinkead-Weekes, M. "*Clarissa* Restored?" *Review of English Studies*, n.s., 10 (May 1959): 156–71.

———. "Pamela." In *Samuel Richardson*, edited by John Carroll, 20–27. Englewood Cliffs: Prentice-Hall, 1969.

———. *Samuel Richardson. Dramatic Novelist*. London: Methuen & Co. Ltd., 1973.

Knight, Charles A. "The Function of Wills in Richardson's *Clarissa*." *Texas Studies in Literature and Language* 11 (Fall 1969): 1183–90.

Konigsberg, Ira. "The Dramatic Background of Richardson's Plots and Characters." *PMLA* 83 (March 1968): 42–53.

———. *Samuel Richardson and the Dramatic Novel*. Lexington: University of Kentucky Press, 1968.

Kreissman, B. *Pamela-Shamela*. Lincoln: University of Nebraska Press, 1960.

Krutch, Joseph Wood. *Five Masters. A Study in the Mutations of the Novel*. New York: Jonathan Cape & Harrison Smith, 1930.

Lefever, Charlotte. "Richardson's Paradoxical Success." *PMLA* 48 (September 1933): 856–60.

Lyles, Albert M. "'Pamela's Trials.'" In *Twentieth Century Interpretations of Pamela*, edited by Rosemary Cowler, 103–4. Englewood Cliffs: Prentice-Hall, 1969.

Lynch, Lawrence W. "Richardson's Influence On the Concept of the Novel In Eighteenth-Century France." *Comparative Literature Studies* 14 (September 1977): 233–43.

McAdam, E. L., Jr. "A New Letter from Fielding." *Yale Review* 38 (December 1948): 300–310.

Macaulay, G. C. "Richardson and His French Predecessors." *Modern Language Review* 8 (October 1913): 464–67.

Macey, Samuel. "Richardson's Grandison and Austen's General Tilney: Contrasting Authorial Views on Clockworklike Efficiency." *Transactions of the Samuel Johnson Society of the Northwest* 14 (1983): 1–16.

McIntosh, Carey. "Pamela's Clothes." In *Twentieth Century Interpretations of Pamela*, edited by Rosemary Cowler, 89–96. Englewood Cliffs: Prentice-Hall, 1969.

McKillop, Alan Dugald. *The Early Masters of English Fiction*. Lawrence: University of Kansas paperback, 1968.

———. "Epistolary Technique in Richardson's Novels." In *Studies in the Literature of the Augustan Age*, edited by Richard C. Boys, 199–217. Ann Arbor: George Wahr Publishing Co. for Augustan Reprint Society, 1952.

———. "On *Sir Charles Grandison*." In *Samuel Richardson*, edited by John Carroll, 124–38. Englewood Cliffs: Prentice-Hall, 1969.

———. "Richardson, Young, and the *Conjectures*." *Modern Philology* 22 (May 1925): 391–404.

———. "Richardson's Early Writings—Another Pamphlet." *Journal of English and Germanic Philology* 53 (January 1954): 72–75.

———. *Samuel Richardson. Printer and Novelist*. Chapel Hill: University of North Carolina Press, 1936.

———. "Samuel Richardson's Advice to an Apprentice." *Journal of English and Germanic Philology* 42 (January 1943): 40–54.

———. "Supplementary Notes on Samuel Richardson as a Printer." *Studies in Bibliography* 12 (1959): 214–18.

Moler, Kenneth L. "The Balm of Sisterly Consolation: *Pride and Prejudice* and *Sir Charles Grandison*." *Notes and Queries*, n.s., 30 (June 1983): 216–17.

Moore, Robert Etheridge. "Dr. Johnson on Fielding and Richardson." *PMLA* 66 (March 1951): 162–81.

Newcomb, Robert. "Franklin and Richardson." *Journal of English and Germanic Philology* 57 (1958): 27–35.

Noel-Bentley, Elaine. "An Allusion to 'Sir Charles Grandison' in Jane Austen's Letters." *Notes and Queries*, n.s., 24 (July–August 1977): 321.

Park, William. "Fielding and Richardson." *PMLA* 81 (October 1966): 381–88.

Pierson, Robert Craig. "The Revisions of Richardson's *Sir Charles Grandison*." *Studies in Bibliography* 21 (1968): 163–89.

———. "A Study of the Text of Richardson's *Sir Charles Grandison*." Ph.D. diss., University of Arkansas, 1965.

Poetzsche, Erich. *Samuel Richardsons Belesenheit.* Kiel: Verlag von Robert Cordes, 1908.

Rabkin, Norman. "*Clarissa:* A Study in the Nature of Convention." *English Literary History* 23 (September 1956): 204–17.

Reid, B. L. "Justice to *Pamela.*" In *Twentieth Century Interpretations of Pamela,* edited by Rosemary Cowler, 33–41. Englewood Cliffs: Prentice-Hall, 1969.

Rudnick-Smalbraak, Marijke. *Samuel Richardson: Minute Particulars Within the Large Design.* Chapter 4. Leiden: Leiden University Press, E. J. Brill, 1983.

Sabor, Peter. "*Amelia* and *Sir Charles Grandison:* The Convergence of Fielding and Richardson." *Wascana Review* 17 (Fall 1982): 3–18.

—————"Richardson's Advice to Novelists." *Transactions of the Samuel Johnson Society of the Northwest* 13 (1982): 60–71.

—————. "Richardson's Masculine Dreamers." Paper presented at the Johnson Society of the Central Region Meeting, Milwaukee, 1982.

—————. "Samuel Richardson's Correspondence and His Final Revision of *Pamela.*" *Transactions of the Samuel Johnson Society of the Northwest* 12 (1981): 114–31.

Sale, William M., Jr. "From *Pamela* to *Clarissa.*" In *The Age of Johnson,* edited by Frederick W. Hilles, 127–38. New Haven: Yale University Press, 1949.

—————. *Samuel Richardson. A Bibliographical Record of His Literary Career with Historical Notes.* New Haven: Yale University Press, 1936.

—————. *Samuel Richardson: Master Printer.* 1950; reprint, Westport, Conn.: Greenwood Press, 1978.

Sherbo, Arthur. "Time and Place in Richardson's *Clarissa.*" *Boston University Studies in English* 3 (Autumn 1957): 139–46.

Sherburn, George. "Samuel Richardson's Novels and the Theatre: A Theory Sketched." *Philological Quarterly* 41 (January 1962): 325–29.

—————. " 'Writing to the Moment': One Aspect." In *Samuel Richardson,* edited by John Carroll, 152–60. Englewood Cliffs: Prentice-Hall, 1969.

Shoup, Louise. "The Use of the Social Gathering as a Structural Device in the Novels of Richardson, Fielding, Smollett, and Sterne." Ph.D. diss., Stanford University, 1950.

Sklepowich, Lois Anne. "Providential Labyrinth: The Development of Richardson's Christian Comedy." Ph.D. diss., University of Virginia, 1963.

Smidt, Kristian. "Character and Plot in the Novels of Samuel Richardson." *Critical Quarterly* 17 (Summer 1975): 155–66.

Smith, Phyllis Patricia. "The Eighteenth-Century Gentleman: Contributing Theories and Their Realization in Sir Charles Grandison." Ph.D. diss., Radcliffe, 1947.

Smith, Sarah Winthrop Robbins. " 'Mastering the Heart': From the Moral Novel to a Theoretics of Value in the Works of Samuel Richardson." Ph.D. diss., Harvard, 1975.

———. *Samuel Richardson.* Boston: G.K. Hall, 1984.

Stephen, Leslie. "Prefatory Chapter of Biographical Criticism." In vol. 1 of *The Words of Samuel Richardson,* ix–lv. London: Henry Soteran and Co., 1883.

Talburt, Nancy Ellen Brown. "The Use of Family Relationships for Dramatic Effect in the Novels of Samuel Richardson." Ph.D. diss., University of Arkansas, 1967.

Thomson, Clara Linklater. *Samuel Richardson.* London: Horace Marshall & Son, 1900.

Ulmer, Gregory L. "*Clarissa* and La Nouvelle Héloïse." *Comparative Literature* 24 (Fall 1972): 289–308.

Vaid, Sudesh. *The Divided Mind: Studies in Defoe and Richardson.* New Delhi: Associated Publishing House, 1979.

Van Ghent, Dorothy. "On *Clarissa Harlowe.*" In *Samuel Richardson,* edited by John Carroll, 49–66. Engelwood Cliffs: Prentice-Hall, 1969.

Varney, Andrew. "Ornamental Turning in *Sir Charles Grandison.*" *Notes and Queries,* n.s., 27 (February 1980): 41–42.

Ward, H. G. "Richardson's Character of Lovelace." *Modern Language Review* 7 (October 1912): 494–98.

Warner, William Beatty. *Reading Clarissa: The Struggles of Interpretation.* New Haven: Yale University Press, 1979.

Watt, Ian. "Defoe and Richardson on Homer: A Study of the Relation of Novel and Epic in the Early Eighteenth Century." *Review of English Studies,* n.s., 3 (October 1952): 325–40.

———. "The Naming of Characters in Defoe, Richardson, and Fielding." *Review of English Studies* 25 (October 1949): 322–38.

———. *The Rise of the Novel.* Berkeley: University of California Press paperback, 1971.

Wendt, Allan. "Clarissa's Coffin." *Philological Quarterly* 39 (October 1960): 481–95.

Wilcox, Frank Howard. "Prévost's Translations of Richardson's Novels." *University of California Publications in Modern Philology* 12 (11 January 1927): 341–411.

Wilson, Stuart. "Richardson's *Pamela:* An Interpretation." *PMLA* 88 (January 1973): 79–91.

Winner, Anthony. "Richardson's Lovelace: Character and Prediction." *Texas Studies in Literature and Language* 14 (Spring 1972): 53–75.

Wolff, Cynthia Griffin. *Samuel Richardson and the Eighteenth-Century Puritan Character.* Hamden, Conn.: Archon Books Shoe String Press, Inc., 1972.

Wood, John August. "The Chronology of the Richardson-Bradshaigh Correspondence of 1751." *Studies in Bibliography* 33 (1980): 182–91.

Wooten, Elizabeth Harper. "Biblical Allusion in the Novels of Richardson." Ph.D. diss., University of Tennessee, 1973.

Zach, Wolfgang. "Richardson and the Dedication to the Earl of Grandison in Ogilvie's *Civil History of the Kingdom of Naples.*" *Archive* 213 (1976): 343–45.

Zirker, Malvin R., Jr. "Richardson's Correspondence: The Personal Letter as Private Experience." In *The Familiar Letter in the Eighteenth Century,* edited by Howard Anderson, Philip B. Daghlian, and Irvin Ehrenpreis, 71–91. Lawrence: University of Kansas Press, 1966.

2. *Courtesy and Conduct Book Criticism*

Allen, E. Sprague. "Chesterfield's Objection to Laughter." *Modern Language Notes* 38 (May 1923): 279–87.

Aronson, A. "The Anatomy of Taste." *Modern Language Notes* 61 (April 1946): 228–36.

Baldwin, Edward Chauncey. "The Relation of the Seventeenth Century Character to the Periodical Essay." *PMLA*, n.s., 12 (1904): 75–114.

Betz, Siegmund A. E. "Francis Osborn's *Advice to A Son.*" In *Seventeenth Century Studies,* 2d series, edited by Robert Shafer, 3–67. Princeton University Press for University of Cincinnati, 1939.

Bobbitt, Mary Reed, comp. "A Bibliography of Etiquette Books Published in America Before 1900." *Bulletin of the New York Public Library* 51 (December 1947): 687–720.

Bogosian, Ezekiel. "The Perfect Gentleman: A Study of an Esthetic Type in the Novels of Richardson, Jane Austen, Trollope, and Henry James." Ph.D. diss., University of California, Berkeley, 1937.

Bornstein, Diane. *The Lady in the Tower: Medieval Courtesy Literature for Women.* Hamden, Connecticut: Archon Books, 1983.

Bornstein, Diane. *Mirrors of Courtesy.* Hamden, Connecticut: Archon Books, 1975.

Bornstein, Diane. "Women's Public and Private Space in Some Medieval Courtesy Books." *Centerpoint* 3 (1981): 68–74.

Brauer, George C. Jr. "Good Breeding in the Eighteenth Century." *University of Texas Studies in English* 33 (1953): 25–44.

———. "The Well-Made Gentleman: A Study in English Theories of Aristocratic Education from 1660–1775." 2 vols. Ph.D. diss., Princeton, 1952.

Defoe, Daniel. *The Compleat English Gentleman.* Edited and introduced by Karl D. Bulbring. London: David Nutt, 1890.

Green, Catherine Sobba. "The Courtesy Novel (1740–1820): Women Writing for Women." Ph.D. diss., Georgia State University, 1983.

Heltzel, Virgil B. "Chesterfield and the Anti-Laughter Tradition." *Modern Philology* 26 (August 1928): 73–90.

———. "Chesterfield and the Tradition of the Ideal Gentleman." Ph.D. diss., Chicago, 1925.

Heltzel, Virgil B., comp. *A Check List of Courtesy Books in the Newberry Library.* Chicago: The Newberry Library, 1942.

Heltzel, Virgil B., ed., "Richard Earl of Carbery's Advice to His Son." *Huntington Library Bulletin,* no. 11 (April 1937): 59–105.

Hemlow, Joyce. "The Courtesy-Book Element in Fanny Burney's Works." Ph.D. diss., Radcliffe, 1948.

———". Fanny Burney and the Courtesy Books," *PMLA* 65 (September 1950): 732–61.

Hildebrand, Ann M. "Jean de Brunhoff's Advice to Youth: The *Babar* Books as Books of Courtesy." In *Children's Literature,* Vol. 11 of *Annual of The Modern Language Association Division on Children's Literature and The Children's Literature Association,* edited by Francelia Butler, 76–95. New Haven: Yale University Press, 1983.

Hodges, James. "*The Female Spectator,* A Courtesy Periodical." In *Studies in the Early English Periodical,* edited by Richmond P. Bond, 151–82. Chapel Hill: University of North Carolina Press, 1957.

Holme, James W. "Italian Courtesy-Books of the Sixteenth Century." *Modern Language Review* 5 (April 1910): 145–66.

Hornbeak, Katherine Gee. "The Complete Letter-Writer in English 1568–1800." *Smith College Studies in Modern Languages* 15 (April–July 1934): iii–150.

Kelso, Ruth. *Doctrine for the Lady of the Renaissance.* Urbana: University of Illinois Press, 1956.

———. "The Doctrine of the English Gentleman in the Sixteenth Century With A Bibliographical List of Treatises on the Gentleman and Related Subjects Published In Europe to 1625." *University of Illinois Studies in Language and Literature* 14 (February–May 1929): 11–288.

———. "Sixteenth Century Definitions of the Gentleman in England." *Journal of English and Germanic Philology* 24 (1925): 370–82.

Lee, Patricia Ann. "The Ideal of the English Gentleman in the Early Seventeenth Century." Ph.D. diss., Columbia, 1966.

Mason, John E. *Gentlefolk in the Making.* 1935; reprint, New York: Octagon Books, 1971.

Millett, Fred B. "English Courtesy Literature Before 1557." *Bulletin of the Departments of History and Political and Economic Science in Queen's University, Kingston, Ontario, Canada,* no. 30 (January 1919): 1–16.

Nicholls, J. W. *The Matter of Courtesy: A Study of Medieval Courtesy Books and the Gawain-Poet.* Dover, New Hampshire: Boydell and Brewer, 1985.

Noyes, Gertrude E. *Bibliography of Courtesy and Conduct Books in Seventeenth-Century England.* New Haven: Tuttle Morehouse and Taylor Co., 1937.

Powell, Chilton Latham. *English Domestic Relations 1487–1653.* Chaps. 4 and 6, Appendix D, Bibliography I. New York: Columbia University Press, 1917.

Quintana, Ricardo. "Notes on English Educational Opinion During the Seventeenth Century." *Studies in Philology* 27 (April 1930): 265–92.

Sinagel, Michael. "Daniel Defoe: The Gentleman Theme, Its Significance in His Life, His Works, and His Age." Ph.D. diss., Harvard, 1963.

Smyth-Palmer, A. *The Ideal of a Gentleman or A Mirror for Gentlefolks.* London: George Routledge & Sons Limited, n.d.

Thompson, Elbert N. S. *Literary Bypaths of the Renaissance.* Pp. 127–71. New Haven: Yale University Press, 1924.

Ustick, W. Lee. "Advice to a Son: A Type of Seventeenth-Century Conduct Book." *Studies in Philology* 29 (July 1932): 409–41.

———. "Changing Ideals of Aristocratic Character and Conduct in Seventeenth-Century England." *Modern Philology* 30 (November 1932): 147–66.

———. "The Courtier and the Bookseller: Some Vagaries of Seventeenth-Century Publishing." *Review of English Studies* 5 (April 1929): 143–54.

———. "The English Gentleman in the Sixteenth Century and the Early Seventeenth Century: Studies in the Literature of Courtesy and Conduct." 2 vols. Ph.D. diss., Harvard, 1931.

Vale, Marcia. *The Gentleman's Recreation, 1580–1630.* Totowa, N.J.: Rowman & Littlefield, 1977.

Vogt, George McGill. "Gleanings for the History of a Sentiment: Generositas Virtus, Non Sanguis." *Journal of English and Germanic Philology* 24 (1925): 102–24.

Wildeblood, Joan. *The Polite World.* London: Davis-Poynter, 1973.

Wright, Louis B., ed., *Advice to a Son. Precepts of Lord Burghley, Sir Walter Raleigh, and Francis Osborne.* Introduction. Cornell University Press for The Folger Shakespeare Library, 1962.

3. Other Criticism and History

Abbey, Charles J. *The English Church and Its Bishops 1700–1800.* 2 vols. London: Longmans, Green, and Co., 1887.

Abbey, Charles J., and John H. Overton. *The English Church in the Eighteenth Century.* 2 vols. London: Longmans, Green, and Co., 1878.

Adams, Percy G. *Travel Literature and the Evolution of the Novel.* Lexington: University of Kentucky Press, 1983.

Altman, Janet Gurkin. *Epistolarity.* Columbus: Ohio State University Press, 1982.

Anderson, Howard, and Irvin Ehrenpreis. "The Familiar Letter in the Eighteenth Century: Some Generalizations." In *The Familiar Letter in the Eighteenth Century,* edited by Howard Anderson, Philip B. Daghlian, and Irvin Ehrenpreis, 269–82. Lawrence: University of Kansas Press, 1966.

Anderson, Judith Lawrence. "The Development of the Novel of Manners In the Eighteenth Century, As Seen in Representative Novels of the Period." Ph.D. diss., Harvard, 1970.

Armistead, J. M., ed., *The First English Novelists.* Knoxville: University of Tennessee Press, 1985.

Armstrong, Anthony. *The Church of England, the Methodists and Society 1700–1850.* London: University of London Press, 1973.

Babcock, R. W. "Benevolence, Sensibility and Sentiment in Some Eighteenth-Century Periodicals." *Modern Language Notes* 62 (June 1947): 394–97.

Baker, Ernest A. *Intellectual Realism: from Richardson to Sterne.* Vol. 4 of *The History of the English Novel.* London: H. F. and G. Witherby, 1930.

———. *The Later Romances and the Establishment of Realism.* Vol. 3 of *The History of the English Novel.* London: H. F. and G. Witherby, 1929.

———. *The Novel of Sentiment and the Gothic Romance.* Vol. 5 of *The History of the English Novel.* London: H. F. and G. Witherby, 1934.

Baker, Martha Cathey. "The Philosophical Seducer." Ph.D. diss., Yale, 1971.

Barker, Gerard A. *Henry Mackenzie.* Boston: Twayne Publishers, 1975.

Beasley, Jerry C. *Novels of the 1740s.* Athens: University of Georgia Press, 1982.

Bernbaum, Ernest. *The Drama of Sensibility.* Boston: Ginn and Co., Publishers, 1915.

Black, F. G. "The Technique of Letter Fiction in English from 1740 to 1800." *Harvard Studies and Notes in Philology and Literature* 15 (1933): 291–312.

Blanchard, Frederic T. *Fielding the Novelist.* New Haven: Yale University Press, 1927.

Bliss, Isabel St. John. *Edward Young.* New York: Twayne Publishers, Inc., 1969.

Bossy, John. *The English Catholic Community 1570–1850.* London: Darton, Longman & Todd, 1975.

Boyce, Benjamin. *The Benevolent Man: A Life of Ralph Allen of Bath.* Cambridge: Harvard University Press, 1967.

Brooks, Van Wyck. *The Flowering of New England 1815–1865.* New York: E. P. Dutton & Co., Inc., 1936.

Brown, Laura S. "Drama and Novel in Eighteenth-Century England." *Genre* 13 (Fall 1980): 287–304.

Burns, Landon C. *Pity and Tears: The Tragedies of Nicholas Rowe.* Salzburg: Institute für Englische Sprache und Literatur, 1974.

Champion, Larry S., ed., *Quick Springs of Sense.* Athens: University of Georgia Press, 1974.

Clark, Sir George. *The Later Stuarts 1660–1714.* 2d ed. Oxford: Clarendon Press, 1955.

Clifford, James L., ed. *Man Versus Society in Eighteenth-Century Britain.* Cambridge: Cambridge University Press, 1968.

Crane, R. S. "Suggestions Toward a Genealogy of the 'Man of Feeling.'" *English Literary History* 1 (December 1934): 205–30.

Crane, Thomas Frederick. *Italian Social Customs of the Sixteenth Century and Their Influence on the Literatures of Europe.* New Haven: Yale University Press, 1920.

Culler, A. Dwight. "Edward Bysshe and the Poet's Handbook." *PMLA* 63 (September 1948): 858–85.

Davis, Herbert. "The Correspondence of the Augustans." In *The Familiar Letter in the Eighteenth Century,* edited by Howard Anderson, Philip B. Daghlian, and Irvin Ehrenpreis, 1–13. Lawrence: University of Kansas Press, 1966.

Day, Robert Adams. *Told in Letters.* Ann Arbor: University of Michigan Press, 1966.

Dooley, Roger B. "The Catholic in the Eighteenth-Century Novel." Ph.D. diss., Catholic University, 1956.

Duckworth, Alistair M. *The Improvement of the Estate. A Study of Jane Austen's Novels.* Baltimore: Johns Hopkins Press, 1971.

Dussinger, John A. *The Discourse of the Mind in Eighteenth-Century Fiction.* The Hague: Mouton, 1974.

Elliott-Binns, L. E. *The Early Evangelicals: A Religious and Social Study.* Greenwich, Conn.: The Seabury Press, 1953.

Fergus, Jan. "The Clay Circulating Libraries." Paper presented at the New York Eighteenth-Century Seminar Meeting, New York City, 22 March 1984.

Folkenflik, Robert, ed. *The English Hero, 1660–1800.* Newark: University of Delaware Press, 1982.

Ford, Boris, ed. *From Dryden to Johnson.* Vol. 4 of *The New Pelican Guide to English Literature.* Harmondsworth, Middlesex, England: Penguin Books Ltd., 1982.

Fowler, Marian Elizabeth. "Patterns of Prudence: Courtship Conventions in Jane Austen's Novels." Ph.D. diss., University of Toronto, 1970.

Frantz, R. W. *The English Traveler and the Movement of Ideas 1660–1732.* 1934; reprint, New York: Octagon Books, Inc., 1968.

Gill, Richard. *Happy Rural Seat.* New Haven: Yale University Press, 1972.

Goldgar, Bertrand A. *Walpole and the Wits.* Lincoln: University of Nebraska Press, 1976.

Greene, Donald. "Latitudinarianism and Sensibility: The Genealogy of the 'Man of Feeling' Reconsidered." *Modern Philology* 75 (November 1977): 159–83.

Hagstrum, Jean H. *Sex and Sensibility.* Chicago: University of Chicago Press, 1980.

Hamlyn, Hilda M. "Eighteenth-century Circulating Libraries in England." *Library* series 5, no. 1 (1947–48): 196–222.

Harding, Alan. *A Social History of English Law.* Baltimore: Penguin Books, 1966.

Heidler, Joseph Bunn. "The History, From 1700 to 1800, of English Criticism of Prose Fiction." *University of Illinois Studies in Language and Literature* 13 (May 1928): 1–187.

Hemphill, Dom Basil. *The Early Vicars Apostolic of England 1685–1750.* London: Burns & Oates, 1954.

Hibbard, G. R. "The Country House Poem of the Seventeenth Century." *Journal of the Warburg and Courtauld Institute* 19 (January–June 1956): 159–74.

Hnatko, Eugene. "The Failure of Eighteenth-Century Tragedy." *Studies in English Literature* 11 (Summer 1971): 459–68.

Hughes, Helen Sard. "The Middle-Class Reader and the English Novel." *Journal of English and Germanic Philology* 25 (1926): 362–78.

Hughes, Philip. *The Catholic Question 1688–1829.* London: Sheed & Ward, 1929.

Humphreys, A. R. " 'The Friend of Mankind.' (1700–60)—An Aspect of Eighteenth-Century Sensibility." *Review of English Studies* 24 (July 1948): 203–18.

Hyamson, Albert M. *A History of the Jews in England.* London: Chatto & Windus, 1908.

Kievitt, Frank David. "Attitudes Toward Roman Catholicism in the Later Eighteenth-Century English Novel." Ph.D. diss., Columbia, 1975.

Koller, Katherine. "The Puritan Preacher's Contribution to Fiction." *Huntington Library Quarterly* 11 (August 1948): 321–40.

Leys, M. D. R. *Catholics in England 1559–1829.* New York: Sheed and Ward, 1961.

Litz, A. Walton. *Jane Austen.* New York: Oxford University Press, 1965.

MacCarthy, B. G. *The Later Women Novelists 1744–1818.* Cork: Cork University Press, 1957.

McClung, William A. *The Country House in English Renaissance Poetry.* Berkeley: University of California Press, 1977.

Malins, Edward. *English Landscaping and Literature 1660–1840*. London: Oxford University Press, 1966.

Maresca, Thomas E. *Epic to Novel*. Columbus: Ohio State University Press, 1974.

Marlowe, John. *The Puritan Tradition in English Life*. London: The Cresset Press, 1956.

Marr, George S. *The Periodical Essayists of the Eighteenth Century*. New York: D. Appleton and Co., 1924.

Marshall, Roderick. *Italy in English Literature 1755–1815*. New York: Columbia University Press, 1934.

Massingham, H. J. *The English Countryman*. London: B. T. Batsford, Ltd., 1943.

Mathew, David. *Catholicism in England*. 2d ed. London: Eyre & Spottiswoode, 1948.

Miller, Nancy. *Readings in the French and English Novel, 1722–1782*. New York: Columbia University Press, 1979.

Mingay, G. E. *English Landed Society in the Eighteenth Century*. London: Routledge and Kegan Paul, 1963.

Moorman, John R.H. *A History of the Church in England*. London: Adam and Charles Black, 1953.

Morgan, Charlotte E. *The Rise of the Novel of Manners: A Study of English Prose Fiction Between 1600 and 1740*. New York: Columbia University Press, 1911.

Newlin, Claude M. "The English Periodicals and the Novel, 1709–40." *Papers of the Michigan Academy of Science, Arts and Letters* 16 (1931): 467–76.

Park, William. "What Was New About the 'New Species' of Writing"? *Studies in the Novel* 2 (Summer 1970): 112–30.

Parnell, Paul E. "The Sentimental Mask." *PMLA* 78 (December 1963): 529–35.

Paulson, Ronald. *Satire and the Novel in Eighteenth-Century England*. New Haven: Yale University Press, 1967.

Plumb, J. H. *England in the Eighteenth Century*. Vol. 7 of *The Pelican History of England*. Harmondsworth, Middlesex, England: Penguin Books Ltd., 1963.

Pollard, Hazel M. Batzer. *From Heroics to Sentimentalism: A Study of Thomas Otway's Tragedies*. Salzburg: Institut für Englische Sprache und Literatur, 1974.

Porter, Roy. *English Society in the Eighteenth Century*. Harmondsworth, Middlesex, England: Penguin Books Ltd., 1982.

Poston, Mervyn L. "The Origin of the English Heroic Play." *Modern Language Review* 16 (January 1921): 18–22.

Praz, Mario. *The Romantic Agony.* Translated by Angus Davidson. London: Oxford University Press, 1933.

Preston, John. *The Created Self. The Reader's Role in Eighteenth-Century Fiction.* London: Heinemann, 1970.

Price, Cecil. " 'The Art of Pleasing': The Letters of Chesterfield." In *The Familiar Letter in the Eighteenth Century,* edited by Howard Anderson, Philip B. Daghlian, Irvin Ehrenpreis, 92–107. Lawrence: University of Kansas Press, 1966.

Rawson, C. J. "Some Remarks on Eighteenth-Century 'Delicacy,' With A Note on Hugh Kelly's *False Delicacy* (1768)." *Journal of English and Germanic Philology* 61 (January 1962): 1–13.

Reynolds, E. E. *The Roman Catholic Church in England and Wales.* Wheat-hampstead-Hertfordshire: Anthony Clarke Books, 1973.

Reynolds, Myra. *The Learned Lady in England 1650–1760.* Boston: Houghton Mifflin Company, 1920.

Richetti, John J. *Popular Fiction Before Richardson. Narrative Patterns 1700–1739.* Oxford: Clarendon Press, 1969.

Røstvig, Maren-Sofie. *The Happy Man—Studies in the Metamorphoses of a Classical Ideal 1600–1700.* 2 vols. Oslo: Akademisk Forlag, 1954.

Rothstein, Eric. *Restoration Tragedy.* Madison: University of Wisconsin Press, 1967.

———. *Systems of Order and Inquiry in Later Eighteenth-Century Fiction.* Berkeley: University of California Press, 1975.

Sacks, Sheldon. *Fiction and the Shape of Belief: A Study of Henry Fielding With Glances at Swift, Johnson and Richardson.* Berkeley: University of California Press, 1966.

Sams, Henry W. "Anti-Stoicism in Seventeenth- and Early Eighteenth-Century England." *Studies in Philology* 41 (January 1944): 65–78.

Schöffler, Herbert. *Protestantismus und Literatur.* Leipzig: Verlag von Bernhard Tauchnitz, 1922.

Schücking, Levin L. *Die Familie im Puritanismus.* Leipzig: Verlag und Druck von B. G. Teubner, 1929.

Shroff, Homai J. *The Eighteenth Century Novel.* New Delhi: Arnold-Heinemann, 1978.

Singer, Godfrey Frank. *The Epistolary Novel.* Philadelphia: University of Pennsylvania Press, 1933.

Smith, John Harrington. *The Gay Couple in Restoration Comedy.* Cambridge: Harvard University Press, 1948.

Spacks, Patricia Meyer. "The Dangerous Age." *Eighteenth-Century Studies* 11 (Summer 1978): 417–38.

Spector, Robert Donald, ed. *Essays on the Eighteenth-Century Novel.* Bloomington: Indiana University Press, 1965.

Steeves, Harrison R. *Before Austen. The Shaping of the English Novel in the Eighteenth Century.* New York: Holt, Rinehart and Winston, 1965.

Stephen, Sir Leslie. *History of English Thought in the Eighteenth Century.* 3d ed. Vol. 2. New York: G. P. Putnam's Sons, 1902.

Stone, Lawrence. *The Family, Sex and Marriage in England 1500–1800.* New York: Harper and Row, Publishers, 1977.

Streeter, Harold Wade. *The Eighteenth Century Novel in French Translation.* New York: Publications of the Institute of French Studies, Inc., 1936.

Sykes, Norman. *Church and State in England in the XVIIIth Century.* 1934; reprint, New York: Octagon Books, 1975.

————. *The English Religious Tradition.* London: SCM Press, Ltd., 1953.

————. *From Sheldon to Secher. Aspects of English Church History 1660–1768.* Cambridge: Cambridge University Press, 1959.

Tave, Stuart M. *The Amiable Humorist.* Chicago: University of Chicago Press, 1960.

Todd, Janet. *Women's Friendship in Literature.* New York: Columbia University Press, 1980.

Trumbach, Randolph. *The Rise of the Egalitarian Family: Aristocratic Kinship and Domestic Relations in Eighteenth-Century England.* New York: Academic Press, 1978.

Turberville, A. S. *English Men and Manners in the Eighteenth Century.* Oxford: Clarendon Press, 1926.

Turberville, A. S., ed. *Johnson's England. An Account of the Life & Manners of his Age.* 2 vols. Oxford: Clarendon Press, 1933.

Van Eerde, Katherine S. "The Creation of the Baronetage in England." *Huntington Library Quarterly* 22 (August 1959): 313–22.

Walsh, John. "Origins of the Evangelical Revival." In *Essays in Modern English Church History,* edited by G. V. Bennett and J. D. Walsh, chap. 6, pp. 132–62. New York: Oxford University Press, 1966.

Ward, Addison. "The Noblest Work of God: Studies in Augustan Social Ideals." Ph.D. diss., Yale, 1957.

Ward, Bernard. *The Dawn of the Catholic Revival in England 1781–1803.* 2 vols. London: Longmans, Green and Co., 1909.

Wasserman, Earl. "Johnson's *Rasselas:* Implicit Contexts." *Journal of English and Germanic Philology* 74 (January 1975): 1–25.

Watkin, E. I. *Roman Catholicism in England from the Reformation to 1950.* London: Oxford University Press, 1957.

Wearmouth, Robert F. *Methodism and the Common People of the Eighteenth Century.* London: The Epworth Press, 1945.

Williams, Basil. *The Whig Supremacy 1714–1760.* 2d ed. rev. C. H. Stuart. Oxford: Clarendon Press, 1962.

Williams, J. Anthony. *Bath and Rome: The Living Link.* Oxford: TRUEXpress, 1963.

INDEX